GOOD

THINGS

HAPPEN

SLOWLY

GOOD
THINGS
HAPPEN
SLOWLY

A LIFE IN AND OUT OF JAZZ

FRED HERSCH

CROWN
ARCHETYPE
NEW YORK

Copyright © 2017 by Fred Hersch and David Hajdu

All rights reserved.

Published in the United States by Crown Archetype,
an imprint of the Crown Publishing Group,
a division of Penguin Random House LLC, New York.
crownpublishing.com
crownarchetype.com

Crown Archetype and colophon is a registered trademark
of Penguin Random House LLC.

Photograph credits appear on page 306.

Library of Congress Cataloging-in-Publication Data is
available upon request.

ISBN 9781101904343
eBook ISBN 9781101904350

PRINTED IN THE UNITED STATES OF AMERICA

Book design by Anna Thompson
Jacket design by Cardon Webb
Jacket photograph by Matthew Sussman

2 4 6 8 10 9 7 5 3 1

First Edition

For Scott

After the dazzle of day is gone,
Only the dark, dark night shows to my eyes the stars;
After the clangor of organ majestic, or chorus, or perfect band,
Silent, athwart my soul, moves the symphony true.

—WALT WHITMAN

Start where you are.

—PEMA CHÖDRÖN

CONTENTS

GOOD

THINGS

HAPPEN

SLOWLY

KINGS ISLAND

I f you drove out of Cincinnati on Interstate 71 and went north for about twenty miles, you'd see the Eiffel Tower—actually, a one-third-scale model that stood at the entrance to the Kings Island amusement park. Rural Ohio was years ahead of Las Vegas in the art of erecting cheesy replicas of iconic architecture for the vacation trade. In 1975, when I was living back in Cincinnati after dropping out of Grinnell College, Kings Island was a fairly new park, open for only three years. It gleamed in its brown-and-olive-green seventies splendor, and it was vast, filling hundreds of acres of paved-over cornfields with roller coasters, kiddie rides, souvenir shops, snack stands, and more souvenir shops. At the center of the main grounds, not far from the Eiffel Tower, stood an inflatable-dome theater that seated a couple of hundred people on benches. In '72, *The Partridge Family* shot an episode there. That's how perfectly the place exuded middle-American wholesomeness. The following year *The Brady Bunch* came and filmed a show. The year after that, I was playing there.

Kings Island, like most major amusement parks in those days, put together a short musical revue every summer. The idea was a throwback to the tent shows that, early in American musical history, traveled the country bringing entertainment to people living on farms such as the ones Kings Island had replaced. I remember reading once that Lester Young, the tenor saxophonist who became known for his radically beautiful, lyrical improvisations, had started out as a child musician in a family band that worked the tent-show circuit. But that fact had nothing to do with my decision to take a job as the pianist in the orchestra pit of the Kings Island revue that summer. I did it for the work. It was a well-paying gig—a professional job when I was just beginning to see what it was like to be a professional musician. I got $500 a week, as I recall, for playing seven thirty-minute shows per day, one every hour on the hour, six days a week.

The show was called *Hit-Land USA!* The exclamation point was part of the title, as in *Oklahoma!* and exclamatory exuberance was the mode of the singing in the production. It was a revue of mainstream pop hits, skewed somewhat toward the older crowd of parents and grandparents who came to these shows to sit for half an hour while the kids were flipping upside down on the rides. We did things like "Up, Up and Away," the Jimmy Webb tune, and "I Don't Know How to Love Him" from *Jesus Christ Superstar*. Not my favorite music, but not the absolute worst shit ever written, either.

There were two groups of performers in this show: the singers and the musicians in the pit. The singers were either gay boys right out of the local conservatory or straight girls with dreams of going to Broadway and starring as Marian the Librarian. They were all terrifically talented in the musical-theater way. They were young and full of fire and hope, and so was I. The musicians were all older, more seasoned, and jaded. These guys—and they all were guys—were solid working pros or local high school music teachers from the Cincinnati jazz scene. They were making a buck, but they all really loved jazz. Many of them thought of themselves as jazz musicians, and so did I. I was nineteen years old.

I didn't get to know the gay boys in the show—I didn't let myself—even though I was gay too. For me, so far in my life, being gay meant being romantically obsessed with a couple of my friends in school and fantasizing about messing around with one of them. I didn't really understand what it meant to be gay. I had no one to talk to about it, and I barely knew a thing about the gay subculture.

One night late that summer, the boys in the show invited me to a party at somebody's house near the University of Cincinnati. I was jittery and went by myself. As I walked in, the first thing I saw was a guy in a blond wig with bangs and a ponytail. He was dressed like a bobby-soxer, in a short pink poodle skirt and saddle shoes with the socks rolled down. Another guy was dressed like Rita Hayworth in *Gilda*, with that amazing red Rita Hayworth hair and the elbow-length gloves. I had never seen men in drag before other than straight old show-biz people such as Milton Berle or Bob Hope going for cheap laughs on TV. I thought to myself, *Is this what gay men are supposed to do?* My head was spinning, and I left in a hurry without talking to anyone.

I had more interaction with the musicians in the show, because I was already playing in the local jazz clubs and getting known as a young cat on the scene. I saw the guys around. Some of us gigged together. I was beginning to be accepted as a jazz musician—one of them.

The jazz guys didn't know I was gay, and I hadn't directly admitted it to the boys in the show, either. But now and then during a performance one of the boys would look down into the pit and catch my eye and give me a wink, just to mess me up. And the guys in the band would watch the singers as they did a little twirl or a time-step, and they'd mutter to me, "Get a load of those fags!" This incessant banter made me nervous.

Between shows we took our break in a pair of trailers set up behind the theater. They were attached to each other and arranged in an *L* shape, with one trailer for the singers and one for the musicians. At the elbow of the *L* there was a tiny common area, and that's where I would sit. To my left, I could watch the jazz guys as they rested and refueled. They'd huddle on the metal folding chairs, munching on sandwiches and chitchatting about their women, cars, and the Cincinnati Reds. To my right, I could see the gay boys entertaining themselves and the girls as if the real show were only starting—lip-synching to Bette Midler and Judy Garland records, dishing one another in catty ad libs, calling one another Mary. Could either group really have been such a socio-logical cliché? Or was that just the way I saw them?

The internal conflict of knowing I didn't completely fit into either group took me many years to resolve. That summer I sat alone between them—wondering where, if anywhere, I belonged.

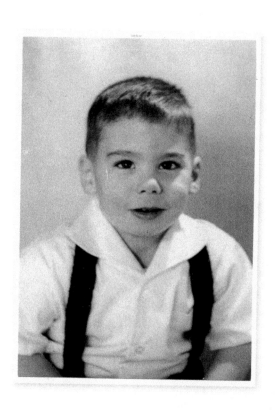

CHAPTER 1

SHORT ARMS

These days I rarely make a set list. Whether I'm performing solo piano in a concert hall or playing a set with my trio in a jazz club, I prefer not to plan what I'm going to play too thoroughly. I like to work spontaneously, organically—in the moment. Though I might have an idea of the tune I want to open with for any given set, as I'm walking onto the stage I start to pick up a feeling for the audience. I sit down, settle onto the piano stool, and see what kind of mood I'm in. Sometimes when playing with my trio I will ask them what they feel like starting with—a nice surprise for me, as I tend to play better if I don't overthink things. If I'm playing with the group, I get a thousand cues from the bassist and the drummer, and I send my own cues back to them. The music is like a rhythmic and harmonic river rushing along, and each of us jumps into it in our own way as it flows by. We are making spontaneous music *together*—and the fact that we are speaking the same musical language gives the music power and a feeling of pure joy. When we are in sync with one another it's unlike anything I have ever experienced. The music, and each evening, takes on a shape of its own. Every night, every performance, every tune—every moment—has its own character, its own life. I believe in honoring that.

I've never been a big fan of overplanned, tightly constructed show business—nor of the practice of some jazz musicians stuffing generic licks and patterns they've worked out in advance into whatever tune they are playing. I can admire the craft involved, but it doesn't move me. This "one size fits all" approach is pretty uninteresting; for me, each piece should occupy its own specific and considered musical world. I have always been most interested in the kinetic, almost magical spontaneity of improvisation, the open give-and-take among musicians. I love *jazz*—and great jazz has to have the element of danger, even if it doesn't sound wild or crazy. Sometimes just changing one tiny detail in the moment can open a musical door.

There are many reasons for my aversion to elaborate constructions of theatrical show, and one of them is surely that I grew up in an environment of carefully planned and meticulously executed artificiality. I spent my childhood in a household that would have appeared from the outside like a model of middle-class American excellence. Everything about it adhered to the script of midcentury domestic rightness. But it was essentially a grand charade, more than a bit like the film *Ordinary People*—and I felt lost in it all.

I was raised in a handsome older neighborhood of Cincinnati

called North Avondale. It was a gaslight district, literally. The streets were spotted with flickering gas lamps set atop cast-iron poles, conjuring something of an old-world atmosphere in the modern Midwest. The houses were well designed and sturdily built in an eclectic range of styles, with Tudor, Victorian, and Gothic Revival elements artfully employed and sometimes combined. They were homes that sought to show the sophistication, and not merely the prosperity, of the people living in them. North Avondale was one of the first suburbs of Cincinnati proper—not one of the super-fancy, newer, snooty ranch-house suburbs where the richie-rich families lived but a neatly tailored community. Each house had a real personality, and the oak, maple, and gingko trees lining the winding streets were enormous. It was a postcard image of the ideals of social aspiration and assimilation that midwestern Jews such as my parents upheld. It was racially integrated and religiously diverse; incomes ranged from solidly middle class to upper-middle class.

Both of my parents had grown up in West Virginia, not known for its large Jewish population. They met in Charleston, married there in 1952, and decided to settle in Cincinnati, where my father helped build a prominent legal practice in corporate law and my mother served, for as long as she could, as a good lawyer's wife. I came along in 1955, followed by my brother, Hank, just over two years later. My mom, a petite, smart, poised, attractive, and eternally optimistic woman, educated at Smith College, has always had a strong sense of what should be done and how things ought to be, though I'm not sure if she could always tell you *why*. My dad, a graduate of Princeton and Yale Law School, was also intelligent and good-looking in a fifties movie-magazine way, and he exuded the competence and self-confidence expected of successful males in the *Mad Men* era.

As I entered the double digits, I realized that my parents' marriage was an unhappy one. In the midst of their marital difficulties, neither one of them was available to teach me life skills and discipline. My father was largely disengaged from his family—none of us knew until many years later that he had a problem with alcohol. He was a member of "the greatest generation," who lived through the Great Depression and fought in World War II, but he didn't talk to me or Hank about those experiences until he was in his late eighties and I persuaded him to write down what he went through as a nineteen-year-old army sergeant in the trenches of France. He was a small-town kid who saw unimaginable horrors that no doubt scarred him for life and may have led to his self-medicating by drinking. And though I have tried many times, I can barely remember an instance of the two of us doing anything together when I was growing up.

My mom seemed to always be busy doing *something*, though I am not completely sure how she filled her days given that she didn't work and had help at home during the week. An energetic woman then, as now, she did do a good amount of schlepping Hank and me to and from various after-school activities. But until I was able to drive myself at age sixteen, I do remember her taking me out after school to run errands with her in a somewhat conspiratorial way—"Don't tell your father, it's our secret." I think she was lonely at home and needed an ally.

In addition to her involvement in groups such as the temple sisterhood, my mother was part of a group of women who had all gone to elite eastern colleges and needed a reason to keep their minds sharp. They held meetings they called "Current Topics"; rotating among their homes, each meeting two women would read a "paper" they had written on a subject of their choosing— followed, of course, by "luncheon" featuring elaborately shaped Jell-O molds, tomato aspic, and other sixties buffet foods. Shortly after we moved to a bigger house in 1965, my mom wrote a paper entitled "My Life with HHH" (my father's initials). In a happy, sitcom manner she described our home life, with the cute, high-spirited kids, the obligatory dog, and my father's constant volunteer work. She was putting a comic face on what she must have known, deep down, was anything but funny.

So I ended up creating my own life, without much guidance. My parents were committed to showing the world a rosy, almost WASPy model of a marriage—though it was bankrupt in the important, emotional ways.

Thank God there was music, my great escape from the unbearable tension in the house. Music had come down on both sides of my family in my grandparents' generation, and my folks appreciated it through their parents even though they didn't play themselves. My paternal grandmother, Ella Hersch, was a skilled amateur pianist. When she turned twenty-one and graduated with a music degree from Pittsburgh's Chatham College, her parents gave her a six-foot, mahogany 1921 Steinway Model O piano—an instrument built during a high point in Steinway history. After I inherited it in 1997, I have had it at various times in my New York home. And as I have upgraded instruments, I have lent it to some of my best students who needed (and couldn't afford) a grand piano. My grandmother emigrated from Russia in 1904 and lived until 1996, experiencing almost all of the twentieth century.

She always did what she could to encourage my interest in music. She also, touchingly, went out of her way to show me that she welcomed the multiple ways in which I was *different*. Later in her life she would always ask me if I had a "special friend." For a person of her time and place, she had an enlightened attitude.

On my mother's side, my grandfather Fred Bloomberg, whom I was named for, was a semiprofessional violinist. He was first generation, born in Brooklyn of Lithuanian and Russian heritage. He made his living in furniture sales but was passionate about classical music and helped found the Charleston Symphony Orchestra. I adored my grandfather and was broken up when he died, in 1974. He had a dignified appearance, with a mane of white hair combed straight back. We visited him often in Charleston when I was a child, and I was fascinated watching him practice the violin. I myself have always hated practicing, but I loved to watch him do it. His wife, Roslyn, née Thalheimer, was a descendant of German Jews who came to the Deep South in the mid-1800s. She was the granddaughter of the mayor of Selma, Alabama, where she grew up in a Victorian household complete with a staff of five. Coddled as she was, though well read and highly intelligent, she was much better at arranging for those in her employ to boil her an egg than making one herself.

When my parents married, one of the things they made a point to buy with their wedding money was a piano—a five-foot Lester baby grand in ebony. By the time I was four I had discovered it. I started picking out little tunes—nursery rhymes and cartoon-show music like the themes from *The Huckleberry Hound Show* and *The Flintstones*, which I learned later is actually fairly hip and is based on "rhythm changes," the harmonic structure of George Gershwin's "I Got Rhythm."

When my parents saw me doing this, it struck them that I seemed to have some talent. They put me in class piano lessons at the age of five. To their credit, after it was clear that I was outgrowing the class lessons, my parents rather quickly arranged for me to study with the best teacher they could find in Cincinnati, a woman named Jeanne Kirstein, who was the local heavyweight. She was a New Yorker—she had that cachet—and had won the prestigious Naumburg Piano Competition. Her husband was Jack Kirstein, the 'cellist in the LaSalle Quartet, a group well regarded for its important early recordings of music of the Second Viennese School: Schoenberg, Berg, and Webern. Jeanne was a serious musician and a lovely person, and I liked going over to her house and playing. And lying on the floor of their house and hearing the string quartet in rehearsal made me forever love music in four parts—I would try to hear the viola against the second violin or one of the two violins against the 'cello. But I didn't practice much and never went to my lesson fully prepared. I would get to a tough passage and either fake it or close my eyes and grit my teeth and hope that I could get through it. Unfortunately for my discipline but fortunately for my development as an improviser, I often got away with winging it.

Looking back, I wish Jeanne had pushed me harder. She could have kicked my ass to make me better than I was, and I think that she should have. She should have explained why learning scales and arpeggios would be of service to me later on. But she held back, partly in deference to my mother, who had heard horror stories of overzealous, shrewlike parents pushing their kids too hard. She didn't want to turn into a stage mother. She told my teacher, "I know he's a talented kid, but he should enjoy himself. I don't want his piano lessons to be drudgery." So Jeanne didn't push me that hard. Under the cover of my best interests, I think that my mom was more concerned with what she might become than she was with what I could grow up to be.

I enjoyed my piano lessons but avoided pieces that would challenge me technically—I favored slower, lyrical pieces over flashy and more difficult ones. I derived a lot more satisfaction from sitting at the piano at home making up music of my own. By early elementary school I was starting to create music—improvised pieces in the vein of the classical works I was playing for my lessons. I would follow my intuition, and the music would come out in the style of Bach or Mozart or Schumann, because that's what I had been playing and listening to. My mother would hear me, and for a moment or two she would think I was playing a piece from the classical canon, but she knew well enough what the written pieces sounded like and soon realized that I was inventing the music myself. She would yell out from the kitchen, "You're not practicing!" But making things up was a lot more fun, and she couldn't have conceived that what I was doing was practicing at a way of making music that neither one of us knew much about. I had not yet learned that anything like jazz existed.

But my parents must have seen my persistence in creating my own music and realized that it might be enhanced by systematic nurturing. When I was eight, on Jeanne's recommendation they set me up with a private theory and composition teacher in Cincinnati, Walter Mays. It was the single best thing they ever did for me.

Mays was a doctoral composition student at the local conservatory. A lanky Texan in his late twenties, he was very friendly and kind, and lived with his wife in an old gloomy brownstone apartment in the student neighborhood near the school. He had never taught a child before—let alone one hour every week or two. Unlike Jeanne, he didn't need my mother's consent to push me because I applied myself ardently to the material he was teaching me. It involved the creation of original music, rather than the techniques necessary to reproduce music someone else had composed long ago. From third grade through seventh grade, I received an advanced musical education. I learned music notation (with an Osmiroid pen and India ink), how to compose in different styles, four-part writing, counterpoint, and score analysis. By the time I got to sixth grade I had done everything a first-year student would have done at a conservatory. He gave me the musical tool kit that I use to this day every time I pick up a pencil. (And, yes, I write only with a pencil and staff paper—my favorite pencil is the legendary Palomino Blackwing. I have never used any computer notation programs.) Mays's lessons had an indelible impact on me. They taught me how to channel the creative impulses that I had been applying intuitively in the service of composition.

When I wasn't making music, I felt a little lost. I was small for my age and not particularly athletic. I liked swimming and diving, sports that didn't rely on physical heft and aggression, but couldn't really compete and wasn't interested in the rough-and-tumble team sports. I felt alone in the world in some ways that are common to young life—being a little lost is normal for kids, part of the process of taking form as a person and finding your place in the world. At the same time, I felt different in ways that I could not yet identify, much less overcome.

My parents, whose communication with each other was severely strained, were not always attuned to my needs. After kindergarten at North Avondale Elementary, I was pulled out of the public school and enrolled in a private school, Lotspeich. I enjoyed the new school and would have liked to stay there, but I was taken out after two years and put back in North Avondale. I've never understood the reasons for this upheaval. And that year, third grade, my mom got me my first pair of glasses. They had little sheriff's stars on the front corners—totally embarrassing.

I know only that I felt like it was all somehow my fault. I came home from elementary school one day and I told my mother that on the playground all the kids were touching their toes but that I couldn't do it. She said, matter-of-factly, "Your arms are too short." Though she didn't remember saying it when I asked her about it many years later, this was one of the many things that she said off the top of her head that had a huge impact on me. She may have believed the statement in the moment, but I don't think she ever took the time to question whether it was actually true.

I know now that she meant no harm, but "Your arms are too short" defined me going forward. For years after that, those words would echo within me whenever I faced a daunting challenge. *I'm just not built for this. I'm innately inadequate.* Could I learn to play that long, complex piano piece? Could I master recording technology? Could I attempt to learn computer music notation? I would think, No—*I'm too limited. My arms are too short. Why try?* Without quite acknowledging it, I began to set only the most modest goals for myself. I believed that I inherently lacked self-discipline, and outside of music I didn't have good role models so there was no one to boost me up when I needed it most.

On top of my piano lessons and the composition and theory sessions with Walter Mays, I played the violin at school for five years, from fifth grade to tenth. I've always liked stringed instruments, and I wanted to play the 'cello. But my grandfather was a violinist, so I played the violin, to honor him. I was given an old family violin and a cheap violin case. It was truly hideous—rectangular and covered in gaudy fake-alligator plastic. I was embarrassed to be seen with it. I was a scrawny, nerdy little kid with glasses to begin with, and carrying this ridiculous violin case along with my books didn't help matters. A bully shoved me down a flight of stairs at high school one day. After that, to my horror and shame, I began to develop a crush on him—even though he was a tough, straight kid who was totally unavailable to me and probably would've treated me far worse if he'd known.

I played the violin in the high school orchestra but never practiced. Just to make it sound decent was hard work, and holding it properly was uncomfortable. It didn't come naturally to me as the piano did, so I felt that I wasn't cut out for it—my heart just wasn't in it. I kept the instrument in its awful case in my locker, and pretty much only pulled it out to play in the orchestra. The only benefit of playing the instrument was, for me, the satisfaction in playing with other musicians, making my own intonation, following a conductor, and being a part of a musical whole that was larger than each individual participant. I also got a lot out of being a member of an a cappella vocal ensemble, accompanying the choir and both singing onstage and playing in the pit for the musicals. This kind of group music making started in elementary school when I joined the Cincinnati All-City Boys Choir.

As the choir was organized, two fifth- and sixth-grade boys from each public school were accepted, based on auditions, and I was one of the two from North Avondale. We met on Saturday mornings at the Washburn School downtown and sang for three hours. There was a conductor and a piano accompanist. Among the pieces in our repertoire was a buoyant little sea chanty called "Away to Rio." I remember that as the accompanist played it, I knew that *I* could play it, just from having heard it a few times. And so not long after I joined the choir, when I was ten years old, I walked up after choir practice and said to the adult accompanist, with complete confidence, "I could play that piece."

He chuckled and said, "Really? Okay—go ahead."

I had never seen the music, but didn't need to. I sat down and played the accompaniment I had heard him playing, note for note. It felt as natural as breathing. After that, I was named the assistant accompanist, and for the next several years I alternated between singing and accompanying the choir.

The age of ten was a breakthrough time for me as a young musician. It was the period when I first entered the public sphere in Cincinnati and began to be known as one of the city's home-grown musical prodigies. There was an instrumental competition for young people sponsored by the Cincinnati Music Scholarship Association, and I entered it, performing Bach, Mozart, and a composition of my own titled "A Windy Night." I won first prize. When I played my piece at the winner's concert, it looked as if I was playing it from memory—but I was making parts of it up as I went along, hoping no one would notice and that I would get away with winging it once again. It was thrilling.

The same year, I was invited to appear on a local Sunday-morning program for kids on WKRC-TV, the CBS affiliate, called *The Skipper Ryle Show*. (The station has a companion radio station that was the inspiration for the seventies sitcom *WKRP in Cincinnati*.) The titular Skipper was a jovial sea captain played by a local broadcaster with a cartoonish hound-dog face and an appropriately bushy mustache. He was a superstar on the playgrounds of Cincinnati, and my appearance on his show, playing "A Windy Night," boosted my standing at school, though I'm not sure my brother and his friends, not into classical music, were particularly impressed.

It was a blessing—or perhaps inevitable—that Hank and I would grow up with very different personalities and strengths. He was a model student and got top grades in every subject. I did well on standardized tests but excelled in the classroom only when I was interested in the subject. I didn't have the discipline to push myself to master things that bored me, such as trigonometry. Hank also had the perfect personality for team sports, such as basketball, which he played passionately even though he wasn't that tall. He tried hard, and he could get along with everybody, even the biggest asshole on the team. I was more socially awkward.

Both of us were competitive at what interested us, but not terribly so with each other. We found our own areas early in life and sped along on separate but roughly parallel paths. We both ended up making a living in the arts—me in jazz and he as a gifted writer who became the assistant managing editor of *Sports Illustrated*. I know Hank thought that I was self-absorbed when we were young—I could have been a better big brother. In my defense, all I can say is that I thought a great deal about myself because I was still an enigma to myself. Though I knew I was talented, I didn't have the framework to understand how I was able to do what I did musically, and I was attracted to boys, but had no idea of what the ramifications would be. My parents didn't relate to me as *me*. But neither did I.

Television became a large part of my life—it provided an escape from the subconscious pain of my family dynamic, and it opened my world to music beyond classical. Cincinnati was one of the last bastions of live TV, and I watched talk shows such as *The Bob Braun Show* and Ruth Lyons's *50-50 Club* and—believe it or not, a Sunday night square dance show called *Midwestern Hayride*, featuring yodeler Miss Bonnie Lou, a caller named Estil McNew, and a live band, the Midwesterners. There were only three TV channels in those days, and jazz-inflected singers such as Dean Martin, Andy Williams, and Perry Como—in addition to the must-watch *Ed Sullivan Show*—introduced me to the mainstream pop music of the sixties as well as to such artists as Ella Fitzgerald and Frank Sinatra.

Through TV I also got my first visual exposure to nonclassical piano playing. On *The Lawrence Welk Show* there was a honkytonk pianist, Jo Ann Castle, who would smile and look at the camera while she pumped her arms. I was also aware of a fourteen-year-old jazz piano prodigy, Craig Hundley, who appeared with a teenage bassist and drummer on national TV shows; he was also a child actor, and I remember seeing him in an episode of *Star Trek*—super cool. In junior high and high school, TV became more and more of a compulsion for me—instead of practicing or doing my homework, I zoned out on *Gilligan's Island, Green Acres, The Beverly Hillbillies,* and other early (and fairly terrible) sitcoms. I was also glued to *The Rifleman* and *The Wild, Wild West,* both shows featuring good-looking cowboys. I would watch *anything,* really. But my brother could sit and half-watch while doing his homework and get straight As, while my grades began to get shaky.

When I was ten, our fifth-grade class put on a production of *Peter Pan,* and I asked the music teacher if I could work up a score of background and incidental music to set up the scenes, like I'd seen in TV. I used some fellow students to create a small ensemble: piano, flute, violin, and 'cello. The teacher was impressed but wanted to change some of what I'd written. I said no on the spot. Didn't even need to think about it. It was the first moment in which I felt protective of something I'd written.

"I wrote what I wrote," I told her. They could use it as I wrote it or not use it at all. I gave them the choice. In the end, they used what I wrote. My parents didn't take me to task for this insubordination, though they certainly would have been justified.

Musically advanced but still a kid, I exhibited a combination of youthful bravura and ill-defined feelings of insecurity. As a result, for many years as an adult I have vacillated between grandiosity and low self-esteem. My parents—especially my mother, since my father, like many family men at the time, was not present in his own household—nurtured my musical development to the extent that doing so would be recognized as praiseworthy parenting by their friends. Neither of them seemed to fully understand—or know how to handle—this curious creature in their midst. I was precociously talented and somewhat of a social misfit—not your normal kid. So they reasoned that they should try to make me more "normal."

For six years I was sent to a summer camp in Maine for an eight-week program of outdoor normalization. My mom had gone to camp in Maine for eight weeks a summer when she was a child, and my father had gone, too. It was written in the Torah that you go to Maine in the summer—that's what good Reform Jewish kids do. So there I was, a nonathletic musician, at a jock boys' camp with a bunch of rich Jewish kids from the East Coast, so I could go hiking and canoeing and play tennis and do all that normal, healthy stuff. I would have fit in much better at a music or arts camp, but nobody asked my opinion. Naturally, I ended up focusing on the camp shows, playing piano and also performing. Given that it was an all-boys camp, the kids dressed in drag for the camp productions. I did this on occasion, but I don't remember getting any charge out of it—I was not a "campy" camper and did my best to fit in. In that bucolic setting I discovered a love of nature that has stayed with me all my life.

AS I entered adolescence, I experienced the awakening of sexual impulses appropriate to my age, and I found that it was boys I was attracted to. By the time I was thirteen, I knew I was gay, though nobody in my world was using that term. Summer camp was a totally male environment, with lots of nudity—naked early-morning laps in the freezing lake, mature counselors who were very attractive—and as I began to become fully sexual, I was highly stimulated. These feelings were the most exciting thing in my life, and yet I knew instinctively that I had to keep them secret, although I did have some furtive, never-again-discussed encounters with other campers.

I was alone with my feelings, and there were no healthy gay role models to look to. When I was young and beginning to come to terms with my sexual identity, it was a very different time. There was very little understanding of homosexuality in America. People were still throwing around hoary slurs such as "fairy" and "fag" with impunity. There were no gay role models for young people—no celebrities or actors or politicians who were out. There were no gay-straight alliances at high schools as there are today. I couldn't have imagined that we would come to a time when declaring oneself as gay, in most places in America, would be received as about as interesting as whether or not one wears glasses—in other words, a nonissue.

The predominant image of male homosexuality at the time was a demeaning caricature of mincing, preening, flustery queen-ishness, as embodied by Paul Lynde. On rare occasions I would overhear adults saying something serious about someone being gay, and what I heard was just as off-putting as the flouncy comic stereotype. I'd hear whispers about such-and-such being caught doing "something with boys" at the bus station or so-and-so being arrested in the park at night. Everything I picked up from the world I occupied in the 1960s associated homosexuality with clownishness, pedophilia, or criminality. It was not an easy time for a young person to be thinking, *Well, I guess I'm attracted to boys. Now what?*

MY father became more prominent in Cincinnati Jewish society and a partner in his law firm. By the mid-sixties, he was the president of our temple, Rockdale, and a leader of several organizations, including the Jewish Welfare Fund Drive and the Jewish Family Service. For us, religion was a social, not a spiritual, matter. My father had a strong sense of charitable responsibility to his community, which overlapped conveniently with his desire to get out of the house most evenings. We subscribed to the *American Israelite*, the well-known Jewish newspaper published in Cincinnati—we called it "Jews in the News"—and it seemed as if my father's name and photo were in it every week. My parents needed a home to suit their standing, and so during the summer of 1965 they bought an elegant three-story brick house with room enough to accommodate large parties; we had a housekeeper four or five days a week.

When we moved into our new home, my father's mother, Ella, offered to replace the Lester piano I had been using with a superior instrument. It was high time that I had an instrument appropriate to my skills, my seriousness, and my potential. At age eleven, I was evolving fast as a musician and needed a piano that I could continue to grow with. I also had the fantasy that if I had a better piano, I would practice more. (This search for the ultimate piano has led me to swap out and to constantly tinker with various vintage pianos over the years, though it has not led me to being more of a practicer.) I was tremendously excited to know I would be getting a new instrument, hopefully a Steinway. My friend Mark Hornstein down the street had one, and so did my grandmother. I used to love playing my grandmother's piano, with its excellent responsiveness to touch and a rich, warm tone that befitted the music I was playing. And I could hear that special sound on all of the recordings of the great pianists that I was constantly listening to.

When the new piano arrived, it was a baby-grand mahogany Baldwin. Curious why my parents had chosen to buy a mid-level instrument, I asked them, "Why didn't we get a Steinway?" It must be said here that I am truly grateful that I grew up an upper-middle-class child having all my material needs provided for and being given what I asked for, within reason, and I don't want to come off as totally spoiled. But even at that age I was old enough to know the difference between an okay instrument and a high-quality instrument. My grandmother had the means to pay for a Steinway, without a doubt, and there was plenty of room for one in the new, larger living room. Plus, the piano was *for* me; I was the one who'd be communing with this new instrument, and yet they'd never even asked me about it, never involved me in the selection process.

My mother, put off by the question, said they thought the Baldwin was perfectly fine, and I should be happy with it. Supposedly, my teacher selected it. Though Jeanne herself had a Steinway, she was on the Baldwin artists' roster, and the Baldwin factory was in Cincinnati at that time. I don't know whether my parents asked her about a Steinway. And my mom made the excuse that the local Steinway dealer was anti-Semitic. I have a hard time believing this knowing the many piano dealers I do today and their eagerness to sell pianos to whoever wants them. The message was plain: I was lucky to be getting this piano, because there were many youngsters who didn't have any grand piano to play. At any rate, my teacher said it was a fine piano, and my grandmother paid for it. If I wasn't happy to have this piano, there must be something wrong with me.

I tried my best but could never get the classic Steinway sound I wanted from that piano. It became frustrating to play, and every time I made the effort it reminded me that my parents didn't consider me worthy of the same high-quality instrument that other serious musicians around us had. I felt hurt. From that day on, for as long as I lived in that house, I got less and less enjoyment from practicing classical music.

But there was a nice stereo in the den, and I loved to sit there and listen to records. Being alone was not always easy for me, and it would remain a challenge well into adulthood. I was attracted to boys but had no validation of gay identity in my life. I knew my musical ability and my interests in mythology and Renaissance art history were unusual among youngsters my age, and at the same time I felt inadequate and had a difficult time connecting with my peers. The message that my arms were too short echoed endlessly in my mind. I was not terribly comfortable with myself. When I was alone with music, though, I didn't feel quite so alone.

When I turned eleven, I got *Horowitz at Carnegie Hall: An Historic Return*, the celebrated double LP from 1965, for my birthday. The whole album is extraordinary, but I was especially taken by Horowitz's performance of Chopin's Etude in F Major, op. 10, no. 8. I heard that, tried to play it, and thought, *Well, there's no point in my trying to do this. It's already been done. And it's not easy!*

I was familiar with the classical piano repertoire from the score analysis I had done in my music studies and also from attending the Cincinnati Symphony with my parents, who went weekly and often brought me with them. I saw most of the heavies of the 1960s in their prime: David Oistrach, the thrilling Russian violinist, and Byron Janis and Gina Bachauer, two titans of the piano. Listening from the center balcony of the Music Hall, I had a deep appreciation for classical music from firsthand exposure to it on a high level, but I had no idea how to make it my life given my lack of a work ethic.

Not that I had any other ideas. I was floundering—succeeding in highly visible ways as a young pianist but without much in the way of emotional grounding or focus. And I had no idea that being a composer—let alone an improvising pianist—was a career path that was open to me. I had memorized most of the biographies in *History's 100 Greatest Composers,* and it seemed to me that many of them had either emerged fully formed or died young and penniless—these tragic stories seemed very romantic to me. But I couldn't wrap my head around the effort involved to compose music on a high level.

At one point in my high school years, my teacher, Jeanne, played a house concert in our living room of prepared piano music by John Cage, which she had recorded for Columbia Records—with Cage himself in attendance. These pieces involved precisely placing screws, bolts, rubber bands, and other objects on or between the strings of the piano, thereby creating otherworldly, non-pianistic sounds. Cage stayed at our house for two nights, and I remember eagerly showing him my compositions. This was around the time of a big *New York Times* feature on him that had me very intrigued. At that time I was not a great listener, and I remember talking more about my music than asking about his. But he was very sweet about it, and I think he got a kick out of me. For a larger man, there was something elfin about him. I remember a distinct twinkle in his eye as he enthusiastically shared with me his non-musical interests of foraging for wild mushrooms and designing neckties. He just seemed like a kind, somewhat kooky, unpretentious older man. I had no idea of his prominent place in music history or that he was gay. I wish I could sit down with him now.

When I was in high school, of course, I listened to a lot of the music that other people my age were listening to, and the early seventies were an insanely great time for pop music. There was Janis Joplin, connecting rock to Bessie Smith and the ballsy blues queens of the early twentieth century. There was Crosby, Stills and Nash, with their lush harmonies and songs about the natural world. I loved Aretha Franklin, Motown, the Beatles, James Taylor, and Joni Mitchell. Because their music was keyboard-based I listened to Traffic and Emerson, Lake and Palmer. I liked Elton John for the same reason—he was a piano player, and I tried to ignore the trite gibberish that his lyricist, Bernie Taupin, wrote for him. As my hippie friends and I rode around stoned in one of our parents' cars, the AM radio poured out the Carpenters, the "Philadelphia sound" of the Stylistics, and the disco predecessor Isaac Hayes's "Theme from *Shaft*." I got my own stereo at fourteen and two years later, when I was able to drive, went to the record stores often after school, spending all my allowance on albums, when I wasn't spending it on weed.

As a Christmas gift around that time, I received *The New York Times Great Songs of the Sixties*, an anthology of sheet music with piano arrangements by Milton Okun. Since it was from the *Times*,

I assumed that these songs were indeed "the best," and I eagerly learned many of them. As I remember, the collection included multiple songs by Burt Bacharach, some European art-house movie themes, and "By the Time I Get to Phoenix" as sung by Glen Campbell. I played the notes as written but also began to change the chords based on what I was hearing and using the music theory that I acquired from Walter Mays. I began to make my own money playing background music at parties given by my friends' parents out in the suburbs.

While most boys were busy dating or chasing girls, I just hung out with my straight guy friends, suppressing many aspects of my personality, trying to fit in. Meanwhile, I found kindred spirits in the social misfits who were in the stage crew from the school productions. By ninth grade, I was especially tight with my buddy Jim, a bright-eyed kid who was good-looking, naturally athletic, and super-cool. Even at a young age, he had an acute awareness of his sex appeal. We would get stoned and listen to rock records, or hang around Calhoun Street, near the university, where the hippie culture flourished, and chow down at Skyline Chili—one of Cincinnati's two great contributions to our national cuisine, the other being Graeter's ice cream. I was smitten with Jim, though of course he was straight. We fooled around once when we were high on acid. We didn't talk about it until many years later—and when we did, he said he didn't know at that time whether to enjoy it or beat the crap out of me. I not only had a crush on him, I wanted to *be* him—he was that self-assured.

Then, during the last couple of years of high school, I grew closer and closer to my friend Ron, who was into the same music I was into. While the two of us were on an eight-week backpacking trip in

Western Europe the summer after high school, I was barely able to contain my attraction to him. But Ron was straight, too. Our connection was real emotionally, but it went only one way physically.

There was sweetness in this adolescent budding of ardor and eros—though looking back, I have come to know these as romantic obsessions. Both Jim and Ron were nice guys, but the relationships were intrinsically imbalanced in a way that only fed my insecurity about being gay. I had to erase a large part of myself when I was around them to try to act as cool as they were. After a while I didn't enjoy getting stoned all that much, but I kept getting high, as I didn't want to miss out on anything or seem weak. My attraction to both Jim and Ron was strong, but the lack of reciprocity and inability to talk to anyone about it left me feeling small.

Despite my social awkwardness, I was fairly popular and was invited to lots of parties. More often than not, I would end up at the piano, playing Elton John and James Taylor songs for the other kids. I began to see music as my social currency.

Starting in ninth grade, I vented my multiple frustrations by acting out, indulging in increasingly reckless behavior. Like most of the kids I knew, I smoked a lot of pot, trying to be "in," and then I started to smoke more and more and more. I dropped acid and took speed. I smoked more pot. I skipped classes. I got high in school. I shoplifted and got arrested. I dropped Quaaludes. I drove while stoned. My grades plummeted. I was subconsciously begging for attention, hoping my parents would *see* me.

Toward the end of high school, I began to discover jazz. Having been demoted from studying with Jeanne because I wasn't "serious" enough, in ninth grade I had started studying with Bill Cammarota, one of her graduate students. He was a hip young guy and an accomplished classical player who showed me a few jazz chords and some simple tunes such as Herbie Hancock's "Maiden Voyage." And he was the first person who mentioned the name Bill Evans to me. I joined the high school jazz ensemble, a pretty primitive group that played some forgettable funk charts and songs by the rock group Chicago, which was thought of as *jazzy* because it had a horn section. I had only a couple of jazz albums then: Dave Brubeck's wildly popular *Time Out* and Ramsey Lewis's funky *Wade in the Water*.

In 1972 I bought *Miles Smiles*, the seminal album of Miles Davis's second great quintet, with Herbie Hancock, Wayne Shorter, Ron Carter, and Tony Williams, with that bright orange, almost pop art cover. I also had *Cannonball & Coltrane*, which featured the Miles Davis sextet of 1959, without Miles—Cannonball Adderley and John Coltrane on saxophones, with Wynton Kelly, Paul Chambers, and Jimmy Cobb as the backing trio. It had an abstract cover featuring black orbs in an array like billiard balls against a gold background. I bought both records for twenty-five cents apiece at a yard sale, because I liked the covers, without knowing that much about the musicians or the music. Alone in my room, I put *Miles Smiles* on the turntable and listened to it stoned. I found it totally enigmatic. The players were communicating with one another in what seemed to me like a musical code. Herbie Hancock hardly uses his left hand and doesn't exactly *accompany* the soloists. To this day, I'm not sure what they're doing on parts of that album, but I found myself compelled by it. The deeply felt yet highly intellectual music on that record confirmed that there were more levels to this art form than I understood. It came out of my speakers like a miraculous new language I wanted to learn.

DIMINUENDO AND CRESCENDO

When it came time to plan for college, everyone assumed I would apply to the big music conservatories. I went to the guidance counselor's office at Walnut Hills, and as I looked over the brochures for Juilliard and Oberlin and Eastman, the sound of Horowitz at Carnegie Hall played in my head. I thought to myself, *Why am I doing this?*

I didn't want to be another Vladimir Horowitz. Horowitz had been doing that job rather well. I wanted to be Fred Hersch—I knew that much. I just didn't know who Fred Hersch was, as a musician or a man.

Besides, I wasn't really prepared to apply to the major conservatories. I had a Beethoven sonata in my repertoire and could play some Bach, but I had never buckled down to memorize a big Chopin *ballade* or *scherzo*. It's not just that I didn't have the discipline; I didn't have the interest. I felt guilty about it at the time, because there were well-established, long-standing expectations for musicians who could play as well as I could at my age. You were supposed to choose a couple of impressive audition pieces and practice them for months until you had them down cold, so you could spend the rest of your life doing the same thing, over and over, as a classical concert pianist. I didn't want to do that. At the same time, I didn't know what I wanted to do instead. So I felt ashamed and lazy, like I was chickening out, and there was nobody giving me the guidance that might have made me feel better about myself.

I decided to go for a liberal arts education. Even though my grades were spotty, I did well enough on the SATs, and I was a National Merit Scholarship semifinalist. I visited Grinnell College in Iowa with my friend Ron and got accepted there. It helped that Ron was going to attend as well. I thought, *No better place to figure out what I want to do than in Iowa in the middle of the winter—nothing to distract me.* Although I didn't know it at the time, Grinnell has a small but notable jazz legacy. Herbie Hancock had attended the school briefly, as an engineering student, and Gary Giddins, the jazz critic and biographer, had graduated the spring before I arrived.

Living away from home for the first time since my summers at jock camp in Maine—other than a summer semester at Andover, the prep school in Massachusetts, where I studied film and art history—I felt a tinge of the nervous anticipation that's surely typical of college freshmen. I wondered if I would meet many other guys like me, attracted to men. I was hopeful but tentative, uncertain of what to expect and how to handle whatever I would find. And soon after my arrival at Grinnell I saw my first example of a gay male couple, out and proud, students strolling around the campus hand in hand. Blown away by their boldness, I was too awed by their self-confidence to speak with either of them.

Not long after I settled into my dorm, I met an upperclassman, a hot-looking athlete I'll call Paul. To my disbelief, I found out that he was having sex with another guy on my floor. Upon close inspection of his room, I noticed that he had an extensive collection of cute stuffed animals and figurines—something that would make my gaydar go off today. Over time, I would come to feel my attraction in the secret, unspoken language of gay men conditioned to communicate in code. You meet another man, and your eyes lock for a nanosecond longer than they would with someone else; the message is clear.

I would often go to Paul's room to "study," though he was older and we were not taking any of the same courses. Basically I just wanted to moon around him, as I had in high school with my friend Jim. One night he grabbed me, beginning what I was excitedly hoping would become the first fully mutual, grown-up sexual experience of my life. Instead, he quickly and firmly took command. He forced me to lie on my belly, and he raped me from behind. No explanation and no tenderness.

I had never before thought about anal sex and, believe it or not, had no idea that it was conventional sexual practice for gay partners—and, for that matter, many straight partners as well. I certainly didn't consent to what Paul did to me. He did it *to* me, not *with* me. I stuffed away this memory until the term "date rape" came into the lexicon many years later.

I left his room quaking but never confronted him. Though we

lived in the same dorm, I never talked to him again, and he ignored me, making me feel completely defective. Like many victims of campus rape, straight and gay, I told no one what had
happened. I was ashamed and confused. I didn't know how to
process what had taken place. Was that supposed to be *okay*? Was
I wrong to think it was wrong? Was it my own fault for letting it
happen? I felt powerless and ignorant, and hated myself for feeling
that way, nearly as much as I hated Paul. For many years afterward, when I was rejected by a man I would always assume that
there was something wrong with me.

IT was at Grinnell that my eyes began to open to jazz in a more
significant way. The school had a charismatic professor, Cecil
Lytle, an imposing African American man who taught classical
piano and could play credible jazz as well. He had won first prize
in the International Liszt Competition and recorded ragtime for
Nonesuch. In addition to our piano lessons, he introduced me
to Amiri Baraka's book *Black Music*, a groundbreaking treatise
on African American aesthetics that had been published a few
years earlier. I haunted the college record store for the music
Baraka had written about—Coltrane, Ellington, Pharoah Sanders, Mingus—and began to understand jazz as a lineage, how
it had synthesized the blues, Creole music, ragtime, and other
genres. I read books on jazz with the same fervor that I had read
History's 100 Greatest Composers and found everything about it
fascinating.

Meanwhile, I was playing in a chamber music trio at Grinnell—
piano, violin, and 'cello—and that, in a strange way, primed me to

want to play jazz. Chamber music is a communal music, played *with* other people. And jazz, I was discovering, was a language that, once you learned it, enabled you to tell spontaneous musical stories with other musicians in real time. It made me realize what had been missing in my musical life: the satisfaction of making music in a cooperative way with musical equals. Playing classical piano is usually a solitary thing, with lots of hours spent alone at the keyboard, torturing oneself. The atmosphere with the trio was light but stimulating. We debated how to interpret the pieces. Playing together was *fun.* I loved it.

The so-called energy crisis hit in late 1973, and that winter, Grinnell panicked over the cost of heating the buildings and closed the school, extending the winter break for six weeks. I went home to Cincinnati, and it was there that I had my jazz epiphany. I would go back to Grinnell only once—to accompany the musical *Once Upon a Mattress,* which I had committed to, and to pack up my things.

It happened on a night in December 1973. I knew of a folkie club near the university called the Family Owl and went in expecting to catch some bluegrass music in the basement. But at the club entrance I noticed a sign that said LIVE JAZZ UPSTAIRS and made a spur-of-the-moment decision. Instead of heading down, I climbed the stairs to the second floor, where a local saxophone quartet was playing. I sat at a table near the front, ordered a beer— though I was eighteen, under the legal drinking age in Ohio at the time—and listened. I was mesmerized.

The leader was a tenor saxophonist named Jimmy McGary, a fiery little man in his forties with a reddish-gray beard and sparkly eyes. He was a strong player with a full tone and a hard-swinging feel. As I learned later, he was revered by all of the local jazz musicians in Cincinnati, and he had earned that admiration.

The bassist was a wiry guy of indeterminate age named Bud Hunt—a solid player but not quite on McGary's level. The drummer was a hulking, mad-looking bear of a man named Grover Mooney. He played in the mode I would later associate with Elvin Jones, with a broad downbeat and a kind of rolling approach to jazz timekeeping. The pianist was playing a Fender Rhodes electric piano.

I listened as they played a set of some standards, some of which I knew, and some jazz tunes. There was no sheet music on the stage, and they seemed to be creating the music out of thin air. Nervously, on the break at the end of the set, I worked up my courage, went up to McGary, and asked if I could sit in. He said, "Know any tunes?"

I said, "I think I can play 'Autumn Leaves.'" McGary nodded, and when it was time to start the second set he waved me on. Though I had been in the jazz band in high school, playing with a professional rhythm section is a very different thing, as I would discover. I took a seat at the Rhodes, trying to look casual about it, and played "Autumn Leaves." Actually, I overplayed it and messed up the form of the tune without knowing it. After the number, my adrenaline rushing, I went to the bar and listened to the rest of the set. There, a local bass player kindly introduced himself to me as "Alex Cirin—but you can call me 'the Dancing Bear.'" That was the coolest thing I had ever heard.

When it was over, McGary came up to me at the bar and said, "Hey, come with me, kid." He brought me to a small musicians' break room in the back of the club. There was a table in the corner that held a portable record player and a few LPs stacked next to it. Jimmy lit a joint and passed it over to me—this I took as a good omen. While I was taking my hit, he pulled an album out of a sleeve and put it on the turntable. "Now listen to this," he said. "Don't talk—just listen."

The LP was *Ellington at Newport*, the live recording of the performance by Duke Ellington and His Orchestra at the 1956 Newport Jazz Festival. That concert—and the subsequently released recording—was such a sensation in its day that *Time* magazine made it a cover story. Jimmy picked up the tone arm and dropped the needle on the second track of the second side: "Diminuendo and Crescendo in Blue," the number that made the performance a sensation, with twenty-six improvised blues choruses by the tenor saxophonist Paul Gonsalves. I sat and watched the record spin and listened intently. The energy was extraordinary, building with every chorus Gonsalves played. You could feel Ellington and the rest of the band egging him on, and you could hear the crowd going wild. People were hooting and hollering like it was a rock concert. It was absolute hysteria. But beneath it all you could hear the fabric holding it all together, the shared sense of swing that brought the musicians together—the basic rhythm of jazz. At the end, Jimmy picked up the needle and looked me in the eye. "That's *time*," he said.

"Now, you have to have *time*. And you have to know some tunes. So, as soon as you've done some listening and you've worked on your time and you know some tunes, you can come back and play."

Excited, later that week, I went to Mole's Record Exchange, a cluttered store near the campus of the University of Cincinnati that sold used albums for a buck or two. With nothing to guide me except my intuition, I rifled through the jazz bins, working my way from A to Z, and bought every album that had a version of "Autumn Leaves" on it: records by Miles Davis, Ahmad Jamal, Bill Evans, Oscar Peterson, Erroll Garner, Stan Getz, Chet Baker, Cannonball Adderley—thirteen in all. I brought the pile home and played each version of the tune, skipping all the other tracks. Then I played them all again, one by one. It was a revelation. Some were subtle, some virtuosic, some brisk, some meditative. They all had a mastery of *time*. I realized that each version was unique, and all of them were great.

I thought about my reluctance to devote myself to the classical repertory after hearing Horowitz play canonical pieces so spectacularly, and it struck me: In jazz it's individuality, not adherence to a standardized conception of excellence, that matters most. With this music, musicians are completely free to be themselves within the tune. Difference matters—in fact, it's an asset, rather than a liability. There is no describing how exhilarating this epiphany was for me, as a person who always felt different from other people. In jazz, difference is the key element that makes the artistry possible.

Listening to all those versions of "Autumn Leaves," I not only recognized the value of individual expression in jazz, I also saw that the music has a standard framework—melodic and harmonic structures that facilitate collaboration. All the recordings I played had a few things in common. They all had formal integrity, harmonic sophistication, and, at their heart, a deep pulse. And they were *all* wonderful on their own terms—I couldn't say that one of them was "the best." I could feel in my bones what Jimmy McGary meant when he talked about *time*.

Fueled by the thrill of discovery, I set out to learn all I could about jazz from the musicians on the scene in Cincinnati. To appease my parents, who might not have approved of this pedagogical strategy, I enrolled in the University of Cincinnati College-Conservatory of Music as a classical piano major. But I thought of that as an extracurricular activity. The education I was after would take place in and around the jazz clubs, playing and hanging with the older musicians. For the first time in my life, I was involved in music that my parents knew very little about. It was *mine*.

Setting up my new life—in Cincinnati but away from my parents—I moved into a clapboard house in the conservatory neighborhood with four other guys, all musicians studying at the school. I didn't spend much time with them. I was focused on working my way into jazz. I made myself a fixture in the clubs, got to know the musicians, and soaked everything up.

In the 1970s the jazz scene in Cincinnati was fringy and tenuous, kept alive by people who played and supported the music for the love of it. No one was making much money being a jazz musician. Over the years since then, as I got to know musicians from all over the country, I learned that this was the norm in most American midsize cities at the time. Jazz, in the era of Top 40 stars such as Barry Manilow and the Eagles, was far from the center of American popular culture. Jazz education had not yet become a fixture in music schools, so there wasn't an audience of young musicians—and jazz musicians couldn't get daytime teaching jobs to support their evening jazz habit. In fact, jazz had not had much in the way of mainstream visibility since West Coast "cool jazz" was popular, a generation before. Musicians were not playing jazz for glory and riches in the 1970s. They were playing jazz for the sake of playing jazz.

There were rarely big jazz concerts in Cincinnati then. But there were jazz-circuit clubs in Cincinnati and nearby Dayton that regularly brought in many of the living legends. I heard the elegant pianism of Teddy Wilson and Bill Evans; the hard-hitting post-bop of drummer Art Blakey and the Jazz Messengers; the organ trios of Shirley Scott and Richard "Groove" Holmes, and the more spiritual jazz of saxophonist Pharoah Sanders.

Sometimes these shows took me to the outer reaches of jazz, to the most distant orbit. The first time I went to Gilly's in Dayton, I sat at the front table with my friend Eric listening to Sun Ra and his Intergalactic Arkestra. There must have been nine or ten musicians onstage, and I use the term "musician" loosely, as many of them seemed stoned beyond words and were mostly banging on things and making deliciously bizarre sounds. The great tenor saxophonist John Gilmore was in the band, and he played at a level surpassing everybody but Ra himself. There were slide projections behind the band, and two nubile dancers who for the most part slithered around and occasionally wandered through the audience. Sun Ra was seated at a Farfisa combo organ, dressed in a sequined kaftan and wearing an oversized headpiece with glittery stars affixed to it. At one point during his iconic number "Space Is the Place," Ra got up from the organ and came to our table. Standing over us, he intoned repeatedly, "Saturn is the planet of discipline." Eric and I were both high on weed, and even had we not been, the music was trippy enough to qualify as psychedelic. We felt transported to another dimension.

Though I was under the legal drinking age, the proprietors of these clubs were happy to have another warm body listening to the music and buying a beer or two. I went as often as I could. One night I introduced myself to pianist McCoy Tyner (who had been a member of the groundbreaking John Coltrane Quartet) at the Viking Lounge and discovered that we were both vegetarians, which was not as common then as it is today. I boldly asked him to lunch the following day, and to my surprise he said yes. He was good company and put me right at ease, so much so that when we'd finished lunch I invited him over to my rather funky student digs, where I had a DeKalb baby grand piano. I played a few tunes for him. Tyner was in his late thirties by then, and even though I was just nineteen, I'd like to think he saw something in me as a player. We sat and talked, and I peppered him with obvious questions. "What was it like playing with Coltrane?" "Can you give me some insight into how you approach jazz piano harmony?" He was very kind and patient and did his best to answer my questions, but he wasn't prepared to give me an on-the-spot piano lesson. Still, spending time with one of my idols, eye-to-eye, gave me a sense that what he had accomplished might be possible for me. And it made me see him, a major jazz artist, as just a really nice guy who happened to do what I did—but a whole hell of a lot better.

Cincinnati local jazz was an underground phenomenon and not particularly remunerative. Gigs in clubs paid $40 a night, if that. More often than not, the band would split the proceeds from the door—say, a $5 cover charge multiplied by the twenty people who showed up, divided by the four people in the group: $25 per person for playing three sets. The only way to make a reasonable living was to do studio session work or land a hotel job, tinkling cocktail piano

in the restaurant or the lounge, along with playing parties and weddings on the weekends. There were jazz musicians in Cincinnati
who cobbled together a livelihood this way. I was very impressed
by them.

The bassist Bud Hunt, I learned, had a side business selling
marijuana. If you were looking for pot, you'd go to Bud Hunt. His
name sounds like a gag from a Cheech and Chong movie, but this
is the truth. The hitch was that you could buy from Bud only if he
accepted you as a musician—you had to be able to *play*. When I
copped my first bag from Bud after a few months playing around
town, I knew I had arrived as a jazz musician in Cincinnati.

Bud was bony and earthy-looking, with a prematurely wiz-
ened face like Chet Baker in his later years. He may have been in
his thirties, or he may have been in his fifties. He had a farm in
Evansville, Indiana, and reminded me of the dust bowl sharecrop-
pers that Walker Evans photographed for the Farm Security Administration. He grew his pot on that farm, and it was named for
the location. Nobody ever referred to it as marijuana or reefer or
pot. It was always Evansville—as in, "Want a hit of Evansville?" or
"I could go for some Evansville tonight." It was bright green and
had a character unlike any other pot I have ever smoked. It never
made you feel wigged out or paranoid. It made you want to *play*. I
have always found pot to be a terrible performance drug, with the
singular exception of Evansville. You had to be able to play to get
it, and it rewarded you by making you want to play more.

The musicians I got to know and play with in Cincinnati were all
kind to me, even if their kindness took the form of jazz-world tough
love. I was learning on my own as I went along. I picked up one of
those one-thousand-song fake books with the melodies and lame

chord changes that wedding bands use. I watched up close and listened to the other musicians, played records constantly, and started to come up with chord substitutions based on hearing other musicians do it and by using the foundations in harmony I had learned from Walter Mays. Some of the musicians would give me pointers now and then, and Jimmy McGary, by being a non-teacher, was the best teacher of all. We'd start to play some tune I'd never heard before. I'd make my way through the opening melody—the "head"—and I'd be floundering with the harmony. Jimmy would walk over to me and say, "Now, figure it out. You're a jazz musician. Use your ears." Then he would walk off the bandstand.

Around Cincinnati at that time there were two camps of jazz pianists. One was led by a hard-swinging pianist named Frank Vincent. Vincent and his crowd were the Oscar Peterson worshippers. Oscar was a direct musical descendant of the blind Toledo-born pianist Art Tatum—even Horowitz was awed by Tatum's virtuosity, his musical imagination, and his round, pearly sound. I understood why these guys bowed before Peterson—his technique was indisputably impressive, and he was a dazzling player, if a bit stiff. But even then, when my ears were still developing, I wasn't much impressed by impressiveness. I was more drawn to playing that stirred a feeling or evoked a mood or had a more creative edge, some danger to it. I respected Oscar Peterson but wasn't the least bit interested in learning to play like him.

The other camp was clustered around the highly eccentric pianist Ed Moss. Moss and his followers were the avant-garde. Moss owned two businesses, a coffeehouse called the Golden Triangle and a jazz club named Emanon, after the Dizzy Gillespie tune—"no name" spelled backward. *So conceptual.* Moss was a self-absorbed alpha-male cult-leader type. A largish man with a larger ego, he sported a beard and a ponytail and a huge collection of hats (think Thelonious Monk), drove an early-sixties Cadillac hearse, and always wore vintage suits from the forties. All the men who worked for him also had beards and ponytails and drove old Cadillacs. He had a harem of women who worked at his establishments whom we called the Mossettes, many of whom bore his children out of wedlock. Late at night, when the gigs were over, the staff and the musicians would hang around the Golden Triangle, sipping Turkish coffee or cognac and smoking high-quality hashish till dawn. There would be fantastic music playing on the stereo, and that's where I first tuned in to Ahmad Jamal and Erroll Garner and got deeply into Monk. Listening to that music, stoned on hash, in this communal way allowed me to hear not only the notes being played but the space *around* the notes. "The scene" was seriously kooky and kookily serious. I much preferred it to the Frank Vincent–Oscar Peterson contingent, despite my discomfort with Moss himself. I was one of the few people who would call him on his pseudo-intellectual bullshit or his musical opinions. I'd say, "Ed, uh . . . I don't think you're right," and everybody would gasp.

I played anywhere I could get hired, with anybody half-decent. At one point I got a months-long booking in a trio backing a jazz and blues singer, James "Popeye" Maupin, in a place called Robert's Neoteric Lounge. The walls were painted black and decorated with Day-Glo posters. The owner was a double for Isaac Hayes, and Popeye could have been his larger and even wilder-looking brother. He was enormous and bald and had a goatee; occasionally he performed in a gold lamé cape. He got the name Popeye because he had a glass eye he could pop out for dramatic effect. He wasn't a great singer technically, but he was a marvelous entertainer and could really swing. I was playing with him and having a good time at it when my parents came one night to watch. They were there with another couple after a night at the symphony, all dressed up. Robert's Neoteric Lounge was not their scene, though they may have thought themselves a bit hip for showing up there. I loved being in a world they knew very little about. I couldn't imagine what they thought, and I didn't ask them. They could see that I had talent as a jazz pianist, and it was clear that I was having fun, so they left me alone about it.

In 1974 I took my first gig on the road—with the South of the Border Revue, a two-bit Mexican family circus. There was a dog act (the featured performers sometimes peed on the stage), jugglers, a contortionist. The musical ensemble consisted of trumpet, drums, and me on Fender Rhodes. We wore sombreros and ponchos and made $75 cash per night—each—playing seedy arenas and run-down theaters in such Ohio glamor spots as Youngstown, Akron, and Lima. They had no book of music for the band, and after "Guantanamera," "The Mexican Hat Dance," and "Tico Tico," we ran out of appropriate material. So we would just make up long "Latin-sounding" vamps and hope for the best.

One night the three of us in the band were near Cleveland on a rare evening off. I had heard that there was a club there called the Smiling Dog. Miraculously we found it, pulled up in front, and read the marquee: OPENING TONIGHT: MILES DAVIS. We were stunned. We got high in the car, walked right in—the club wasn't two-thirds full—and sat two tables from Miles for two sets. His band at that time had the same personnel as his extraordinary album *Get Up with It,* which he dedicated to Duke Ellington right after his death in 1973—including drummer Al Foster, percussionist James Mtume, saxophonist Sonny Fortune, and guitarist Pete Cosey. I guess it was fated that I took that circus gig— this experience was the real payoff. Miles was in his high-fashion period, rail thin with an expensive scarf, flared slacks, knockout shoes, and of course his huge square tinted glasses. The music was hypnotic, not as much about people taking solos as it was about creating a trippy fabric of sound. Miles prowled back and forth in front of the band, at times weaving in on trumpet but mostly letting the musicians use their imagination. He'd let things percolate and then pick just the right moment to play a phrase or two to move things forward. When he did play it was so compelling that everything else kind of melted away. This was the only time I heard Miles in person, and experiencing his powerful, mysterious presence at close range was a watershed moment for me.

My life was completely centered on jazz—both the music and getting high, which at the time to me seemed of a piece. I hung out on the scene, listened to records all night, and slept during the day. I was feeling my way on my own without guidance any more specific than Jimmy McGary telling me, "Now, figure it out." I learned by experimenting, fucking up, and making my mistakes, whether I was rushing the time or turning the beat around, or if I didn't know the harmony or all the substitute chords that were possible in a progression. And I learned by listening, to other musicians both live and on records. It was then that I developed the habits of an autodidact. It never occurred to me to ask one of the older jazz pianists around town for lessons; I don't know if any of them even taught young pianists. Though I might have saved myself a few steps by asking questions, in the end I think just following my instincts during these developmental years may have helped me evolve my own style.

One of the beautiful paradoxes of jazz as an art form is that it is spontaneous music, invented on the spot every time it's played, and also a music with canonical works—masterpieces of improvisation documented on records and not on printed music. The vast history of this improvised music is accessible for appreciation and study on recordings. I didn't transcribe other pianists' solos note for note—common practice for budding jazz musicians now—but I would sit down, play a tune I associated with them, and try to channel them as I played. I hoped to get inside their musical minds by inexact imitation.

In Cincinnati I started collecting Duke Ellington records, and I made an important discovery. I realized that Ellington always got the same piano sound, whether the music was recorded in the forties, the fifties, or the sixties. One record could be solo piano and the other a full orchestra, one could be mono and the other stereo, and Ellington's playing always had a consistent sound. It was stunning to me that a musician could have a sound not dependent on the specific piano or the style of recording. His sound was round, clear; it seemed chiseled out from everything going on around it. This got me considering sound in a deeper way. From Duke, I started thinking about what it was that made Thelonious Monk's sound and Ahmad Jamal's sound and Herbie Hancock's sound and Bill Evans's sound. I was a long way from finding a sound of my own, but I began to see it as a possibility.

Records had a profound effect on my early development. I can still recall vividly the moment when I decided to fully commit myself to being a jazz musician. I was seriously stoned and listening to records with some older musician friends, and I heard two albums on the same night. One was Miles Davis's *In Person Friday Night at the Blackhawk*, the great live quintet set from 1961 with Wynton Kelly on piano. The way Wynton accompanies Miles is wondrous. He knows just where to place the chords behind Miles to complement his solo and help the music groove, and he swings with a truly joyous time feel. The other was *Mingus Mingus Mingus Mingus Mingus*, Charles Mingus's 1964 album of soulful modernist compositions for an ensemble of eleven pieces—it sounded to me like Ellington in a fever dream. I thought, *This shit is just too cool. This is all I want to do for the rest of my life. I want to swing like Wynton Kelly and write like Charles Mingus.*

I took the work I could get, playing as much jazz with good musicians as possible but also doing gigs of lesser seriousness for the sake of the work, because that's what the jazz musicians I knew had to do. It was during the summer of my second year back in Cincinnati that I took that gig in the band at Kings Island amusement park and found myself sitting alone between the two trailers, with the jazzmen on one side of me and the gay boys on the other.

Like all practitioners in the apprenticeship stage of their art, I was absorbing the influences of my tutors and the masters they had learned from. My conception of what I could do in the future was framed by what others were doing around me and what their predecessors had done. I wanted to be like Wynton Kelly and like Charles Mingus but had only the vaguest conception of how to be Fred Hersch.

CHAPTER 3

BOSTON

When I discovered jazz in Cincinnati, I saw a world of possibilities—a place where I could escape the rigidity of classical music as I came to know it from my piano lessons and evenings at the symphony with my parents. Before long, though, I began to see more limits than possibilities.

I mean no slight to Cincinnati or the musicians I got to know there. I made good friends in the local jazz scene—the great guitarist Cal Collins, the pianist Steve Schmidt, and others. I came to care dearly for them and respect them very much. I just started to feel like I couldn't do what I wanted to do and be what I wanted to be if I stayed in Cincinnati. At every gig, the leader would just call out whatever commonly known tunes he felt like playing at the moment—no one seemed interested in expanding their repertoire beyond the standards and basic jazz tunes, and nobody rehearsed a band or played original music. The audience seemed content with this casual approach to a set. So I had to get out before I ended up settling comfortably at a hotel lounge or in the house band for *The Nick Clooney Show.*

One of the pianists I was fascinated with, along with Wynton Kelly and Ahmad Jamal, was Jaki Byard. Jaki was well known for his ability to internalize and express every historical style of jazz piano imaginable in a way that was completely his own, sometimes combining multiple styles in one solo. He had played sophisticated "composer's piano" with Charles Mingus's ensembles, made his own albums, and was an electric—and eclectic—virtuoso. I was startled to learn that he was teaching in a new program in jazz studies at the New England Conservatory in Boston. *Jazz studies? What?!* I thought I was doing jazz studies the only way it could be done, buying records and playing the music following the advice of Jimmy McGary: "Figure it out—you're a jazz musician."

I decided to investigate the program Byard was teaching in. I wrote a letter of inquiry to the conservatory and got a brochure in the mail. The program it described was unique in the world: an accredited conservatory degree in jazz taught by working masters of the music at an elite conservatory—in a major metropolitan center over seven hundred miles away from Cincinnati, at that. It was one of only a handful of music schools in the country that acknowledged jazz as a valid musical art form at that time.

Gunther Schuller, the conductor, composer, and French-horn player who straddled the spheres of classical music and jazz, had assumed the presidency of the New England Conservatory in 1967, and he instituted a jazz studies program two years later, with a faculty including Byard, jazz composer George Russell, and the brilliant and underappreciated improvising pianist Ran Blake. Schuller had played horn on Miles Davis's *Birth of the Cool* album, the famous manifesto of postwar musical hybridization and intellectualism, recorded in 1949 and 1950. Along with the arranger Gil Evans (who had done some of the writing on *Birth of the Cool*) and the pianist John Lewis (with the Modern Jazz Quartet), Schuller emerged in the fifties as one of the leaders of the third-stream movement, entwining elements of both jazz and Western classical music. For example, Schuller's "Transformation," perhaps the first third-stream piece, starts as a twelve-tone row, morphs into a twelve-bar blues, then ends back at the twelve-tone row. The Charles Mingus album that had such an impact on me, *Mingus Mingus Mingus Mingus Mingus*, with its dense compositions by Mingus and orchestrations for large ensemble by Bob Hammer, could have been thought of as third-stream music, and though I've never been a big fan of the term or the intellectual pretensions associated with it, I relished the way composers and arrangers such as Mingus and Evans were expanding the jazz palette without sacrificing human feeling.

When Schuller launched the program at NEC, it was called Afro-American Music, in the proudly postcolonial lingo of the day. Its implicit mission was to elevate the status of jazz in the culture by welcoming it into the academy alongside music in the white European tradition. In that conservatory brochure, published in 1975, Schuller proclaimed: "Students are instructed in the art of jazz with the rigor associated with classical training." I appreciated that the school was treating jazz as an art form, and I wasn't too frightened by the threat of rigor in the training. I knew my parents would support my going to a prestigious conservatory, even if the curriculum was in jazz.

In April 1975 I set up a road trip to Boston with Grover Mooney, the crazed drummer from the Family Owl, and his girlfriend, Roxy. Trading off the driving in his beat-up 1964 Oldsmobile Cutlass, we did the ride in one very long stretch. The night I arrived I went out to catch an emerging young guitarist at a small club in Central Square: Pat Metheny. The next day I found the main building of the conservatory, Jordan Hall—a grand structure that housed the classrooms, faculty offices, and rehearsal spaces as well as an exquisitely ornate, acoustically superb concert hall—and I wandered around, hunting for Jaki Byard. I only knew him from record covers, and when I found him, in a hallway on the floor that held the piano teaching studios, I was surprised to see not the clean-cut figure I had expected but a heavyset man with a wild mass of soft, gray-and-black hair. (He was part Cherokee, a fact that I didn't know at the time but that became apparent as we spent time together.)

"M-Mr. Byard," I stammered, "I drove here all the way from Cincinnati, I love your playing, and I really want to come to school here and study with you, and . . ."

"All right," he said, looking me over. "I think I have fifteen minutes." He took me into a nearby room with two pianos. I sat and played two or three tunes—I don't recall what they were, I was so nervous—and when I was finished he said, "Okay, you're in."

And that was basically it. The school's catalog may have promised the rigor of classical training, but the admissions process was pure jazz, as loose as a club date.

I enrolled in the fall of 1975 as a sophomore in the four-year bachelor of music program with a major in Afro-American studies. I had saved a little money playing gigs in Cincinnati, but my family came through with support; for all our squabbles over the years, they could see I had found my passion and was following it in a serious way, by getting a conservatory degree. My grandmother Ella covered the tuition, and my father helped me secure an apartment, covering my rent until I could earn my own money in Boston. The curriculum included undergraduate courses in the liberal arts, which I certainly benefited from—I took a poetry class and delved into Walt Whitman and Wallace Stevens for the first time. But in terms of my musical education, I felt as if I was in graduate school. I had done my undergrad work at the Emanon and at Robert's Neoteric Lounge in Cincinnati.

Jaki Byard was in his fifties and still active as a player, though owing to a fondness for alcohol and a stubborn personality his career was never what it could have been. He was a living encyclopedia of jazz piano, skilled in every style from ragtime to stride to swing to hard bop. He could play like Fats Waller or Bud Powell and demonstrate the mechanics of each technique. He had a profound and detailed understanding of why each pianist sounded the way he did—to this day, I'm not sure where he got such vast knowledge. For that ability alone, he was ideally suited to teaching. He was also funny as hell and great company. He taught from the deep well of experience he had accumulated over many years as a professional musician—he had a lot to teach. But he was somewhat unorganized and would sometimes show up late for a lesson or come clutching a bottle of cheap wine, or not show up at all. As an educator, he didn't do much to refute the trope of the jazzman as brilliantly creative but unreliable.

I learned a lot from Jaki simply being in his presence. As a musician and as a person, his spirit was fearless—he didn't let stylistic constrictions get in his way of playing whatever he felt—and he was not the least bit ostentatious. He had an unmanicured view of jazz and life in general. At NEC he counterbalanced Gunther Schuller.

NEC wasn't a jazz studies "program"—we didn't even have the benefit of the small, faculty-led student ensembles that are at the core of modern jazz education today. Jazz was simply one of many departments in the school. Other than George Russell's *Lydian Chromatic Concept of Tonal Organization*—an early attempt to make theoretical sense of what jazz players hear naturally—and a big-band arranging class, we took the same courses the classical students did. And for that I am boundlessly grateful. Though I went to NEC for Jaki, I didn't go to study jazz as much as I went to open my ears and become a better musician. The faculty comprised almost exclusively creative, working musical artists. For example, my favorite theory teacher, Joe Maneri, never graduated high school but could play crazy, Eastern European–influenced, microtonal jazz just as well as he could guide me through Schoenberg's *Theory of Harmony*. Students would get to learn music history from someone who wrote music himself, not an academic.

It was Jaki who sparked my interest in solo piano, something that would absorb me for the rest of my life. He introduced me to the solo work of Earl "Fatha" Hines, James P. Johnson, Fats Waller, and Teddy Wilson. He was an aficionado of stride and got me into a stride-piano kick for a while. (Stride, a descendant of ragtime, with its loping, "striding" left hand that alternates low bass octaves with chords in the middle register, was the dominant jazz solo piano style in the first half of the twentieth century.) I couldn't get enough of Hines especially—his solo work, even by today's standards, is some of the most commanding and creative jazz piano music ever recorded. I had always had a good left hand, having played a lot of Bach, and I liked to do more with it than rudimentary "comping" block chords. This inclination had gotten me into trouble in Cincinnati. Once, when I was playing with Jimmy McGary, I was doing some independent, contrapuntal things I thought were interesting with my left hand, and Jimmy snapped at me, "What's that shit?" I have always heard music as based on four independent voices—going back to listening to string quartets and playing Bach chorales and fugues—and thought that the left hand should be active. To me, what was revolutionary about Bill Evans was the voice leading in his left hand. I loved moving things around down there instead of playing chord "voicings."

When I was at the conservatory, the living North and South Poles of solo piano in jazz were Cecil Taylor and Keith Jarrett, both of whom I loved. I've always been fascinated by how Cecil's music sounds so free and kinetic and chaotic when it's actually meticulously structured—something you can only appreciate if you take the time to study it. Keith's music can be the near opposite, sounding like he's playing a structured composition when he's really just playing what occurs to him in the moment. I was more familiar with contemporary figures such as Cecil and Keith than I was with Earl Hines or Teddy Wilson until Jaki showed me the lineage behind them. I began to see solo piano as a long and deep tradition.

Jaki was the first great solo pianist I had ever had the opportunity to study at close range. He would sit down, and off he'd go. In the course of a lesson with me, he might play in half a dozen styles. But no matter what tune he played or what style he played in, the music was definitely his. Jaki had his own approach to line, to rhythm, to color, and to touch. I learned quite a lot from watching him over the keyboard, playing piano duets with him, and just simply listening to him—thank God, because I didn't get very much out of the exercises he gave me. He would hand out worksheets—exercises where you would do things in twelve keys or take different chords through the circle of fifths, so you'd always have those techniques under your fingers. Though I regret it now, I didn't bother much with any of that. I had never been good at doing things I didn't want to do, and that didn't change at NEC. What I took away from Jaki was what I learned from being next to him while he played, watching him use the whole instrument, top to bottom, style by style, in a way that always had his own musical signature.

Working with Jaki was the first time I connected directly to someone who had been a part of major moments in jazz. He had played with Charles Mingus on *Mingus Mingus Mingus Mingus Mingus* and on *The Black Saint and the Sinner Lady*. He had worked with saxophonist and flutist Eric Dolphy and the legendary drummer Art Blakey. I asked Jaki about Mingus, but he didn't want to talk about him. I got the clear impression that something had gone on between them, but I never knew what.

Jaki was much more comfortable talking about Dolphy. He played with Eric in Mingus's sextet in the early sixties, and on Dolphy's beautiful album *Far Cry* from 1960. Jaki had been shaken badly by Eric's death in 1964. Talking about it with me more than twenty years later, Jaki would still get upset. Dolphy had been in

Berlin at the time and collapsed from an undiagnosed diabetic condition. At the hospital the attending physicians assumed that because he was black and a jazz musician, he must have passed out from drug use. They let him lie there on the bed, waiting for the drugs to run their course. But Dolphy was in a diabetic coma and died within hours, untreated.

In June 1964 he recorded what would be released as *Last Date* with Dutch musicians in Holland. At the end of the album he is heard saying, "When you hear music, after it's over, it's gone in the air; you can never capture it again." This could be a definitive statement about great live jazz—each performance is unique and lives on only in the memory of the people who were lucky enough to be there to hear it.

It's hard for me to think about this without thinking of Jaki Byard's own death some years later, early in 1999. The history of jazz is laced with tales of unnecessary or mysterious deaths, but Jaki's had particular resonance for me, in part because of his importance in my early development as a jazz musician and in part because the fragility of human life was very much on my mind in the late nineties—I was thinking, even at a fairly young age, about my own mortality. Jaki had left NEC in the mid-eighties, recruited to teach at the new jazz program at the Manhattan School of Music, which was closer to his home base in Hollis, Queens. One night in his house he was murdered by a single bullet shot through his nose. There were no signs of forced entry, and his two daughters, in their beds on the second floor, heard nothing unusual until the gunshot. The case is unsolved to this day. By this time, Jaki and I had been out of touch, and I was having quite a bit of success as a jazz pianist. I wish I could have had the

chance to tell him outright how much he'd taught me. But I think
he probably knew.

In the two years I spent at NEC, I did practically everything
a pianist could do there, playing in the contemporary music ensemble, the wind ensemble, Gunther's ragtime ensemble. Just as
in high school, I was an all-around music jock, open to almost
anything and excited about the opportunities to try new things
and have unique musical experiences. Schuller was a demanding
taskmaster as a conductor and his ears were legendary—though
we were still students, we were expected to play on a professional
level, and mistakes were not tolerated. As part of his program to
bring the stature of classical music to jazz, Schuller was actively
advancing Duke Ellington as "the American Bach." To establish
Ellington's music as a canon, he made exact transcriptions of some
of Ellington's works and conducted them in repertory, performed
by the NEC jazz orchestra with me at the piano. I was among the
first pianists to play this music note for note since Ellington himself performed it, a fact that Schuller made sure I knew.

I was fascinated by Ellington's programmatic, almost visual approach to structure and voicing. He had the luxury of composing
directly for the specific musicians who stayed with him for many
years, and he wrote to their particular sounds and strengths. Some
of his writing looks a bit unconventional on the page, but it works
perfectly with his idiosyncratic players. I tried to honor him by
getting his sound as nearly as possible where there was a written-
out piano solo. That's a challenge, one Ellington himself never
had to face. He played only one way, like Duke Ellington, and
that was more than sufficient. But to my thinking, there was something misguided and even patronizing in the Schuller conception

of Ellington as our Bach, only seeing him—and all of jazz—in relation to European classical music. He was our Ellington. That was a great enough thing to be.

Duke Ellington loomed large at NEC. On Wednesday nights Jaki had a regular gig leading an Ellington-influenced big band he called the Apollo Stompers at Michael's Pub on Gainsborough Street, a few blocks from the school. He stocked the band with NEC students, who in turned stocked the club with their friends. Jaki would conduct the band and play tenor and alto saxophone—he was a quirky sax player—and conjure an atmosphere of high spirits. I played the piano in this group most nights and had a ball doing it. The repertoire was solid swing with arrangements and compositions by Jaki. Playing this music in a band with eighteen pieces, I was glad to have begun my lessons in *time* by studying *Ellington at Newport* in the back room of the Family Owl.

After a year at NEC, I requested a new piano teacher, because Jaki's attendance had become erratic and I also wanted to broaden myself as a pianist. NEC is one of the world's greatest classical conservatories, and I wanted to take advantage of that as much as possible. I am fortunate to play an instrument that has more than four hundred years of masterpieces composed for it, and now, unlike in high school, I wanted to get into some of them. (By contrast, if you are an alto sax player, the written repertoire is largely mediocre French stuff; the greatest alto sax music was created by the jazz virtuosi.) I started studying with an adjunct instructor in the classical division, Irma Wolpe. She was Romanian and carried with her an air of Eastern European severity. Early in her life she had been married to the German composer Stefan Wolpe, who was admired if not known widely for his austere twelve-tone music. (That genre of somewhat severe music never found a wide public audience, though it was avidly dissected in the East Coast music theory community.) That was the credential factoid that students passed around about her, even though she and Wolpe had divorced decades earlier and she had remarried mathematician Hans Rademacher. Her approach was grounded in the Russian school of piano technique, with its emphasis on arm weight and "scraping" the key toward the body. I didn't agree with everything she taught, but she got me thinking about the mechanics of sound in my own playing, and that would become more and more important to me over time.

Along with my awakening to the possibilities of solo piano, I developed a special appreciation for the duo format at the New England Conservatory. There were superb student musicians at the school who would end up having significant careers in jazz: the reed players Michael Moore and Marty Ehrlich; the bassist and guitarist Jerome Harris; the pianists Anthony Coleman and Mike LeDonne, and more. Strangely, though, there were not many first-rate rhythm-section musicians in the jazz program then, so I found myself playing mostly solo piano or duos. The piano practice area of Jordan Hall had a long hallway with rows of rooms equipped with two Steinways. I'd be practicing, and if I saw Michael or Marty—or another of the jazz pianists—walking down the hall, I'd grab him and get him to come in and play some duos.

I had played some duos in Cincinnati, primarily with a superb and underrated guitarist about ten years older than me named Kenny Poole. He was a sensitive musician who, unlike many other guitarists, never overplayed. He was especially good at anything

Brazilian and helped fuel my lifelong interest in the music of Antonio Carlos Jobim and Brazilian music in general. He could play
a bossa nova and sound just like João Gilberto. I lost touch with
Kenny but learned a few years ago that he had died of cancer in
Cincinnati, where he had been playing in his beautiful style in
restaurants. It was in Boston, however, that I began to fully grasp
the potential of the creative duo format.

The duo suited my ability to use the entire keyboard to do multiple things at once. It also let me orchestrate the music instead
of just playing block chords with the left hand. I learned to play
using the piano more like a drum set, having multiple pitches.
I indulged my love of spontaneous counterpoint—two (or more)
independent melodic lines that are going on simultaneously. I can
go from roaring loud to *pianissimo* instantly. It's collaborative and
also intimate—two musicians, close together. Nothing more. You
have to be compatible but also different enough for each musician
to offer something unique. You inspire each other and interact in
the deepest musical way. It's almost sex.

JUST as I was beginning to build my identity as a musician in
Boston, I started to work out what it meant to be a gay man. There
was something of a gay sphere on campus at the conservatory,
populated largely and conspicuously by singers in the opera concentration. They all sat together in the cafeteria and carried on
in the same near-drag you-go-girl way as the show-tune boys in
the trailer at Kings Island. All of us in the jazz department called
these guys the "opera queens." I used the term myself with my
straight jazz friends, to prove that I fit in with them. In retrospect,

I wish I had used more restraint and shown more respect to a group of people who no doubt knew that everybody realized they were gay and had learned to live with that. I wasn't ready.

I had been attracted to men for as long as I'd had any sexual feelings at all. Now, living on my own in Boston, could I act on that in a fulfilling way? What did I need to do to meet other men like me, and then, how should I behave? I knew nothing.

In 1975 the drinking age in Massachusetts was eighteen, and I had turned nineteen shortly after starting the fall term at NEC. College students were going to bars all the time—and when they weren't at bars, they were talking about bars. I knew about all the bars in Boston that my straight friends were going to, as well as which ones they were avoiding, because "queers" went to them. I started going to those bars.

The meat-market atmosphere of gay bars was rattling to me, and I would never be fully comfortable with it. Not since my summers at jock camp in Maine had I found myself trying to navigate an environment where a person's physical attributes established his worth. I had been known as a musician since I was a child, and it was my musicianship that defined me in most other people's eyes as well as my own.

I am not a tall person—not super-short, but just below average. When I was very young, I was pretty chunky, though I lost that extra weight during high school. I'm nearsighted and have worn glasses nearly all my life. None of those physical qualities ever mattered when I sat down at the piano. At the piano stool, my music defined me as someone interesting, someone with a special capacity to reward your attention.

At a barstool, things were different. Men don't go to a gay bar just to have a drink. They go to drink and find men to go home with. A gay bar is a place for gay men to meet other gay men—for the pleasure of being in the company of kindred spirits, yes, and for the comfort that a protective environment provides, absolutely. Still, generally speaking, gay bars—just like straight bars—exist mainly to facilitate attraction between strangers. I'm talking about sexual attraction, and that usually starts with physical attraction.

James Baldwin once said, "I could talk away my looks in ten minutes." At the piano, I could play away my size and my eyeglasses in half that time. At gay bars I had a harder time. Still, I did all right. Before long, I had a neatly trimmed full beard. I was in reasonably good shape, having started working out with weights and swimming regularly at the YMCA. I now wore contact lenses. I was beginning to become comfortable in my own skin. I was outgoing, and as much as any person can gauge such a thing about himself, I think I was likable. I could approach good-looking guys without too much fear—though that meant learning about rejection more than once. Night by night, I got the hang of the pickup scene. Like most people my age, male or female, straight or gay, I was at the point in my life when sex was extremely important, if not quite all-consuming. I learned from the bars that having sex and plenty of it was what defined being a gay man.

The bars generally had plain, inconspicuous, almost off-putting street fronts, under-designed façades that signaled to passersby that there must be shadowy goings-on behind those doors. No windows, or glass panes painted over, sometimes no sign, in the manner of speakeasies in the days of Prohibition. All this had the effect of reinforcing to both the bars' gay patrons and the straights outside that being gay was disreputable, something shameful. I was beginning to grasp how gay men and women had been functioning as a secret society, and this made me feel a little ashamed, which is exactly how the straight world wanted me to feel, but also proud to be part of something outside the mainstream culture. Most of the bars were dimly lit inside, to make it harder to see and hence easier to find the guy sitting next to you attractive.

At the first bar I went to in Boston, a dive called Sporters, a time came near the end of the evening that we called "the racetrack." You had your eyes on Hot Guy X all night, and now he was hooked up with somebody else. It was getting late, so you had to act fast and see if there was anybody left you could still hook up with—so you walked slowly and deliberately in a circle around the bar in the center of the room holding your drink. Close to the 2 A.M. closing time, people would get frantic, hitting on people they wouldn't have bothered with an hour earlier. It was nerve-racking and not exactly uplifting if you were one of the guys who would get picked up at the last minute, in sexual desperation.

The dance clubs were very different scenes. This was the mid-1970s, the early days of the disco craze. I was aware of disco from hearing Top 40 by happenstance now and then—on a streetcar ride, I might hear a song like Barry White's "Love's Theme" or the Hues Corporation's "Rock the Boat" on one of the passengers' radios—but I was concentrating on jazz and contemporary classical music and had not been paying much attention to other genres since my pop-music listening back in high school. It was only later that I learned disco had begun in the underground gay dance clubs of Manhattan, where it was inextricable from the gay subculture. I discovered disco after it had begun to be appropriated and assimilated into mainstream pop music. When I first walked into a gay dance club, I was unprepared.

Shortly after I moved to Boston in August 1975, I found myself passing by a disco near where I lived in Allston, near Boston University. It was called the Land of Oz. It had taken its name, unsubtly, from the dream world in the classic Hollywood musical that had made Judy Garland a star and provided the secret password— "Are you a friend of Dorothy?"—for midcentury gay men who needed to know who was gay and who was not so they didn't get the crap beaten out of them or taken down to the precinct. Steeling myself, I walked into the club from the gray landscape on Commonwealth Avenue, feeling like Dorothy Gale stepping out of her collapsed black-and-white farmhouse to enter the Technicolor fantasy of MGM's Oz. I inched my way to the bar. I stood there nervously clutching a gin and tonic and stared out at an army of men dressed up in open polyester shirts with wide wing collars and crotch-hugging pants, dancing the Hustle. Glitter drizzled from the ceiling, the disco ball was spinning, and the air was thick with cigarette smoke and the sour, intoxicating smell of male bodies sweating. I got picked up by a decent-looking guy and went home with a total stranger for the first time in my life. I was not very comfortable doing this, but I just thought, *If you are gay, this is what you do.* I had no instruction yet from older men in how to embrace my sexuality. But over time, and as I hit the bars more often, I began to develop friendships with some older gay guys who let me into their circle and taught me the ropes of the scene.

The bars and clubs always stocked piles of gay newspapers and flyers for gay-oriented services—massage parlors and gay-friendly businesses such as gyms and hair salons. I picked up the gay papers and noticed the personal classifieds, which were like the meat market of the bars in a more efficient form. It seemed easy—you could shop for a sexual partner as easily as shopping for a sofa or a car. I answered an ad once and arranged to meet a guy at a bar. I'll just say that his self-description in the ad showed exceptional creativity and imagination. That was the first and last time I used the personal ads in Boston.

When I moved to Back Bay, in a sketchy area on Westland Avenue near the conservatory, I was down the block from the notorious Fenway, where men went for nocturnal hookups. A friend took me there once after midnight, and I was amazed—it was like being in a gay Fellini movie, men having sex under the moonlight in couples and in groups. I was titillated, and I went on my own several times just to look, much too frightened to participate. But something in me said that it was not my scene and that it could all too easily become addictive—or that I could get arrested. So I stopped going there.

I had an affair with a handsome graduate composition student my first year at the conservatory. But as it often went in those carefree days, he also had a girlfriend; and she had another boyfriend; and I sort of had a girlfriend too, though our relationship was largely platonic. Somewhere along the way, we all got crab lice and, after a lot of intense conversations and finger pointing, traced the crabs to one of our sofas. The couch was summarily dumped on the street with an appropriate note pinned to it.

But I had not yet had anything close to an actual relationship with an out gay man. There were the close high school friendships with guys I was obsessed with. And when I was living in

Cincinnati as an upcoming jazz musician I had some drunken or stoned sexual experiences with some of my musician friends. Those men were straight but curious, and our sexual intimacy was a secret. It wasn't until the summer of 1976 that I had an ongoing connection to one man, though I wouldn't say we were boyfriends, exactly. I had met Don, a smart, good-looking guy, in a bar. About five years older than me, he had a cute smile, a nice build, and soulful brown eyes. He was wearing a knitted cap the night we met. When we got back to my apartment and he took his hat off, I saw that he was, for the most part, bald, which wasn't a turn-off at all. After a month of spending time together, he told me he needed a place to live, so he moved in with me that summer. We didn't set up housekeeping together. We cohabitated, essentially like friends in a roommate situation, but there was some sex and genuine affection between us. Some evenings we would just hang out together and listen to music. Don was sort of bookish and sweet and had a beautiful, clear tenor voice that was perfectly suited to the folk songs and old Americana material that he loved to sing, accompanied by his guitar.

Don introduced me to the "Calamus" poems by Walt Whitman, which we hadn't studied in my poetry class. He showed me "When I Heard at the Close of the Day," which ends with these words:

For the one I love most lay sleeping by me under the same
    cover in the cool night,
In the stillness in the autumn moonbeams his face was in-
    clined toward me,
And his arm lay lightly around my breast—and that night I
    was happy.

It blew me away that Whitman dared to write this in the mid-nineteenth century. That poem made me believe that love between two men was possible.

The arrangement Don and I had was not an exclusive one. It was just one of those undefined sort of relationships. But it was great to be with him and have a positive one-to-one experience with a man I cared about. For the rest of my life, I've always connected that feeling with the sentiment of "When I Heard at the Close of the Day." I was starting to learn that being gay could mean many things—bars and discos and glitter and sex, of course, but also friendship and warmth and quiet happiness.

I graduated from the New England Conservatory in the spring of 1977, one year early, with honors. My parents came, along with my brother—he was then at Princeton studying English and working as a sports reporter at the college newspaper—to my graduation recital. After so many years of living unhappily together, they were separated, and tension between them was high. I played a trio set with my old bassist friend Bob Bodley, who came up from Cincinnati, and a student drummer. And during my very long solo set I played one classic stride piece, Eubie Blake's difficult "Charleston Rag." I also played a series of duos with my musical friends from NEC. Cincinnati guitarist Cal Collins was in town with Benny Goodman, and he played duets with me as well. I showed, musically, that I had a growing and more confident sense of who I was—both on my own and with another person.

CHAPTER 4

BRADLEY'S

On a Sunday in the spring of 1976, Michael Moore and a couple of other musician friends of mine at the conservatory were talking about how so many of our favorite records had been recorded at the Village Vanguard in New York. There was Sonny Rollins's magisterial *A Night at the Village Vanguard*, a tenor sax trio date with bassist Wilbur Ware and drummer Elvin Jones from 1957, an album that could be sold as a textbook on the art of thematic variation in jazz improvisation. Chorus after astounding chorus, Rollins extracts everything that can be extracted from every tune, and every phrase sounds fresh and alive. There was John Coltrane's *Live at the Village Vanguard* from 1962, a testament to his profoundly fertile creative imagination, followed up by *Live at the Village Vanguard Again!* from 1966. There was Bill Evans's landmark of jazz piano trio, *Sunday at the Village Vanguard* from 1961, and a number of other superb albums recorded at the same location by Dizzy Gillespie, Gerry Mulligan, Elvin Jones, and the Thad Jones/Mel Lewis Orchestra, among others. What was it about the Village Vanguard and its sound that inspired such amazing music making? We needed to know. The next day, five of us packed into a friend's car and drove from Boston to Greenwich Village to hear the revered tenor saxophonist Dexter Gordon, who had recently returned from his long exile in Europe. We were acolytes making a jazz pilgrimage to the most famous basement club in the world.

To picture what the Vanguard looked like in 1977, all you need to do is go to the club today. Max Gordon opened it in 1935, and it has barely changed. The only thing missing now is the cigarette smoke. There used to be a mix of jazz, folk music, and comedy—acts such as Josh White, Lead Belly, Lenny Bruce, and Professor Irwin Corey, along with Monk and Miles—but it has presented exclusively jazz since the late sixties. As I write this in the second decade of the twenty-first century, the Vanguard is still owned and operated by Max's widow, Lorraine, now ninety-four, and her daughter, Deborah.

The Vanguard is an acoustic miracle, shaped perfectly for projecting the sound of almost unamplified instruments. Many, myself included, feel that it is indeed the Carnegie Hall of jazz clubs, the greatest in the world. Dexter's huge, warm tone filled the club with richness and a soulful presence that was a thrill.

Returning to the club a few months later, I heard the Thad Jones/Mel Lewis Orchestra on a Monday night. To this day, I have never heard anything quite like the way that group sounded from my table, fifteen or twenty feet from the Vanguard's tiny bandstand. Mel had a Chinese cymbal that sounded like the greatest, most musical garbage-can lid you ever heard. He was magnificent. He seemed to play effortlessly, with the freedom you would usually associate with small-band drumming. The sound was enveloping, far surpassing the expectations I had had from listening to all those *Live at the Vanguard* records. I watched and studied the pianist, Harold Danko, a fine player in his late twenties, whom I had never heard before, and I thought: *I can do what he's doing. I could play here.*

At the end of the set I went up to Danko and introduced myself. I wrote my name and number on a slip of paper and told him that if he ever needed a sub, he should call me. In my mind that night, I took my next step and moved to New York to set up shop as a working jazz musician.

A week after graduation, on June 1, 1977, I did it for real. A childhood friend from Cincinnati, Eddie Felson, was an up-and-coming bass player and had moved to New York about six months earlier. Eddie was (and still is) tack sharp and resourceful, a sociable, attractive guy with a quick wit. He heard about a loft on East Eleventh Street in the Village, between Broadway and University Place, available for $350 a month and a fixture fee of $4,000 paid to the departing tenant. Back when lofts were lived in by artists of various sorts and before the term "loft" had come to mean any high-ceilinged apartment only affordable for well-to-do workers in the financial sector, they were unadorned commercial spaces. When the artist moved out, he or she would recoup the money spent installing modifications to make it habitable by charging the incoming tenant a fixture fee. Though the lease was a commercial one, landlords often knew that the spaces were being lived in and looked the other way—but in some cases the artists had to keep their residence in the building a secret.

I had access to some cash left over from the education fund my grandmother had set aside for me as well as a fair amount of money I had saved from playing countless private parties through the conservatory gig office. I used it, expecting to continue my education in jazz in the New York scene.

In many ways, this was a dream time to land in Manhattan. The city had been in decline for a decade and was nearly bankrupt, but only economically. Culturally, wild ideas were sprouting from the cracks in the streets. Rents were low and the crime rate was high. Students at New York University, a few blocks south of the loft I rented, were pooling their resources and buying buildings in the East Village, because they could pick up a brownstone for $30,000 or $40,000. Lower Manhattan's SoHo district (for "South of Houston" Street) was a quiet, sparsely populated neighborhood for artists using floor-through lofts in former warehouses to paint huge photo-realist canvases or construct found-object sculpture. There was no major retail shopping in the neighborhood. Times Square was a wasteland of hard-core porn theaters and pimp bars. Manhattan was open to everyone and everything.

Not long after I moved to the city, New York fell under siege to the roaming serial killer the tabloids called the Son of Sam, because he claimed to be acting under orders he received telepathically from a dog owned by his neighbor Sam. It didn't always feel safe to walk home after dark, so you might as well stay out all night and go home at dawn.

The loft Eddie and I moved into was a primitively fitted-out space in a smallish building—it had recently been converted into a living loft by a sculptor. We had the entire seventh floor, 2,500 square feet, with our bedrooms delineated by cheap particleboard walls put up by the previous tenant, who charged us for them, a very basic kitchen, and the funky stall shower he had installed. The elevator opened up right into our living space. There was no air-conditioning, so we kept the windows cracked wide and used fans. That summer the municipal sanitation workers went on strike. Piles of garbage spilled into the streets, and their aroma wafted into our place.

As soon as I arrived in New York, I moved the Baldwin from my mom's house in Cincinnati and sold it to upgrade to a larger German Schimmel grand. Eddie kept his bass next to it. We played a lot of music together and with a floating group of musicians Eddie had gotten to know, as well as others I met as I started gigging around town: bassist Ratzo Harris, tenor player Rich Perry, singers Roberta Baum and Roseanna Vitro, who got romantically involved with Eddie and moved in with us after about six months. People were always coming and going, sleeping on the floor and playing jam sessions at all hours.

My half of the rent was $175—which was chopped down to just $117 after Roseanna joined us—and we had no cable bill or Wi-Fi service provider to pay. I remember spending more than a month's rent—$125—at Crazy Eddie's in the Village to buy an answering machine, the only personal technology available in the days before pagers, cell phones, and home computers. If I got a few gigs that I would have missed by not being at home to receive the call, it would pay for itself.

I didn't have to earn a lot of money to keep myself afloat. It was very important to me to make it as a musician, and I had a deep-seated need to prove to myself that I could make a living at this. That led me to play some gigs that were pretty mundane: weddings, private parties, and restaurant background gigs. I just wanted to be working every night, playing jazz—or some kind of music. Looking back, I know how fortunate I was to know deep down that there was family money available if I needed it and that I wouldn't starve—I never had to wait tables, drive a taxi, or take an office temp job. But my pride in wanting to make a living exclusively from playing music was real.

I vividly remember my first jazz gig in New York, barely a week after I had moved in. It was a quartet date with drummer Jo Jones Jr. that Eddie got me hired for. Though Jo Jo, as he liked to be called, was the son of the groundbreaking swing drummer "Papa Jo" Jones, he had not inherited his father's talent. Still, an actual jazz gig in New York City was a big deal to me, and I was stoked. We played at a place called Barbara's, a block off Washington Square Park on the corner of Thompson and West Third Streets. The piano was painted white (always a bad sign) and was out of tune. It was a door gig, meaning musicians split whatever the club brought in from the cover charge, which wasn't much. At the end of the night, my cut was $7. It was the sweetest money I had ever made.

After we packed up, Eddie and I walked over to Mamoun's, the legendary all-night Middle Eastern joint on MacDougal Street. I got a falafel for seventy-five cents. The experience was exhilarating. I was feeding myself with my earnings as a jazz musician in New York.

Soon after I moved into the loft on Eleventh Street, I got a call from the contractor for the Woody Herman big band, and I signed on to hit the road with Herman and his current configuration of the Thundering Herd. Herman was a smallish, stooped-over man who had recently been in a car accident. That and his need to keep working to pay the IRS back the money that a former manager had absconded with made him particularly cranky, as he had to ride the bus with us rather than travel on his own. He was in his mid-sixties—not old by today's standards but ancient and hardened in his attitudes and practices. He had handed off the musical direction to one of the saxophonists in the band, Frank Tiberi, who would count off the tunes and do the conducting most of the time, while Herman stood there with a paisley ascot under his polyester shirt, glowering at the audience. We played his big swing dance hits "Four Brothers," "Woodchopper's Ball," and "Caldonia"—as well as a quasi-hip big-band arrangement of Aaron Copland's "Fanfare for the Common Man"—every night. The band uniforms were dark blue double-knit leisure suits and lemon-yellow shirts with giant pointy collars that spilled over the lapels. They were suffocating. A lot of guys in the band smoked cigarettes, including me, and many of the uniforms were pocked with holes from ashes dropping on them and melting through the polyester.

We went through three rhythm sections in the first month. Musicians kept coming on the bus, then getting fired. The great tenor player Joe Lovano was in the band then, and we became friends. He was already well developed as an improviser but had to work with cornball conceits such as a "tenor battle" with Tiberi. Most of the guys were miserable, for good reason, and indifferent to the music, or they were drunks. All they talked about were sports and "chicks." I felt like I had fallen asleep in the trailer at

Kings Island, and when I woke up, everybody in the world had become a macho dullard.

We went from town to town, by band bus, all over the eastern part of the country, and I never got a chance to practice. The only time I played piano was onstage. Herman fancied himself a progressive musician, so I had to play a Fender Rhodes electric piano on some of the more modern, non-swing repertoire. My big feature was "La Fiesta," a Chick Corea Latin showpiece that we played really, really fast. The whole experience was hell. The only positive thing Herman did was fire me after five weeks. I wasn't a particularly flashy player who could get lots of applause by playing loud and fast; that and my lack of enthusiasm did me in. But I can't say I was disappointed, as I honestly would rather have driven a cab in New York than play with that band much longer.

I didn't have a manager or a booking agent. I didn't know any musicians who did. I would look through *The Village Voice*, which came out every Wednesday and was the bible for New Yorkers in the days before the Web. It provided all the information you needed to live. Need an apartment? Looking for a job? A date? A good place to eat or hear music? You could find everything in *The Village Voice*. I would go through the listings of the jazz clubs and the bars and restaurants that advertised "music nightly," and I would knock on their doors, bringing my demo cassette tape. Sometimes they'd take your information in case they needed a sub, sometimes they'd say, "Thanks, but no thanks, kid," and sometimes they'd say, "All right, you start next Friday at seven o'clock." And I learned quickly to befriend other pianists so they could throw me jobs that they couldn't take—or didn't want to do.

I became the pianist in the house band of a club called Jazz-mania, which many of us referred to as Jazzphobia. It tried to capitalize on the loft-jazz model of the late seventies—but it was in a safe neighborhood, at Twenty-Third Street near Park Avenue, and the owner also listed it in the personal ad section of *The Village Voice* as a place for cool yuppie singles to meet. I met so many great musicians there, many as new to New York as I was. Each weekend the house trio would play behind a guest artist—these ranged from saxophone avant-gardists such as Arthur Blythe and David Murray to Monk's saxophonist Charlie Rouse, Mingus's trombonist Jimmy Knepper, and baritone sax player Pepper Adams, a mainstay in the Thad Jones/Mel Lewis Orchestra. There were rarely any charts—they just called tunes or brought in the occasional simple lead sheet. This was a great experience that started to get my name around.

I played gigs at the Angry Squire, a dive on Seventh Avenue in Chelsea that had a fifty-six-key spinet piano on an elevated area behind the bandstand. Ten years earlier in Cincinnati I had been distraught over my parents' getting me a Baldwin grand instead of a Steinway, and here I was playing a no-name spinet and glad to have the work. I was too busy hustling to indulge considerations of familial justice. Eventually I was able to play there with the great bassist Sam Jones and the drummer Jimmy Cobb—Wynton Kelly's rhythm section! These two players were some of the best of their generation—the post-boppers who came after Charlie Parker, Dizzy, Monk, and the rest of the bebop pioneers. Jimmy had even played with Miles (the ultimate stamp of approval), appearing on one of my favorite albums, *Friday and*

Saturday Night at the Blackhawk. We managed to make music despite the wretched piano.

I played often with a variety of singers at a restaurant a couple of blocks from my loft, on Eleventh Street between Fifth and Sixth Avenues, called Christy's Skylight Garden. You got $25 a night and a good dinner for six straight nights—a fantastic deal. In one week I would make my rent for the month *and* eat pretty well. I got a weekend job subbing in the house band at one of the old Catskills resorts, the Granit. We played dance music—fox-trots, cha-chas, and merengues—for the cocktail hour, then accompanied the evening touring acts, both musicians and comedians, sometimes having to sight-read nearly illegible arrangements.

In addition to the weddings and private parties, Eddie and I played after hours with the seriously swinging tenor saxophonist Junior Cook at a place called Joyce's House of Unity on Columbus Avenue and Eighty-Third Street, which was a sketchy part of town then. We would go to dinner in Chinatown before the gig started at 4 A.M., and we would play till eight in the morning. There were lots of hookers and pimps, and they were the more respectable, working people in the crowd. When you walked into the club, you got frisked. Junior was a masterful player but always high and, even at that hour, always late. The pay was pretty good—$50—but the hours were hard. My body was beginning to adjust to jazz time. Still, this was rough on the system, and more than once I ended up spending the $50 on coke to get me through the gig. I was learning a lot about what jazz musicians had to deal with for the privilege of practicing their trade.

One afternoon, not long after I moved to New York, I got a

last-minute call to play the piano at a gay bar on the Upper East Side. When I showed up, the manager looked me over and asked me to take off my sport jacket. Then he said to take off my tie and dress shirt. "I want to see what you've got," he said, checking me out in my T-shirt. I was going to the gym regularly and passed the inspection.

"Do you sing?" he asked.

I said, "No."

And he said, "Well, tonight you are going to sing."

Though I knew the lyrics to most of the songs I played, I had no desire to sing "Memory" from *Cats*, the gay anthem "What I Did for Love" from *A Chorus Line*—or anything sung by Barbra Streisand. But needing the job, I played and sang as best I could that night with a tip jar on the piano—in my tight T-shirt, surely looking a bit uncomfortable. It was the first and last time I sang publicly, with or without a T-shirt. I pulled it off well enough, I think, but had no interest in becoming a piano-bar entertainer and stoking the classic image of the gay man singing and playing show tunes.

I went to the Vanguard at least a couple of times a month. When I didn't have the six-dollar cover charge, the door person would let me sit on the steps leading down to the club, and I'd listen from there. In my first couple of years in New York, I saw—or at least *heard*—Bill Evans, Milt Jackson, Joe Henderson, Bobby Hutcherson, and many other great jazz musicians. Though some nights I wasn't even in the room, I was learning by osmosis, by getting as close as possible to the living jazz legends, some of whom I had heard live already, and some only on records.

There was another club in town that was actually the happening place for pianists specifically: Bradley's. A long, narrow store-front bar on University Place just half a block from my loft, it was elegant and woody inside, like an old library, with mahogany wainscoting and modern art on the walls. The owner, Bradley Cunningham, was a gregariously imposing former marine in his early fifties. He had a tousled-hair Robert Redford look and loved jazz, especially piano jazz. He could play a bit himself, in the manner of a talented amateur who never fully applied himself to his instrument but got a kick out of music and knew good piano playing when he heard it. I learned at one point that he had served in the Pacific during World War II, and had interrogated Japanese prisoners of war. Word was that he had extracted some valuable military secrets from captive soldiers. He had a knack with peo-ple, a great asset for a saloon owner. Under Bradley Cunningham, Bradley's was more than a venue of presentation for piano jazz and piano-bass duos; it was a *hang, the* place where jazz musicians went to be with other musicians, to hear gossip, learn material, steal ideas, get drunk, and get high and possibly get laid.

I started hanging out at Bradley's, insinuating myself into the scene. There was rarely a cover charge, and most of the time there wasn't even anybody at the door to take the money. It was at Brad-ley's that I first rubbed elbows with—and played with—some of the great, great musicians of all time. All the heavyweight pianists played there and came in there when they were off for the night—Tommy Flanagan, Jimmy Rowles, Joanne Brackeen, Sir Roland Hanna, Kenny Barron, John Hicks, Cedar Walton, *everybody.* I watched drummer Art Blakey hitting on a young NYU coed at the bar, learned to spot the coke dealers discreetly going in and out of the men's room, and met some of the odd locals who also frequented the Cedar Tavern, the legendary abstract expressionist artists' bar a block up the street.

At the end of the night, pianists who weren't on the bill would take a seat at the piano and show the others a tune or two. There were basses propped up in every corner from the cats who were coming from their other gigs to hear the music and have a nightcap. Fantastic horn players such as trumpeter Woody Shaw and saxophone legends Zoot Sims, George Coleman, Al Cohn, and Phil Woods would sit in and hang out. All these people I knew from records and idolized—there they were, and I was there among them. I saw them drunk. I saw them stoned. I saw them when they were having a bad night and just weren't playing well. I got to see them as people like me, and, just as significant, they got to see *me*.

I came to New York to make it and play with the greatest players in jazz—isn't that why most young jazz musicians come to New York? I was only twenty-one when I started hanging at Bradley's, but I was ambitious and knew what I wanted. I could play and I knew it. I had a good skill set for those days. I knew lots of tunes. I could sight-read. I could accompany in any style. I could swing. I was ready.

Truth to tell, I was pretty full of myself and probably too pushy. I suppose I was a nuisance at Bradley's, in everybody's face a little too much. I could have lain back and taken things more deliberately. If I could go back in time and meet the Fred from those days, I don't know if I would like him very much. He was awfully arrogant for a guy who hadn't done that much yet.

But I know what he would say to me. He would say, *I know what I can do. I have the goods. I want to be playing with the best musicians in the world. Why should I wait?*

I don't know if I was overcompensating for any ongoing feelings of inadequacy, any lingering sense that my arms were just too short, or if I was pushing my way past any intimidation I felt in the company of these masters. But *push* is exactly what I did.

I made sure all the pianists knew who I was, and I constantly asked people if I could sit in. Most of them were nice about it, considering how obnoxious I was. Jimmy Rowles graciously let me sit in a few times, and he showed me some great, obscure tunes after hours. One night Jimmy sat me down and taught me "Lotus Blossom," the beautiful Billy Strayhorn ballad. Strayhorn was the man behind the scenes in the Ellington band—some of the signature tunes we associate with Duke were actually composed by Billy, such as "Take the 'A' Train." He also arranged and orchestrated a great deal of music for the band and could mimic Duke at the piano when Ellington needed to be out front conducting. And he was a major songsmith, writing music and lyrics; "Lush Life" (completed at age nineteen) and "Something to Live For" are among his best-known tunes. There was something of a thing for Strayhorn at Bradley's—a special appreciation for his subtlety and harmonic sophistication. Much of the music Strayhorn wrote was intimate and not that well established in the jazz canon yet, but musicians loved the challenge of playing his tunes, and they were just right for a clubby, jazz-insider setting such as Bradley's. Another night, Tommy Flanagan showed me Strayhorn's "UMMG (Upper Manhattan Medical Group)," written in honor of the staff at the hospital where Billy spent time as a patient.

Tommy was one of my favorites. A bespectacled, light-skinned, and soft-spoken man, he had been Ella Fitzgerald's accompanist for years, had a huge repertoire, and had recorded the very tricky

"Giant Steps" with John Coltrane. With an elegant touch, a graceful swinging beat, and deceptively tricky yet always melodic phrasing, he took a lot of chances when he soloed. That meant that he was not quite as consistent as his Detroit peer Hank Jones but that when he was having a good night, it was something truly special.

I harassed Kenny Barron at Bradley's for so long that he finally let me sit in with the great bassist Buster Williams. Buster grudgingly let me play that time, but as the years passed we played together often and became quite friendly. Eventually, the bassist Red Mitchell, whom I had sat in with a few times, said to Bradley, "Give the kid a gig already."

I was just twenty-two when I was booked to play a full week at Bradley's. It was heady. There was nobody else my age headlining at a place so prominent. Nearly all the other pianists who played Bradley's were twice my age or older. For my first week there, I hired bassist and fellow Cincinnatian Michael Moore (not the Michael Moore from the New England Conservatory), but he took another gig at the last minute, so I hired Bill Evans's former bass player Eddie Gomez. Bradley liked me, and I guess he got good feedback from the other cats and the bar's regular patrons, so for my second weeklong engagement not long afterward I had the good sense to hire Sam Jones, a veteran musician highly respected in the Bradley's circle. In addition to having been the bassist in the band of Julian "Cannonball" Adderley, Miles's alto player of choice, he served significant stints in the trios of Oscar Peterson and Bill Evans. He always played the right note, and he made it look easy. His time was impeccable—his beat had a special lift to it, and it was hard not to swing when you were playing with him.

He also was a sometime bandleader and a composer of numerous catchy tunes, his "Unit 7" being Cannonball Adderley's theme song. The perception of me after that was *Hey, if Sam thinks he can play, he can play.* That was serious cred—I was in.

I was paid $100 per night—a lot of money for me in those days, almost my month's rent. And Bradley offered you free dinner or free drinks—I was doing my small hits of coke toward the end of the night and I never drink on the bandstand, so I took dinner before the gig. I was probably the only person who played there who took that option. Bradley insisted that "this is a saloon, not a concert hall" and as such I had to play what he called "fifty-dollar tunes" during the early dinner sets: Porter, Kern, Gershwin, and maybe a bossa nova or two. Four sets a night—forty-five minutes on, thirty off—from 9:45 to 2:45.

The first time I played at Bradley's I got my first flattering coverage in *The New Yorker.* I think that this, more than anything I had done in my life up to that point, impressed my parents, who, even living in Cincinnati, subscribed to the magazine and read it religiously. The magazine's longtime jazz critic Whitney Balliett put previews of upcoming shows in the magazine's influential "Goings On About Town" section—something close to mini-reviews. In a listing from my first gig at Bradley's with bassist Eddie Gomez, Balliett described me as "a slender, bearded, light-fingered poet of a pianist." To be recognized at my age by someone as highly regarded as Balliett was awfully gratifying, and to be called a poet specifically was a thrill. I couldn't help but bristle a bit at "light-fingered," though. I get that he was saying I didn't have a heavy hand, and that was great. But I thought of *light* as a loaded word. It was a common anti-gay slur to call someone "light in the loafers." Was Balliett trying to suggest something about me in a non-musical sense?

I was paranoid, for sure—secretive about my sexual identity and terrified that the truth would come out and hurt me professionally just as I was beginning to have some success. There was not yet any gay consciousness in the jazz world. I was playing Billy Strayhorn's music but didn't even know that Strayhorn had been gay. Jazz is an intimate art—you're interacting spontaneously with other musicians, expressing yourself and responding to the way they express themselves. As a musician, I have always played with sensitivity and emotionality, qualities Balliett was probably getting at by calling me a "poet." My fear was that if the straight musicians I played with knew I was gay, they would mistake my intense musical connection to them for coming on to them, and I didn't think that would go over well.

One night I went to a gay bar on Christopher Street, and as I walked out, a straight jazz pianist I knew, Jim McNeely, passed by. I thought, *Oh shit—there goes my cover. Now McNeely's going to tell everybody my secret, and I'm sunk.*

MY repertoire expanded at Bradley's as I was introduced to new material through other pianists and composers who frequented the club. I got to know the blind British pianist George Shearing, who came to Bradley's from time to time just to listen. He invited me to his spacious three-bedroom apartment on the Upper East Side for tea with his wife, Ellie. He had a Bösendorfer concert grand in the living room and two nice Yamaha uprights in his music room. George liked to have musician guests play duos with him. We played Bach's Piano Concerto in D Minor on the two uprights with me taking the orchestra part—a lot of fun but a challenge that made me wish I'd kept up my sight-reading after graduating from the conservatory. Ellie was a mezzo-soprano and loved to sing *lieder* and asked me to accompany her on some Brahms and Schubert. I hacked my way through. George turned me on to some fairly obscure tunes that he loved—things like "The Heather on the Hill" and Cole Porter's "Dream Dancing."

As a jazz player who had been hugely popular with his quintet in the fifties, George was business-savvy and quite well off financially. He was also one of the first established professionals to offer me career and business advice. He gave me tips on negotiating fees and told me, to my everlasting gratitude, that I should always hold on to my own publishing rights for my original compositions, calling it "the gift that keeps on giving" in the form of royalties when you (or some other artist) recorded a tune you wrote. He made a small fortune from his hit "Lullaby of Birdland" in its instrumental and vocal versions. He recommended me to an old-school agent who, owing to my lack of name recognition, was only able to get me one weekend gig, playing solo in Schenectady.

One night in 1978 I was playing at Bradley's with a bassist whose name escapes me now when Alec Wilder came in. Wilder was an eccentric composer of classical concert music and had composed a sonata for every orchestral instrument, ensuring that his music would be kept alive in conservatories, since not that much was written for some of the more obscure ones. He also was the author of the classic reference book *American Popular Song*, and his own tunes were popular with the Café Carlyle set. He sat near the piano, at the front table, and listened intently. He stayed for two sets. When I was finished playing, he said nice things about what I was doing and asked me if I'd mind if he sent me his songbooks. That's how I discovered his beautiful compositions "Moon and Sand" and "The Winter of My Discontent." I was twenty-three years old. It had only been a year since I pushed my way onto the piano bench at Bradley's, and Alec Wilder was sending me his music. Naturally, this made me feel like I was heading in the right direction.

Bradley's could be humbling as well. In the fall of '79 I was playing with Sam Jones when Charles Mingus entered the club. This was late in his sadly abbreviated life—he would die from ALS (amyotrophic lateral sclerosis) at the age of fifty-six in less than six months. He was using a wheelchair, aided by his devoted wife, Sue. I saw him start to roll down the aisle toward the piano, and I thought, *Oh my fucking God* . . . Other than Miles Davis himself, nobody could have been more intimidating to me—I had such awe and respect for him. As a master bassist, highly significant composer, and all-around jazz legend, his presence totally freaked me out. I finished the set early, bolted up, ran to the back office, and barricaded myself in. I hid there for about twenty minutes until Sam came in with a glass of sherry and a concerned expression and sat down next to me.

He said softly, "Fred, you have to get a grip on yourself. Listen—there's nothing you can play that that man hasn't heard before. Just play your stuff, do your thing. He came out of his house in a wheelchair because Bradley told him you had something going on. You wouldn't be here if you didn't deserve to be." So when the break was over, I went up to Mingus and nervously said, "It's an honor to meet you. Thanks for coming down to hear Sam and me. Your music has been an inspiration to me for as long as I've been listening to jazz." He just smiled and said, "Thanks." This wasn't the tempestuous *Beneath the Underdog* Mingus of yore, but still, just being in his presence gave me a shiver.

Trying to look cool, I went back up and I played what I played, and Mingus liked it well enough to sit there at his table listening. This may not sound like that big a deal, but it was tremendous validation to me as a new citizen of the New York jazz community. Jazz, after all, is a music steeped in tradition as well as innovation. Every generation of musicians learns the music from the model of its elders—in the oral tradition. And everyone steals ideas from predecessors as well as from peers. The elders carry weight. Mingus's attention was his tacit mark of approval. That night he silently confirmed something I had been telling everybody else but wasn't entirely sure of myself, deep down: I was good enough to be playing there as one of the "cats."

I have always played with my eyes closed. Somehow it helps me to hear the space around the music and feel the piano action better, thus getting a more connected sound. One night at Bradley's I sensed a special presence in the club and opened my eyes. I saw a woman with long blond hair in a Chinese-red silk dress coming down past the bar accompanied by a tall, good-looking African American man. It took me a few seconds to realize that it was Joni Mitchell and her boyfriend, percussionist Don Alias. I was floored. They sat opposite the piano and had dinner. Thinking on it now, I realize that in a strange way, Joni's music, particularly the iconic album *Blue*, helped me get into jazz. I spent hours in high school trying to decipher the chords she was playing on that record (and many of her other ones)—they were not major or minor necessarily. It opened up a whole new harmonic palette for me. After the set, I went up to her like a timid schoolboy and told her how much I dug her. She cracked a broad smile and thanked me.

There was a lot of cocaine at Bradley's. Then again, there was lots of cocaine all over New York in this blithely free and blindly decadent time. Bradley liked coke and would treat the musicians in his inner circle to a few lines in the office, just as a good host of another era would pop a bottle of chardonnay or pour a round of shots. For a time in the late seventies, cocaine was so commonplace as a social lubricant that to spend any amount of time with someone without sharing a line was practically rude. I have always wanted to fit in, so I did my share of coke both inside and outside of Bradley's. I never overdid things, though, and never mainlined cocaine or smoked crack. Pot had been my drug of choice—especially for listening, though I learned back in Cincinnati that it is a terrible performance drug. I was wired by nature, but I enjoyed the extra energy and feeling of confidence coke gave me. Just a small snort made me feel more powerful and in command—at least for as long as I was high.

After establishing myself at Bradley's with Sam Jones, I would play the club three or four weeks a year—with Sam or other great bassists such as Charlie Haden, Red Mitchell, Buster Williams, Ron Carter, and George Mraz. Between those gigs, I would play at the Knickerbocker, a bigger and noisier piano duo room three blocks to the south on University Place, with various bass players. I'd pick up trio dates as I could, and fill in the calendar with odd jobs, playing parties or accompanying singers including Chris

Connor and, later, Sylvia Syms—some great vocalists who taught me the value of knowing lyrics, selling a song, and putting together a set. If I got a decent trio gig and it paid $200, I would hire Buster Williams and Billy Hart, both of whom had played with Herbie Hancock, and I'd pay them $100 each. I didn't make a dime, but I was getting a fantastic free lesson—and it made people believe that I was good enough to hang in there with them. I was becoming one of the cats.

CHAPTER 5

ROLLERENA'S WORLD

The first time I came to New York without my parents, at age eighteen, I drove up in the summer with my Cincinnati roommate Eric Wolfley to go to the Newport in New York jazz festival. We walked along Sheridan Square, a slice of a public space at the three-street intersection of Seventh Avenue, Christopher Street, and West Fourth Street, a few blocks south of the Village Vanguard. I vaguely knew about the area's significance in gay culture but had not yet had any personal experience in the city's mythic gay underground and hadn't yet been to a gay bar. We walked past the Stonewall Inn on Christopher Street, the site of the historic uprising of 1969, when gay men and drag queens (and women, as well as some who rejected either category) fought back against a police raid and lit the torch of gay consciousness in America. When we reached the edge of the square on Seventh Avenue, we found a horde of people gathered on the sidewalk, and I wormed my way to the front of the crowd. In the center of the street was a tall, stalk-thin drag queen dressed in a poofy, faded white taffeta wedding gown. She was wearing a grand dame's hat, sparkling cat's-eye glasses, a wig studded with artificial fruit on one side and a golden tuille veil draped over her face. She was roller-skating in athletic pirouettes and spins, waving a fairy-godmother wand at the crowd, as if she were casting a magic spell—and not just figuratively.

People oohed and aahed, and some called out to her: "Rollerena!" "We love you, darling!"

I flashed on the show boys at Kings Island, lip-synching to Bette Midler records, dressing up as Sandra Dee and Rita Hayworth, and I thought, *Now, this is really gay.*

When I moved to New York a few years later, I didn't do it for the gay culture, though after my experiences in Boston I was eager to check it out. I came to the city for its musical culture, to carve out my place in the jazz capital of the world. It was of secondary importance that Greenwich Village in the 1970s was also the co-capital of gay America along with San Francisco. I was a gay man, after all, and moving to New York helped me come fully to terms with what that meant. As I watched Rollerena, who I later heard was rumored to work daytimes on Wall Street, it hit home to me that *anyone* could be *anything*. I just needed to resolve some issues about what it was that I wanted to be.

I knew I was a jazz musician and wanted to become fully established as a successful one. And I was a gay man and wanted to succeed at that, too, though I wasn't entirely sure what that involved. So I plowed ahead at fulfilling both sides of my identity—but separately, toggling between the two. That was the only way I could conceive of satisfying either part of me. I saw the two as mutually exclusive and elementally incompatible. I had no role models for an integrated life and was aware of how difficult reconciling the jazz cat Fred and the gay man Fred would be. When I first came onto the jazz scene in Cincinnati, I felt like a member of a below-the-radar secret club, accepted as a young, talented, and ambitious player. I was not sure what it would be like to be out on that scene—but I sensed that if I moved to New York, where I knew I would end up, it would have to happen eventually.

It didn't take me long to learn how to make my way around the city's gay scene. There had probably never been a more exciting time and place to be gay than in New York in the late seventies. Over the decade after Stonewall, the long-hidden society of homosexual and sexually fluid men and women had steadily, visibly begun escaping the shadows. The proposition that nontraditional approaches to gender and sexual identity need not be sources of shame was starting to take hold through the bubbling-up gay-pride movement. In Greenwich Village there were gay men, lesbians, and trans-everything people everywhere. There were gay shops, gay restaurants, and gay investment firms. There was an ephemeral but unmistakable gay *feeling* in the air—an energetic sensation of joy in the wonders of *difference*. It was liberating just to walk down Christopher Street, past the leather stores and the Oscar Wilde Bookshop, filled with groundbreaking books from the early renaissance of gay literature: Manual Puig's *Kiss of the Spider Woman*, Andrew Holleran's *Dancer from the Dance*, and the inescapable *Joy of Gay Sex*, cowritten by Edmund White.

There were gay bars outside of which people hung around on

the sidewalk, instead of hiding inside behind painted-over windows, as they would have done a decade earlier. The city was teeming with gay men, or at least that's the way it seemed to me as a young gay man with my eye out for other gay men. People were cruising *everywhere*. They cruised in the aisles of the supermarket and the lines at the bank and the post office. They cruised on the buses and the subways. I remember trudging through the snow in the West Village on a winter afternoon when I got hit on the shoulder by a snowball. A cute guy down the block had tossed it at me. We came up to each other, chatted a bit, got some hot chocolate at a Greek coffee shop, and went to his place together. One night I found myself seated in the Vanguard at the same table with an attractive man, and he started playing footsie with me. At the end of the show I went to his home, then at the infamous Chelsea Hotel.

The seventies were a time of sexual liberation for people of every sexual orientation, of course. Gay men were going to places like the Anvil, where go-go boys danced on the bar upstairs and men had anonymous sex in the dark downstairs. Meanwhile, on the Upper West Side, straight men and women were going to Plato's Retreat, having orgies with a few dozen strangers. It was a time of intoxicating recklessness, of opulent hedonism with few apparent consequences. So you had sex with somebody you had just met in the elevator and would never see again? Why not? What could happen? You might get crabs—or, worst case, God forbid, VD. But there were antibiotics to take care of that. A few pops of penicillin—all better!

I had a good time as a young gay man discovering my sexuality in the late seventies. Yet I was never entirely comfortable with some aspects of the gay male scene in New York. A lot of it was pretty rudimentary. The scene was mostly about sex, and people were largely defined by their physical appeal according to a fairly narrow set of standards, their perceived sexual prowess, or their money. The money came into play mainly as a means to facilitate sex by furnishing booze and drugs. Ultimately, everything boiled down to how hot you looked, how nice your ass was, what you liked to do in bed, and how big you were below the belt. It could hardly have been more basic.

I felt a little alienated in the gay scene much of the time, because I wasn't a he-man, I was a little unusual-looking, and I've never been rich. I was in the midst of figuring out my own way of being gay, just as I was working out my own approach to making music. I wasn't a queen, and I wasn't the Marlboro Man. I was Fred. I had nothing against effeminate men or super-macho men, though I did tend to resist clichés of all sorts, because I'm not interested in clichés—personally or musically. Also, like a lot of gay men in my generation, I had to overcome a degree of internalized homophobia that came with growing up when we did—I wasn't particularly comfortable with obviously effeminate men. I was somewhat resistant to extreme expressions of gay identity, even as I admired those guys—such as Rollerena—for being so brave.

In the summer the entire population of Greenwich Village seemed to migrate to Fire Island, the sliver of rental cottages and beaches off the southern coast of Long Island, where the communities of the Pines and Cherry Grove were de facto gay resorts. As we entered the eighties, I took a quarter share in a house in the Fire Island Pines—I occupied a bedroom with another renter every other weekend—and I was miserable. I felt insecure physically, even though I went to the gym often enough and was in good shape. I just wasn't a big beefy hunk from the cover of *Mandate* magazine. I wasn't a boy toy. I was outside the circle of impossibly good-looking men whom I referred to as "A-gays," though, as I had in high school, I was perversely aching to be "in" with this same crowd who couldn't have seen me as *me*. I was desperate to have an actual conversation about something real with someone, instead of just being all flirty and fucking—though I did some of that too. I was looking for something that was virtually impossible to find there—love. In my experience, Fire Island was like a concentrated version of the bars: a well-constructed, high-functioning marketplace for sex. All the human interaction there was commodified and transactional.

I was ready for something more. I was looking for someone I could talk to about music and books. I wanted to be with someone I found interesting and I respected, and who found me interesting and respected me. By luck, the out-of-control cruising scene of the time worked to my benefit one morning. It was August 1979, and I had just returned from a two-month gig in Tokyo leading a trio with Red Mitchell and drummer Eliot Zigmund. I was standing dazed and jet-lagged on Seventh Avenue South in front of St. Vincent's Hospital, waiting for the light to change. I saw a hot-looking guy getting hassled by a street person. Our eyes locked and we took in each other's looks intensely. I helped free him from the guy harassing him, and we began to talk. His name was Eric Weinmann, and he told me he was visiting from Sacramento, seeing friends and exploring gay life on the East Coast. We went for breakfast and then hooked up. More significant, we *connected* as people and not mere assemblages of body parts.

After a few days he went back to Sacramento, and we started to talk on the phone almost every day. And in a few weeks, he wrote me a touching letter saying, in part, "I've never felt this way before—I think this must be love." I was ecstatic. A few weeks later, I visited him in Sacramento, and we spent time together exploring the San Francisco gay scene. Less than two months after we met, he had sold his pickup truck and his upright piano and moved across the country to live with me. I wasn't even sure if gay men could have what I had with Eric. With Eric, I had my first real adult love relationship, as well as my first mature sexual relationship. And I had my first great gay *friend*.

He had studied classical piano and had an undergraduate degree in music from Sacramento State University. We could talk meaningfully about the great pianists, and he was *hot*. He had the perfect clone look of the era—the mustache, the naturally great build, blue-green eyes, and dark coloring. Other gay men threw themselves at him. A friend of mine once described Eric as the boy next door with a hint of evil underneath, which is a potent combination. I couldn't believe he was with me. Every day I'd ask myself, *What did I do to deserve this smart, sweet, great-looking guy?* It was enough to make me think that maybe my arms were long enough, after all.

Eric found work as a waiter at the Village Green, a two-level restaurant on Hudson Street in the West Village with fancy French dining downstairs and a piano bar at the street level. Murray Grand, a veteran songwriter who had composed the beloved standard of infidelity payback, "Guess Who I Saw Today," in the 1950s, had the piano bar gig, playing show tunes and taking requests. The place was a date destination for upscale gay men and the occasional celebrity who liked the low-key atmosphere there. Eric made good money there. We called it the Village Queen.

A gifted people person, Eric loved to socialize. Wherever we went, he knew somebody. People lit up when they saw him. Bartenders loved him, because when Eric was there people would gather around him, order more drinks, and have a great time. When I was with Eric, I never had to worry about a thing. I wasn't going out to a bar and standing alone in the corner; I was part of the scene, and I became more relaxed as a result. I felt content and better about myself. I know this is elemental stuff, the way people feel when they're in healthy relationships. But it was new to me. I was twenty-four years old and had never been in love before, and I don't think I was unique among gay men at the time. Sex had been easy. Love came harder.

By the time we were together for a year, Eric and I had started wearing rings, simple white gold bands, as a symbol of our commitment. I was half expecting someone at Bradley's to ask me about my ring, but nobody did. I hadn't thought through what I would say if I was asked about it. I was still living two lives—the life of Fred the gay man who went to see *Dreamgirls* on Broadway with his hunky boyfriend, and the life of Fred the jazz pianist who hung around the piano with Tommy Flanagan at Bradley's.

Most nights, when Eric finished his shift at the Village Green, he would go out for drinks and maybe some dancing with some of his pals from the restaurant. Sometimes he would come to Bradley's late at night with his restaurant buddies. They would sit at the bar and just be very gay, dishing and laughing and carrying on. I was horrified. They didn't understand what Bradley's was, and that the regulars—and that always included musicians—didn't

understand why these guys were treating the music so disrespect-
fully. My two worlds were colliding in a way that was out of my
control. I gave Eric a good talking-to. I told him that if he wanted
to bring his friends to the club, fine. But they couldn't be so *obvious* when they were there. It was a symptom of my internalized
homophobia—treating other gay men as I had been treated. I was
trying to control my image as one of the jazz elite, but the cracks
in that façade were slowly beginning to show.

CHAPTER 6

SIDEMAN

G iants of jazz were still among us in the 1980s, and they weren't all dinosaurs. You could go to the Village Vanguard and see Bobby Hutcherson or Joe Henderson, to Fat Tuesday's and see Stan Getz or Chet Baker, to Sweet Basil and see Art Blakey, Art Farmer, or Gil Evans. All of these musicians had been prominent figures on the scene since the fifties or sixties, and they were all still playing at a superb level. For jazz fans, it was an extraordinary time to experience the music as it was created on the bandstand by many of its seminal innovators. For musicians, it was the last time a young person like me would be able to learn directly from this group of masters.

Since the earliest days of jazz, and until jazz performance programs became entrenched in higher education, the music had been taught and carried forward by means of apprenticeship on the job, in the same way artisans or painters had learned their crafts during the Renaissance. Formal music programs like the one I attended at the New England Conservatory started to replace real-world training under the tutelage of working masters, beginning in the early 1980s. But I came up right at the cusp of the two eras and benefited from both a formal musical education and an informal but invaluable one with some of the best musicians in the history of jazz.

Once I established myself as a working pianist in New York, I made it my mission to play with the greatest musicians alive—for the unique opportunity to learn from them, obviously, and also for the status that association with them conferred. I wanted to be thought of as someone who deserved to be working with the best. In other words, I wanted to be perceived as one of the greatest, too. I was essentially willing myself to overcome my own insecurities, proving to the world—and to myself—that I was worthwhile.

I wheedled and cajoled my way into the circle of A-list jazz soloists, asserting myself as a contender to be an A-list sideman. This was the strategy that my slightly older pianist friends had been employing—getting a steady gig with a "name" jazz star. If I was a freshman on the scene, I looked up to these guys as seniors who had hit New York three or four years before me. Being in the band of one of the heavies could lead to sideman work for half the year or more, and there was a decent possibility that a small record label would take a chance on you to record your own project as a bandleader if you had appeared on recordings with the star you were playing with on a regular basis.

There used to be a jazz club called Boomers on Bleecker Street, near Christopher Street, and I was there one night to hear pianist

Cedar Walton playing in a trio with Sam Jones and Billy Higgins. Scouting out the bar, I spotted Charlie Haden, one of the most important bassists in the history of jazz. Charlie, like many jazz musicians, had been a junkie on and off, and though he seemed quietly intense and looked bookish and respectable, during this period his drug use was out of control. I went up to him and introduced myself. I said, "Mr. Haden, I love your music, and I know we're going to play together." He looked me over like I was crazy, but I truly believed that it would happen. And not that many years after that, I hired Charlie as my bassist at Bradley's, and a couple of years later, he played on my second trio album. Our musical relationship was a long and important one, if intermittent.

A conservatory alum asked me to sub for him at a Brazilian nightspot called Cachaça, named after the wickedly strong liquor distilled from sugarcane that is the main ingredient in the Brazilian national cocktail, the caipirinha. It was an upscale joint on the second floor of a building in the East Sixties. I was part of a quartet that played Brazilian music for cocktails and dancing, and I began to work there fairly often. I knew something of Brazilian music from my friend Kenny Poole in Cincinnati, and I had subsequently gotten to know more about it from the younger Brazilian musicians who were around New York when I first arrived. They generously turned me on to the seminal recordings of all the Brazilian greats. The drummer and bandleader at Cachaça was Edison Machado. I didn't know it at the time, but Edison was the inventor of the *samba o prato* style that transferred samba rhythms to the modern drum set. Many describe him as the Papa Jo Jones of Brazilian drummers. He was patient and modest, taught me the repertoire, and helped me feel and play the Brazilian rhythms. I learned there, for the first time, some of the lovely *choros* that were popular in the twenties and thirties. With their multiple repeated sections, they are akin to American ragtime, and their melodies are infectious. Here I was again, lucky to be learning the music from one of the people who invented it—in the right place at the right time—and I include some Brazilian music in almost every solo concert I play today.

In the early eighties only a few megastars had a major-label record contract. Although there were a handful of new, scrappy independent record companies recording musicians on the New York scene, most of the great old jazz labels were out of business. Verve was a dead label. So was Blue Note. CD reissues of their classic albums were not yet part of the picture. The jazz world was loose, and things happened more informally, person to person, by word of mouth. Most business took place in the clubs, where musicians saw and heard and talked to one another. It was the rare artist who had a manager—there were only a few dedicated jazz booking agents—and nobody had a publicist. I watched the way this informal but casually rigorous system worked, and I took advantage of it.

Sam Jones recommended me to Art Farmer, the wonderful flügelhorn player who was in the top tier of jazz soloists in the second half of the twentieth century. Art came in to hear me play with Sam at Bradley's one night as a sort of audition. Sam had given me a heads-up, so I played some tunes that I knew were in Art's repertoire. This scheme must have worked in my favor, because shortly afterward Art hired me to play a two-week gig at a sketchy club called Dummy George's on the outskirts of Detroit, off the notorious 8 Mile Road.

We stayed in a motel with no food service, it was August, and it was miserable. I didn't have a car and had to walk half a mile along the highway to the closest convenience store, where everything—the cashier and all the merchandise—was behind bulletproof glass. You had to point at what you wanted, if you were hungry for chips or a Royal Crown cola, which is pretty much all they carried. Art Farmer had been living in Vienna since the sixties and was starting to come to the States more often but wasn't well enough connected to the American scene to know all the players. As a result, the bass player and the drummer he hired for the engagement were horrendous—he had gotten their names from somewhere and hired them without hearing them. At the end of the two weeks at Dummy George's, I said to Art, "I really love your music, but if this is the rhythm section you're going to go with, I'm afraid I'm just going to step out."

He paused for a few moments, thinking. Then he said, "Who would you choose?"

I said, "Let me think about that," then I helped him put together a much better band for an upcoming tour. We hired the bassist Mike Richmond, who had been working with Stan Getz, and the drummer Akira Tana, whom I knew from the New England Conservatory. Ray Drummond stepped in on bass after a while. I basically became the contractor for Art's band. Since he was living in Europe, he would call me up when he was planning to come stateside and I would round up the rhythm section for all of our engagements. It was a precious opportunity, because I had a hand in choosing whom I'd be playing with, and I could help give a boost to people such as Akira in the same way that Art was boosting me.

I started playing with Art regularly, including the very visible two-week residencies he would do three times a year at Sweet Basil on Seventh Avenue South, off Sheridan Square. The place would be packed every night. The American economy was supposedly weak, not yet having rebounded from the recession of the seventies. New York was still regarded as dangerous. Yet people were eating, drinking, doing drugs, and listening to jazz every night of the week. As I've said, there was a lot of coke flying around then, and I can't help but think that this was a boon to the jazz business. Everybody in town was so wired up, they didn't want to stay home. The high-speed, ecstatic volatility of jazz seemed perfectly suited to the coke-fueled atmosphere of the time.

I learned a lot about how to fit in with a horn player and a rhythm section as a supportive voice in an ensemble. Art didn't make conventional note choices often. As the pianist, you had to be prepared for anything. You had to listen alertly and be able to voice chords in all sorts of ways—and react quickly so as not to confine Art harmonically or come off like an idiot.

Art had a terrifically varied and unusual repertoire, full of interesting and beautiful but offbeat tunes—from "Sing Me Softly of the Blues" by the melodic but unconventional pianist Carla Bley, "The Cup-Bearers" by jazz composer-trombonist Tom McIntosh (a staple of Tommy Flanagan's repertoire), and Michel Legrand's "The Summer Knows," to lesser-known standards such as "Namely You" and "She's Funny That Way." His tastes and mine were compatibly eclectic, and I drew inspiration from the way Art brought unity to such varied material through the individuality of his warm and lyrical approach to the music. He also encouraged me to write my own tunes, something I had been afraid to do. His Viennese pianist, Fritz Pauer, had contributed a few very fine tunes to the book, and Art said one day, "You know, the way you play, there's no reason you shouldn't be writing your own tunes." When I started showing him my first songs, he not only played them, we eventually recorded them, giving me some bit of confidence that I could be a composer as well as a pianist.

In the spring of 1982 I played on one of the five albums I would make with Art Farmer in as many years—a pop-oriented record, unusual for Art, for Creed Taylor's CTI Records, which had become justifiably famous as a contemporary jazz label. There were three keyboard players on it: Don Grolnick, Warren Bernhardt on electric piano and synthesizer, and me. I wasn't a studio heavy like the other guys on the date—I was there because Art insisted I be part of the band. One of the tracks was actually a Bee Gees song, "Stop (Think Again)." Tenor saxophonist Joe Henderson was a co-leader on the date, and it was through that session that I met him. At first I was intimidated. Joe was widely acknowledged to be one of the great sax players of all time, and I was a huge fan. But I knew he was from Lima, Ohio, and after I broke the ice by telling him I was from Cincinnati, he was quite friendly. We bonded over our shared opinion that the repertoire for the album was kind of lame. He didn't have a pianist for an upcoming weekend gig in town, and at the end of the second day of recording, he asked me to play with his quartet.

The first time I played with Joe, we were at Seventh Avenue South, the club owned by Randy and Michael Brecker, and I was so overwhelmed with excitement entwined with pride and insecurity that I could barely function. It helped that I already could play much of his repertoire—most of it consisting of his first-rate original tunes that I had often played at jam sessions and on gigs. Still, this was the sideman job of my dreams, and it put me in a bigger fishbowl.

We started playing regularly at the Vanguard. One night I looked over from the piano at the bandstand, and there were Joe Henderson, Ron Carter on bass, and Al Foster on drums, all living legends. I thought, *What am I doing here? I'm a gay Jewish kid from Cincinnati. How the hell did this happen?* I told myself that I wouldn't be on that bandstand if I wasn't good enough. That's what I had been telling everyone else. Now I had to convince myself.

From my very first set with Joe, I found myself wondering how much I should be playing behind him during his solos. Having studied his classic Blue Note albums back in Cincinnati, I surmised that he had a huge sound and was a pretty aggressive guy. But he actually had a light and flexible approach to the tenor, maintaining a close relationship to the microphone as an integral part of his sound, and he was as mild-mannered as they come. He would play one of his epic-length solos, and at a certain point I would have an instinct to stop playing. He didn't give me a look or say, "Stroll" or "Lay out." There was just a vibe. I just felt, *Okay, I need to let this guy go for a while.* Then, at a certain point, I'd just sense, *Oh, I'm invited back in.* I'd have this experience in almost every set.

I didn't bring it up, because he wasn't much for discussing the work. But then, after a couple of years working together, we had a little downtime backstage at the Vanguard one night, and I finally said to him, "Joe, when I'm laying out behind you and then coming back in, I assume that's cool. I mean, you've never said anything."

He looked at me through his big, thick glasses and said, "If you feel it, it's right. If you *think* it, it's probably not right."

What an amazing lesson—play what you feel! Work from the inside out. Don't apply an external idea that could shake you out of the moment or inhibit you. Don't get into routines. Joe, in his old-school laissez-faire jazz way, had been leaving me to learn that by experience. But it helped me to hear it articulated. Ever since then, I've kept that lesson in my mind on the bandstand, and when I started teaching jazz piano myself, I made a point of passing it on.

Joe was the living embodiment of an old-fashioned jazz cat. He would often leave the club during our breaks, sometimes returning late or only a minute or two before the appointed set time. His nickname was "the Phantom" because you could never find him when you needed him—he would simply vanish. He would leave a message on my answering machine saying he was coming into town and wanted me on a gig, sometimes long in advance. I would try to get back to him to confirm, leaving multiple messages, but I'd get no response. I just had to go on faith—and he never stood me up. Joe liked coke. He also liked smack, and alcohol when he couldn't get either. He didn't do it to excess, at least most of the time when we played together. But he enjoyed it, and knowing that, I tried to have a little blow on hand to offer the boss before the set. For a junior member of the band like me, that was simply common courtesy. Once on a Friday night at the Vanguard my connection hadn't shown up in time, so we went onto the bandstand straight. We played well enough, but I didn't feel like I was doing anything special. Between sets, my connection came. I gave Joe his taste, and I had a little myself. We played the second set, and afterward I thought, *Man, that was killing!*

I was in the habit then of recording my gigs with a Marantz cassette recorder the size of a phone book. (I still have boxes of old tapes from those days, and when I have listened to them I have been amazed at how much talking was going on in the audience—there wasn't the silent reverence for the music that there is in the Vanguard of today.) A week or so after that Friday-night gig in 1983 with Joe, I played the cassette I had made of that evening's three sets, and I was flabbergasted. In the second set, the one I thought was so great at the time, I was rushing and pushing. The phrases went on much too long. I sounded cold. It was an exercise in pointless, unfocused, wasted energy. But the first set, when I was sober, was surprisingly good—grounded, related to the other musicians, and much more interesting. From that day on, I never did drugs on the bandstand. Joe could get a little high before the set, and it never seemed to hurt him. So could plenty of others I've played with. Not me. I'm not making a moral judgment when I say this. I'm just saying drugs aren't compatible with my music making. If I'm playing well—or badly—I want to know that it's really *me* who's up there on the bandstand making the music.

The issue is the same one at the heart of Joe Henderson's comment "If you feel it, it's right." Thinking isn't the only thing that can undermine emotional connectedness. In my experience, anything that takes you too far from authentic feeling carries the risk of taking you out of the music.

That said, I've seen people play spectacularly when they were profoundly fucked up. It's almost as if drugs help some musicians connect—or liberate them from something obstructive inside them. After playing the same music for years, it can get to be routine, so they try to duplicate the feeling of "getting off" with the music like they used to when it was all fresh and new—and they imagine that drugs or booze can help them get there, sometimes the more the better. I'm thinking of Chet Baker, whose addiction to heroin took over his life. His days and nights revolved around getting the money for the fix, getting the fix, and getting the money for the next fix. When I saw him at Sweet Basil after I'd been in New York for a few years, he was physically ravaged—a skeleton with hollow eyes where that beautiful specimen of manhood used to be. He was so messed up that night that his embouchure was shot and he couldn't play the trumpet. But he needed the money, so he scat-sang the whole show, and it was amazing. Delicate melodies of heart-wrenching beauty that sounded just like his trumpet playing. The drugs tore apart his body and, no doubt, his mind, but they could not kill his music.

I encountered Chet half a dozen times before he died, in 1988— still in his fifties but looking twenty-five years older. He struck me as a sweet, fragile man. We were at a jam session once, at a musician's loft in Chelsea. At the beginning of the night someone brought out some heroin—I snorted some for the first time. Chet and some of the other cats shot up. We played together, and it felt like I could do *anything*. My senses and musical instincts were heightened in a new, laser-focused way. When it hit my bloodstream, I felt a rush of delirium like no high I had ever had, and when I came down, I naturally wanted to have that feeling again.

But I thought, *Oh . . . I see how this works.* It was just *too good.* And that was the last time for heroin and me.

OVER more than half a decade of playing with Art Farmer and Joe Henderson, I learned quite a bit. I learned about pacing—how to be patient with yourself night after night, week after week, year after year, taking the long view. I learned how to program a set. Sometimes with Joe, early in the night, I'd hear him do a lot of the same things I had heard him do before. It was like, *Okay, Joe, we know you know how to play that.* Then, five choruses into the tune, it would be like, *Whoa!! Where the fuck did that come from?* A long, steady idle, and all of a sudden, fifth gear.

Art and Joe both taught me about hanging in there during a solo. Sometimes, you need to get through some messy choruses before you get to something good. Sometimes, the good shit is there from the start, and you just say, *Thank you, God.* But there are nights when you have to wallow through some crap or be less than pleased with the way things are going in order for things to get better.

I was a young, hungry man in a hurry and needed to learn to step back, take a breath, and pace myself for the long haul. One day I got a call to fill in for the pianist Jim McNeely on a gig with Stan Getz, a tenor player with matinee-idol looks who had achieved international fame in the sixties playing bossa novas such as "The Girl from Ipanema" and "Desafinado." We were at Fat Tuesday's, a basement club on Third Avenue that booked major acts. I had never played with Getz before and loved his assured way of phrasing, his deep sense of swing, and his warm, huge tone. George Mraz was playing bass, and Al Foster was on drums—master musicians. For some reason, though, I wasn't having a great night. Between the sets I sat in the minuscule dressing room, feeling down. Stan came in, and it was obvious that I was in a funk. I wasn't expecting any comfort from him. It wasn't his job to nursemaid me, and he had a reputation for brusqueness with musicians.

Stan said, "Hey, Fred, man—what's the problem?"

I said, "I don't know—I feel like I'm playing the same shit over and over. I feel I'm not doing anything new."

He said, "Did you play one chord progression different tonight than you played it last time?"

I said, "I'm sure I did."

And Stan said something like, "Well, if you do that once a night, at the end of the year you'll do three hundred sixty-five new things. You don't need to reinvent the wheel every time you play."

That was an important lesson for someone who wanted everything immediately, as I did. I had much more ambition than patience. One of the reasons I love jazz is that it's a music of the moment, the here and now. With some help from people who had been playing the music a lot longer than I had, I started to see that there was something beyond the moment at hand. I began to grasp that jazz careers are built from individual moments, accumulated over time.

Coming up as I did in New York during the late seventies and early eighties, I was among the last jazz musicians to develop on the job the old-fashioned way, figuring it out by fucking up, getting back on your feet, fucking up again, hanging out, learning from the masters. I managed to establish myself as a versatile, in-demand sideman. The job called for deference to the musical personality of the leader, and I repressed aspects of my own playing accordingly. I played one way for Art Farmer, a different way for Joe Henderson, and another way for a singer such as Chris Connor. It was more at Bradley's and other venues where I played piano-bass duos and trios that my own musical personality emerged, and it was a work in progress.

In the early summer of 1979, while I was playing with Art, I got a call from his agent, Abby Hoffer, telling me there was a new club in Tokyo called the Blue Shell that was looking for a piano trio to play for two months. Could I put together a band and go to Tokyo on short notice? I hadn't played much out of the country—only once in Europe with the post-Coltrane *Black Saint* saxophonist Billy Harper (not a great musical experience)—and I was eager to explore Japan and travel internationally as a bandleader. I often played duos with Red Mitchell at the time, so I hired Red. On drums I got Eliot Zigmund, who had just left the Bill Evans trio.

The club was in Roppongi, the nightlife district where the foreign embassies are located, so all the visiting dignitaries could go out clubbing on their government expense accounts. (It was rumored to be owned by the Japanese mafia; what better way to launder some money than to open a pricey jazz club?) Like many of the clubs in Roppongi, this one was on an upper level in an austere, glass-skinned office building. You walked out of the elevator and onto a plexiglass floor with white sand and seashells under the surface, perfectly lit to create the illusion that you're walking on the beach. There was mahogany everywhere and nautical portholes in the walls. Thousands of pieces of Italian glass dangled from the ceiling to create an underwater atmosphere. And there were floor-to-ceiling water tanks embedded in the walls on all sides, with varieties of large, exotic tropical fish swimming around and others lying on the bottom, thrashing about with their fins flapping, dying from some problem with the water or rotten-fin disease. The venue was billed as the Blue Shell: Deep Sea Jazz Experience.

The bandstand was set up inside an enormous mechanical clamshell that was like something out of a Busby Berkeley movie. Red, Eliot, and I would enter through a trapdoor behind the shell and get into position. When I pressed a foot switch, the clamshell would open, revealing the trio, and we would be playing a little ditty that Red wrote called "Clam Time." It was a short series of "Asian-sounding" ascending intervals of fifths; when the set was over we played the series of fifths in descending order and the clamshell closed.

We played four sets a night, from 8 P.M. to 2 A.M., for stretches of ten days straight, with time off when we'd be too exhausted to do anything. After the shows we'd crawl to a bar for a drink or dessert before crashing in the little studio apartments they provided for each of us. We were trapped in a surreal aquatic hell, and the heat and air pollution of Tokyo in August was stifling. I barely saw anything of the city other than the club and my air-conditioned apartment. After a few weeks I could relate to those fish flapping their fins at the bottom of the tanks.

Red had been a mainstay on both the jazz and recording-studio scenes in L.A. in the fifties and sixties—recording everything from major movie scores to one of Ornette Coleman's pioneering early albums. Unusually, he tuned his bass in fifths, like a 'cello (it is normally tuned in fourths), and played some of the most beautiful, lyrical bass solos ever. His lefty politics and increasing cynicism led him to move to Stockholm, where he was living when I had met him at Bradley's. An outspoken liberal, he always railed against the people he called the "me-firsters." I felt I could talk openly to him, so one night toward the end of our underwater ordeal, Red and I were having a late-night dessert, and I told him I was gay. I just blurted it out, and that was that. After all, he had agreed to be a sideman in *my* band, I was getting some musical confidence and positive feedback on the scene, and I had every expectation that I would be able to be honest given his openness about most things. He didn't scream or run in terror, and I thought, *Okay, that went pretty well. Maybe this is something I can tell people without a lot of drama.*

When we returned to New York, we picked up our lives. I didn't play with Red much after that, though I saw him play fairly often at Bradley's, and every time we were together hanging out, he would ask me if I had a girlfriend or if I had gotten married yet. I didn't know if he was joking or what, but he kept doing it. It was weird.

Red left Sweden and moved to Oregon, where he died in 1992. After his death I was in Bradley's one night, chatting at the bar with one of the regular coke dealers and I told him how strange I thought it was that Red was always asking me if I had a girlfriend or if I had gotten married. The dealer said, "Didn't you know? Red told everybody that while you were in Japan together you came on to him."

The jazz world was small, and Bradley's was a gossip den. Without my knowing it, Red had been spreading the word for years that I had hit on him. He was the first jazz musician of his generation whom I had confided in—and this was what he did with my trust? I felt betrayed—and was amazed by his arrogance. But things were different in the eighties, and I was still mainly in the sideman pool—and not "out" to the jazz world as gay. Today, if Red asked me if I had a girlfriend, I would just say, "No, Red, I don't have a girlfriend. I'm in love with a man."

CHAPTER 7

CLASSIC SOUND

have always been fascinated by songs: from the discs on my kiddie record player, hymns I heard at our temple, all of the great pop music of the sixties, and later, classic American popular song. I simply love words and music—that's why I had gotten into that *Great Songs of the Sixties* book. Soon after I learned each song, I would play it in my own way using the rudimentary chord symbols in combination with the book's piano arrangements and my budding knowledge of harmony acquired from Walter Mays. I also began picking up tunes by ear from the radio and from pop and rock LPs—James Taylor, Joni Mitchell, the Beatles, Traffic, and Elton John—and played those too, sometimes for my friends alone or at a high school musical cast party or before or after a rehearsal at school.

Given all of the above, I had a different conception of composition than many of the older jazz musicians I worked with in New York. Since improvisation is a kind of spontaneous creativity, many of the jazz musicians who came up in the era before me were content to apply their creative imaginations to soloing, rather than composing in the traditional sense of planning out and writing down an original tune. They would draw from the existing repertoire—the beboppers often using the harmonic progression of an existing standard and writing their own melody over it so they got to keep the publishing royalties—and maybe compose an original piece every now and then if the impulse struck them, if they got a musical idea they thought was worth developing, or if they needed to fill out an album. Many musicians were content to play others' music—in their own way. Coleman Hawkins didn't write much original music—neither did Art Tatum.

Of course, some of my favorite jazz musicians were also important composers—Duke Ellington, Thelonious Monk, Wayne Shorter, Ornette Coleman, and Charles Mingus foremost among them—and they had highly personal approaches to composition. They drew deeply from their own point of view and their individual aesthetic in the music they usually crafted to be compatible with their own playing style. The great jazz composers' approach to writing music was idiosyncratic and individualistic. It seemed to me of a piece with the way the Beatles, Joni Mitchell, and the other singer-songwriters I grew up with approached their writing. They drew from life to give voice to something meaningful to them—or they wrote something fun, catchy, and seriously grooving. But I have always made the distinction between standards (which have lyrics) and jazz compositions, written by jazz musicians for jazz musicians to improvise upon—even if, in the case of Ellington and others, lyrics were added later for commercial appeal. I believe that a great jazz composition should inspire—and leave room for—the musicians playing it to make it their own. And of course—and this is true of all music—the most important attribute of any composition is memorability.

I had virtually given up composing after writing "A Windy Night" and the score for the fifth-grade production of *Peter Pan* at the age of ten. I didn't realize what was going on with me at the time, but when I reached adolescence and began to confront my sexual orientation, I essentially stopped composing and taking my classical piano lessons seriously. It had never occurred to anyone to mention that being a composer was a career path—it seemed to be concert pianist or nothing. The "classical" music I had been composing as a youngster seemed a distant memory—and I was too insecure at that time to think that I could write jazz tunes of any lasting value.

When I was first playing at Bradley's and spending late nights hanging out with the piano legends of the day, we would often sit around the piano and show one another tunes—or at least share the altered chord changes we were using. Jimmy Rowles taught me his haunting ballad "The Peacocks," and Tommy Flanagan showed me many of Strayhorn's greatest compositions. So when Art Farmer started encouraging me to compose, I wrote my first jazz tune and called it "II B.C."—the title was a play on "I X Love" from *Mingus Mingus Mingus Mingus Mingus*, and the "B.C." was for Bradley Cunningham. It was a thirty-two-bar chromatic ballad in the key of D-flat (the original key of "Body and Soul" and "Lush Life," perhaps the definitive jazz ballads), and I used a lot of the musical language of Mingus and Strayhorn. It was certainly derivative and betrayed my influences at the time, but writing that first tune was nonetheless an accomplishment for me.

During the summer of 1981, Sam Jones grew seriously ill, suffering from lung cancer. He was only in his mid-fifties, but the illness was so advanced that he could no longer play. The word at Bradley's was that Sam didn't have long to live. I cared deeply for him, and after I went to visit him in the hospital in Englewood, New Jersey, seeing him for the last time led me to compose another tune: "One for Sam," a joyful, up-tempo celebration of Sam's ebullient spirit and positive influence on me. I used as a template the sprightly bass-and-piano unison tunes of Sam's contemporary, bassist Oscar Pettiford. Art included it on his new album, *A Work of Art*, along with a second tune of mine, a light samba called "Summersong," inspired by the sunny lightness of spirit that I felt with my first boyfriend, Eric. Art received a Grammy nomination for that album, and I thought that was pretty cool.

Within a year I would write two more tunes for Art's ensembles. "And Now There's You" was my first love song, which I wrote with Eric in mind even though there weren't any lyrics. Art featured it on a mixed-bag album skewed slightly toward romantic numbers, *Warm Valley*, recorded with a quartet of Ray Drummond, Akira Tana on drums, and me, again for Concord Jazz Records. Then, we made a quintet album with the same band plus Art's frequent collaborator Clifford Jordan, on tenor saxophone, for a small label called Soul Note, and Art named the record for a tune of mine on it, "Mirage." A slow bolero with a mournful melody, the music was meant to evoke the image of camels crossing the desert. I wrote the introduction and the A section rather quickly, but it somehow seemed that the tune needed another section; it just wasn't complete as it was. I kept at it from time to time, and one after-noon several months later I played the section I had composed already and the bridge just seemed to come from nowhere—another mirage.

Through these first compositions I was beginning to reconcile my two selves—the gay Fred and the jazz-cat Fred—in music, without any overt plan to do that. I was writing, to some degree, from my heart and from personal experience. At the same time I was trying to figure out how to compose jazz tunes, and one of the ways I did that was to give myself assignments to write with other musicians in mind. This started a practice of dedicating composi-tions to musicians and other people in my life—these dedication pieces now number almost forty. Once again, it's much easier to compose if you have a subject in mind and are not just staring at the manuscript paper waiting for creative lightning to strike. Starting around 2002, when I was feeling artistically stuck I began using a kitchen timer set to forty-five minutes (matching the du-ration of the standard psychotherapy session) and would chal-lenge myself to complete a tune—in scribble—in that time. Often I would randomly pick a starting note, starting key, or specific rhythm to make the game more challenging and get me going faster. This practice—like speed writing for authors—has led to some of my favorite compositions, as the notation occurs as close as possible to the speed of improvisation.

I had avoided writing for years partly out of insecurity. I already had a huge repertoire of great tunes, and I thought to myself, *I'm never going to write anything as good as Thelonious Monk or Billy Strayhorn or Wayne Shorter. Why bother?* When I decided to try to write seriously, I used a technique to impose some structure on the work. I said to myself, *Okay, I'm going to write a post-bop tune in the vein of Sam Jones. It will be my way of honoring Sam and help focus me, too.* I would say, *Now I'll try writing a thirty-two-bar ballad in the style of Strayhorn.* It was a device to get me started, and ironically, working with other musicians in mind led me to write pieces that were very much my own. They spoke of the people I was honoring but in my language.

When Art decided to record those first two songs of mine, someone at Concord Records asked me the name of my publishing company, and I said I would get back to him. I turned to Bob Mintzer, the saxophonist and arranger, who is only a couple of years older than me but had been working solidly in New York for a while and knew the music business better than I did. I had a lot of respect for Bob as an all-around, can-do jazz professional. He told me I needed to sign with a performing-rights organization such as ASCAP or BMI. I asked him, "Which one are you with?" He said, "BMI." So I went up to the BMI offices on West Fifty-Seventh Street to sign on with them as a composer.

The woman at the desk there told me I needed to put the name of my publishing company on the paperwork. I thought about that for a minute, then wrote down "Fred Hersch Music." It felt a bit pretentious—Fred Hersch Music? Who is *Fred Hersch?*" But I couldn't think of anything else to call it. After all, what kind of music was I making? It was *Fred Hersch* music.

Around this time, just as I was taking my first steps to develop a voice as a composer, I took an equally important step in my development as a pianist. I knew how to get around the piano, of course, but I had yet to find a completely integrated personal sound as a pianist. I had facility and speed, could swing and play in most styles, and didn't lack for musical ideas. But I did not quite yet have a *sound* of my own. I was honing in on it, but I needed someone to unlock the secret for me.

I had heard that the wonderful bebop pianist Barry Harris was studying piano with an older gentleman named Joseph Prostakoff, and I was intrigued. Prostakoff lived in a cavernous apartment on the Upper West Side and agreed to take me on—only if I would do exactly as he told me. Normally I would have resisted this dry, technical, and dogmatic approach, but something told me to take a leap of faith. He gave me no say in what pieces I was to work on, and in turn he showed me how piano playing doesn't use the fingers as much as I had thought.

The method Joe taught was originated by a renowned American piano teacher of the mid-twentieth century, Abby Whiteside, with whom he had studied from 1948 until Whiteside's death in 1956. I studied with Joe, as he mandated, three times a week for a month at first, then once or twice a week thereafter—in those days, this was a huge drain on my resources, but I kept at it. Around that time I heard that Joe had a colleague, Sophia Rosoff, who was his fellow student and teaching assistant under Whiteside, and a while after I met her, I decided to study with her. She and I would work together for the next thirty-five years. (As I write this in the middle of the second decade of the twenty-first century, Sophia, at ninety-six, is still teaching sporadically.)

Joe and Sophia could have not been more different from each other in personality and outlook. As dry as Joe was, Sophia was warm and brimming with life. They both told me, in different ways, about Abby's holistic approach to musical performance—a way of thinking that considers the whole body, as well as the mind, and not merely the fingers.

As Sophia recalled to me, she had been working with some success as a concert pianist in New York but was growing increasingly uncomfortable at the piano. Her joints were stiffening, and her body ached when she played. She mentioned this to Artie Shaw, the jazz clarinetist, literary dilettante, and serial husband who had intellectual aspirations and nurtured associations in the classical-music world. (When he gave up jazz to play classical music, she was his accompanist—and later in life he asked her to marry him; she preferred his friendship.) Shaw had made friends with the conductor and pianist Morton Gould, a student of Whiteside's. Shaw recommended Whiteside to Sophia, and Sophia found studying with her to be a life-changing experience, just as I found studying with Sophia.

Sophia, by way of Abby Whiteside, taught me how sound is produced not by the fingers alone but by the entire body. Much piano pedagogy starts by building up the individual finger muscles, but in Abby's world, the fingertip is at the end of an integrated chain that starts farther back in the body—this eliminates the need for some very tedious and mindless exercises. You need to have some finger strength and coordination, of course, but these things are not as important as many would have you believe. And I will always love her for saying, "Don't use the word 'practice'—it sounds like a chore. Think of whatever you are doing as an *experiment*—that's much more fun and interesting."

If you look closely at the way jazz drummers sit when they play, you can see how this approach works. Drummers are constantly shifting their body weight. They sit on a seat that swivels for good reason. Sophia taught pianists to approach sitting at the bench the way a drummer might approach sitting at the stool, with flexibility and freedom of movement in their lower bodies. She said pianists have to get into the optimum postural position to allow the mechanics of producing sound to come naturally. The piano is part of the percussion family—something is struck (the hammer by the key), and the sound always fades from the initial attack but doesn't fade as quickly if you find that sweet spot in the piano's action to get the best sound, not overplaying. And the tip of your finger—like the tip of the stick for drummers—is the end point of a longer chain that starts much farther back. A great drummer can't swing at a brisk tempo on a ride cymbal by only playing from the wrist down.

Working with Sophia, I learned to come forward when I play. I put my left foot back, almost on the ball of my foot. That brought my torso forward, hovering over the keyboard. To play on the upper registers of the keyboard, my left foot pushed me up there, giving me support, and allowed my right arm to stay relaxed instead of becoming extended as if I was reaching from the center of the bench. When I moved down to the bottom of the keyboard, my left foot kept me balanced. Her point was always to be anchored to the floor and adjusting to the keyboard, because it cannot adjust to you.

I think a clear and singing piano sound comes when the fingers are working sensitively and efficiently; gliding on the pads of your fingers allows for more control than pushing down hard with curved fingers. By this I don't mean that a pianist can get away with not using the fingers at all. I just mean that you may get a better sound with less effort if more of your body is involved. And the more relaxed (yet alert) you are, the better the music will flow. After all, if you want to pick up something heavy, you don't use just your hands and wrists—you lift the object using your legs and back. You need to play connected to the floor. Just because your fingertip is the point of contact with the key doesn't mean that it should do all the work—it needs something lined up behind it in order for it to have any tonal quality.

There are various schools of piano technique, some that stress finger strength and others that emphasize arm weight. But this way of playing is closer to yoga than to weight lifting. For a jazz pianist, who doesn't know what's coming next, flexibility is more important than brute strength. The approach I learned from Sophia involves playing from the upper arm, allowing the larger muscles to "draw" the big rhythms and phrases. If you were to place your left hand under your right elbow as you play, the elbow would be "drawing" the shape of the phrase. The fingers and arm simply transfer these into sound with a flat hand and a minimum of effort. You might think of a violinist's bow arm, which can play many notes with a single large motion. Since a jazz pianist is making up the content of the music in each moment, flexibility is what matters.

Sometimes in a lesson with Sophia her students wouldn't play the piano at all. She'd have them sit down and balance an egg on the carpet for concentration. Or she'd tell them to walk around the room slouching like Groucho Marx, relaxing their lower bodies. Sometimes she would ask me to shake out all of my limbs like I was a skeleton—with no muscles at all. I realize how this sounds, like the quack work of a cult figure. But Sophia's methods were carefully designed to impart an understanding of the relationship of the parts of the body to one another, with a focus on balance. Through Sophia and her methods, I began to understand the physicality of sound production.

I can usually tell an individual pianist by his sound, just as a drummer can hear someone playing a ride cymbal and say, "Oh, that's Tony Williams" or "That's Billy Higgins." Drummers can choose their cymbals and sticks, but pianists don't always have that option—we mostly have to play the piano we're given. For us, our eighth note and our touch define our rhythmic signature, much like a great drummer's distinctive ride cymbal beat. When Herbie Hancock plays an eighth note on the piano, it sounds different from an eighth note by Chick Corea. Herbie and Chick both have great sounds, but they're *different*. A Chick Corea eighth note is *thinner* than Herbie's, probably owing to his background in Latin music, where a brighter sound is the norm. You can hear the influence of McCoy Tyner in Chick's sound. A Herbie Hancock eighth note is much *fatter*. You can hear his antecedents—the more solid sounds of classical pianists as well as Miles's pianists Wynton Kelly and Bill Evans. When I play an eighth note, I do think that it sounds like me—there's a note length, a space between each note, an approach to rhythm and pianistic color that's distinctively mine—regardless of the music or the piano I'm playing. I could be playing a ballad out of time or something swinging, but that eighth note will sound like me.

I believe in a "sound first" approach to the piano. No matter how much a pianist can do using harmonic devices, patterns, and scales, it will be meaningless unless it is put into sound in a way that grabs the listener. A useful analogy is that of a stage actor's voice. With experienced stage actors, you can always understand what they're saying without feeling as if they're shouting at you or trying too hard. (That's why the Broadway debuts of many famous film actors are often not successful; they are best at speaking while being closely miked and acting for the camera, not projecting in a naturalistic way to a large theater audience.) If you have a good, clear, relaxed sound as a pianist, you can draw listeners in rather than bludgeoning them, banging the crap out of the piano in the process. And your sensitivity to touch, sound, and the strengths and limitations of whatever piano you're playing will enable you to be more emotionally involved with the music instead of struggling with technique. Though there is no one right way to get piano tone—and there are a wide variety of great jazz piano sounds—music that isn't alive as pure, connected sound (often with the lyrics in mind if there are any) is just a bunch of notes.

An important part of the Whiteside method that Sophia taught me is its emphasis on rhythm. The idea is to absorb the pulse underlying a piece of music—be it classical, jazz, or an Appalachian folk tune—and progress from there. When Sophia talked about the importance of rhythm, she liked to quote Virginia Woolf in a letter to the writer Vita Sackville-West:

> Now this is very profound, what rhythm is, and goes far deeper than words. A sight, an emotion, creates this wave in the mind, long before it makes words to fit it; and in writing (such is my present belief) one has to recapture this, and set this working (which has nothing apparently to do with words) and then, as it breaks and tumbles in the mind, it makes words to fit it.

When you listen to certain pianists, you always have a sense of where the music is *going* and what it's *saying*. There's a forward motion to their playing that transcends the fingers. The music is propelled by a complete internal rhythm rather than simply being a collection of individual notes typed out by the fingers. To my mind, the work of all the truly great classical pianists has this quality. I think of Arthur Rubinstein, Martha Argerich, Glenn Gould, and Josef Hofmann, just to name a few. Among jazz pianists, Herbie Hancock, Paul Bley, Ahmad Jamal, early Bill Evans, Art Tatum, and Tommy Flanagan all have that special ability to communicate through their instrument by using their senses of sound, touch, and internal rhythm so that they're really *talking* to us though their playing. The content of the music is what is foremost in their performances, not the mechanics that achieve it.

Once you have the rhythm of the music in your bones, you think of it as an outline, and you then fill in the musical details one by one. (If you were to paint a landscape, you would most probably start with a horizon line, then add clouds, trees, and grass. You wouldn't start in one corner with all of the details in place.) Pianists who play jazz are almost always working from an outline—though they may not think of it that way. The chord changes (harmonic sequence), in combination with the melodic material, provide the basic structure to which we then add our personal improvisations. This structure is harmonic but also rhythmic—time moves forward on a continuum, and certain harmonies are the signposts.

It's as if the form of each tune is like a glass mixing bowl: solid but clear. In each chorus, you can put different "content" into the bowl—Jell-O, a goldfish in water, rocks, or M&M's—and it will look different depending on what you put into it, though the shape itself will not change. This way each chorus or section of a tune becomes a variation on a theme—and the best jazz performances are continuous storytelling experiences. If I am playing five 32-bar choruses, I want it to sound like 160 bars of music, not the same 32 bars repeated five times. This effect is even more achievable with solo piano—which is one of the reasons I love playing solo. You can blur the beginnings and endings of bar lines and choruses— and obscure the harmony—thus making for a more continuous musical expression.

Rhythm is the very essence of jazz and something I value greatly in every kind of music. On and off the bandstand, I like music that *moves*—and makes me want to move. Sophia said quite rightly, "Sound plus rhythm equals music." That's a definition that can apply to any kind of music at all. A lot of jazz does that, though some jazz can also be contemplative or cerebral—or formatted and predictable. As a musician, I'm interested in the wide range of ways that music can work on the body, the mind, the heart, and the soul. As a listener, though, I'm often attracted to music that is made not just for listening but for dancing. I love Earth, Wind and Fire and all the great R&B music, which you cannot listen to without moving, unless there's something deeply wrong with you. (I suggest to some of my more intellectual, rhythmically challenged students that when they are alone, they put on some loud dance music they love, move with abandon, and get the rhythm into their bodies.) I love Brazilian music, with its special, earthy groove. In Western formal music, rhythm is often underemphasized. Part of the genius of the method Sophia taught is the way it leads you to focus on rhythm in whatever you're playing. For me, Sophia's lessons built beautifully on one of the first lessons I learned about jazz in Cincinnati, when Jimmy McGary played Ellington for me and said, "That's *time.*"

IN the summer of 1979 I moved out of the loft I had been sharing with Eddie Felson and into another loft, one of my own, on the fifth floor of an old building on Broadway between Prince and Spring Streets in SoHo. The district was still undergoing its transition from industrial use to residential occupancy by artists, would-be artists, and others who liked being associated with artists. Its subsequent transition into an upscale shopping district was still in the future and would have been inconceivable to anyone in SoHo in the seventies and early eighties. Most of the buildings were still occupied by wholesalers and distributors of materials for the garment trade and backroom supplies of every kind, but that was changing fast. The loft I moved into was in the Charles Nathan Building, so named for the seller of office furniture and business equipment who had been operating out of the ground floor since the early twentieth century, when the building was new. Before the fifth floor was broken up into open-plan spaces for private renters like me, it had been occupied by wholesale distributor Liberty Electronics, which specialized in reselling tubes and diodes acquired as military surplus. When I moved in, only the second of the ultimately ten tenants on the floor, it was still a construction site and there was a lingering wisp of electrochemicals in the air.

The loft was a clean, New York white space with a good amount of room, fourteen-foot ceilings, a large skylight, two north-facing windows, and an open plan like most commercial lofts. Since technically I had a commercial lease and was scared of being discovered living there, I kept the furniture to a minimum; it was all student-style except for my rather nice stereo, my large LP collection, and the 1896 Steinway B piano that I acquired in 1982 from jazz pianist Richie Beirach after selling the Schimmel. After years of selling, then trading up pianos, I finally had one I really loved. I felt fairly grounded in a place that suited me well and was very cheap to maintain. The fixture fee was on the high side, but the rent was negligible and I got a fifteen-year lease, important to one with a large piano. I could practice, teach, and have jam sessions there—there were other (mostly visual) artists living in the building as well. The fifth floor of 548 Broadway was certainly nothing like my parents' house on Rose Hill Avenue in Cincinnati. That was my home of origin. This was my home for living my life.

Eric had joined me there a few months after I moved in. There was a sleeping loft above the clothes closet, reachable by a ladder; we slept on the then-requisite futon. We settled into a groove and set up housekeeping, chipping in on the expenses, dividing the chores, cooking together sometimes, and hanging out at home when we weren't working, all in a place that felt genuinely like a home to us. We were comfortable with each other. We took turns playing the piano, and we had an active social life—mostly after we both got off work in the evenings, sleeping in most days.

But after two years or so, Eric and I were having problems. Though I would have preferred monogamy, we had established rules that allowed him to sleep with other men when I was out of town—only one time, not in our home, and no boyfriends on the side—but he was not able to abide by them. That year we broke up at my instigation. Model-boy handsome and super-sexy, Eric could always have all the men he wanted. Over time, I got frustrated that our once-fulfilling relationship was not progressing in a healthy way; in fact, it was slowly falling apart. Alcohol and recreational drugs were too much a part of our (especially his) life. Not long after, I learned that he moved in with one of his boyfriends-on-the-side, and I started going out again.

As I approached my thirties, newly single, I started to wish that my professional life was more firmly grounded. There was a certain excitement in the precariousness and habitual contingency of life as a gigging jazz musician. But it could be harrowing never to be sure what was coming next.

I was doing the right things—beginning to compose seriously while finding my personal voice at the piano—at the wrong time in jazz history. By the early 1980s, the music had become splintered into three predominant factions, and I didn't quite fit into any of them. ECM, the German record label founded by Manfred Eicher in the late 1960s, had reached full bloom with its brand of pristine jazz art music—recorded in Europe with a more classical approach, it sounded more like it was played in a concert hall than in a recording studio. Keith Jarrett, Paul Bley, Pat Metheny, and John Abercrombie were among its artists. They made a lot of serious music—almost all original compositions—that I appreciated for its ambition and high audio standards. I adored a lot of their work, but my music didn't fit neatly into the ECM category. I wasn't composing the floating, atmospheric music like most of the artists on the label, and I had no presence on the European scene.

At the same time there was a more commercial strain of jazz-rock fusion—fast, loud, but grooving music centered on synthesizers and electronic effects. This music was largely created by descendants of Miles Davis's electric albums and featured many of his alumnae. Weather Report (Wayne Shorter and Joe Zawinul) and Return to Forever (Chick Corea)—along with Herbie Hancock's efforts along these lines—were wildly popular, understandably. Putting aside the light shows and three-octave keyboards on shoulder straps that you played like a guitar, I genuinely dug them. (I had actually opened for both Weather Report and Return to Forever as a budding young pianist in Cincinnati with the Jimmy McGary quartet—quite a musical contrast.) But the technology involved was way beyond me, so I just enjoyed it from a distance.

The third strain was a kind of Upper East Side jazz, a meticulous and elegant but aesthetically conservative school of music that included the swing revivalists who were emerging in the wake of the campaign by Gunther Schuller and others to canonize jazz. *New Yorker* jazz critic Whitney Balliett was the authority and main cheerleader for this kind of jazz. Concord Records occupied a part of this sphere, with all its albums by mainstream veterans such as Mel Tormé, George Shearing, and Rosemary Clooney, and younger musicians with retro styles such as saxophonist Scott Hamilton, cornetist Warren Vaché, and the singer Susannah McCorkle. I respected most of them, though I didn't find the music very engaging—but I had gotten to know Shearing very well from Bradley's, and I enjoyed visiting his apartment for afternoon tea with George and Ellie. I genuinely loved the old standards and could have gone in that direction, but deep down I was not interested in being a mainstream revivalist of styles of yesteryear.

Great elders of bebop and post-bop were still among us, of course, and I had been working steadily with some of them for several years. There were audiences of varying sizes for varying kinds of jazz. It was clear, though, that most of the attention and most of the money was being paid to Euro jazz, fusion, and mainstream revivalism. Nearing age thirty and concerned about my job security, I decided to open my own recording studio, conceiving of that as a way to generate regular income without relying on gigs, while providing a mechanism for me to make my own records—my own music, made my way. In my grandiose way of thinking, Glenn Gould was my main inspiration—he walked away from a hugely successful concert career at thirty and only made studio recordings until the end of his life.

I worked up a plan to convert the loft at 548 Broadway into a professional recording studio with living quarters upstairs in a low-ceilinged room that replaced the sleeping loft of the original design. For the new design and technical advice on all of the equipment needs, I went to engineer Paul Wickliffe, owner of the very successful Skyline Studios, who was married to Roseanna Vitro. Though at first I wanted to do something fairly modest, the project got out of hand. I insulated all the walls, built soundproof drum and vocal isolation booths, and installed very expensive custom-built studio monitors in a fully stocked control room with the requisite plate-glass window. I purchased a twenty-four-track tape recorder, Dolby noise-reduction modules, and a large assortment of microphones, many of them classic ribbon and tube models. Paul worked up plans for the space, and I helped the contractors who built it by stapling insulation and getting lunch and coffee. For funding, I used savings I had accumulated from the remains of my college fund set up by my grandmother Ella, and my parents and brother all contributed. I was excited by this new adventure and approached it with a lot of energy, but I was a bit in denial about the complexities of it and how running a studio would change my life.

Looking back on this time, I feel as if I'm watching a documentary film about someone else. It's hard for me to conceive of myself as a businessman, though I've always been responsible with money—and jazz musicians, except for the big stars, do all their own business. From the start of my life as a professional musician in New York, I had made sure to take care of the financial side of things, in order to sustain myself and maintain my independence. The decision to open a studio made practical sense, giving me a way to record my own music as well as a hedge against the financial insecurity of the jazz life.

I called the studio Classic Sound, a name that implied a longer history than the operation actually had, and incorporated the company with the state. It opened for business in mid-1983, after about a year of construction. I can't remember what the first record we made in the studio was, but over the five years of its existence we made close to two hundred albums for independent jazz musicians and respected small labels.

I was thrilled, at first. Classic Sound kept me busy. It was a great value in those days, anchored by my superb Steinway and low prices; I did my best to market the studio, sending out brochures to musicians and engineers. I needed to earn back the cost of all that equipment and construction—but I soon learned that jazz records are usually done in two days of live recording, maybe two days to mix, and that's that. Many are done "live to two-track," with the sound being mixed live as the music goes down, eliminating the postproduction mixing process as well as sales of expensive multi-track tape and thereby reducing overall profit. The successful studios had big-name pop and rock clients who would "lock out" a studio for weeks and months at a time, sometimes spending one whole day to get the snare drum to sound just right. As time went on and I realized that I was not technically wired to be an engineer, I found myself answering the phone, taking bookings—and making coffee and running out for sandwiches for other pianists who I thought were not nearly as good as I was. All the costly equipment needed constant upkeep, and the various engineers constantly clamored for new gear, eroding the small bits of money I might have made.

To fill in the calendar and keep the books balanced, I took a few money jobs for commercial clients, composing and recording anonymously. I wrote jingles for watch companies, shirt manufacturers, and sporting equipment. I wrote and produced the jingle for *Woman's World*, a B-grade supermarket magazine published on the Jersey side of the George Washington Bridge. The magazine was no worse than many others like it, actually, and neither was my jingle. In my newfound role as Fred Hersch, businessman, I saw no shame in keeping my company afloat with some work that nobody would ever associate with Fred Hersch, jazz pianist. That said, I rarely talked about my commercial work with my jazz colleagues until I started working on this book. David Hajdu, the music critic and cultural historian, once told me during a late-night conversation about our early careers that he had been writing articles for *Woman's World* under a pseudonym at the same time I was writing the magazine's jingle.

Through the studio I met producers Ettore Stratta and Mike
Berniker. Berniker was a longtime fixture as a house producer at
Columbia Records. He produced Barbra Streisand's first albums,
signed the popular group Duran Duran, and produced most of
Columbia's mainstream older pop artists. Through him, and
back when there were budgets for such things, we went often to
London to record classical/jazz crossover albums, big orchestra
records with artists such as Johnny Mathis and Jack Jones, and
schmaltzy records of songs from the British invasion of Broadway
in the 1980s: *The Phantom of the Opera, Me and My Girl,* and *Les
Miserábles.* We stayed in fancy hotels and ate well on CBS's dime.
Berniker was a blast to work with, and it was at his urging that I
did my first arrangements for string orchestra, a musical skill that
became more a part of my life as time went on.

The end of Classic Sound came one night in 1988 when I was
playing with Joe Henderson at the Village Vanguard. It seemed
like every musician was coming up to me on the set breaks with
some variation on "Hey, Fred, how's the studio?" I went out
after the last set for a few drinks at Bradley's, arrived home a bit
wasted, turned on the control room lights, and looked at all the
gear there—some of which I didn't quite know the purpose of.
I said to myself, *That's it.* Within a month I had sold the tape
recorder, microphones, and console and started sleeping in the
control room. I never looked back—the adventure had lasted five
years and put me in debt for the first time in my life. Through
the studio I learned about sound and producing records while becoming quite comfortable in the recording studio environment
as a musician. I also met a lot of people who would figure in my
life as I went forward. But I was living a double life in my musical

ventures of jazz pianist at night and studio owner by day. How many lives could one person live at the same time?

Back a few months before the studio was under construction, toward the end of my relationship with Eric, I was preparing to work with Stan Getz for the first time. He came to the loft one day to rehearse late in the afternoon. He buzzed the buzzer on the ground floor, and I let him into the building. While he was coming up the elevator to the fifth floor, I looked over the place to make sure everything was in place for the rehearsal. He got out of the elevator and buzzed another buzzer to get onto my floor, and I buzzed him in again. There's a long hall from the elevator to my loft, which is at the rear of the building. While Stan was walking down the hall, I was doing some final tidying up before meeting him at the door—and it suddenly hit me that if Stan used the bathroom in the back of the loft, he would be able to see that there were two toothbrushes on the sink: mine and Eric's. I panicked.

Acting cool, I showed Stan into the main room. As he put his saxophone case down, I darted to the bathroom, grabbed Eric's toothbrush, and hid it in the bathroom drawer. I made a quick pass around the room to make sure there was nothing "gay" out where it could be seen.

When the rehearsal was over and I was alone in the loft, I went into the bathroom to put Eric's toothbrush back where it belonged. I held it in my hand, and I froze. I just stood there and stared at the toothbrush. I thought to myself, *What am I doing? This is my home. This is my life. Eric is part of my life. Why am I hiding? Why am I pretending?*

It would have to stop.

CHAPTER 8

HORIZONS

Before there was a medical term for it, gay men knew something very, very bad was happening in the early 1980s. The first signs appeared in 1981 and '82, as word spread through the gay community that previously healthy people were suddenly developing strange symptoms and, before long, dying. First there was a report of gay men on the West Coast who had come down with what appeared to be a rare strain of pneumonia—or getting Kaposi's sarcoma, a cancer that until that time had only been seen in elderly men from the Mediterranean region. Then came stories about men in cities around the country who seemed to be falling gravely ill for no apparent reason. In less than a year's time, the disease—whatever it was—was inescapable.

You'd be at a bar or on Fire Island, and the guy you had seen not long ago looking totally sexy—hardy, energetic, and bright-eyed—

was almost unrecognizable. Now his skin was gray and loose on his bones, his eyes were dim and set deep in their sockets, and his face was splattered with purple lesions. Then you would never see him again. I had an unrequited crush on a man prominent in gay circles, Paul Popham, who was warm, smart, and drop-dead handsome. But when I saw him last, right before his death, there was just a shell of a man, stooped over, walking with a cane, and wheezing.

Nobody knew what the problem was, how it started, how it spread, or if there was any way to treat or contain it. The only thing the victims seemed to have in common was that they were, in the majority of known cases, homosexual and male, Haitian, or drug-addicted. (In time, terms such as "victims" would be supplanted with the less stigmatic designation PLWA—people living with AIDS.) It was a pandemic in process, and one of seemingly devious selectivity. With no other name for it, people were calling it the gay plague; its first acronym was GRID (gay-related immune deficiency).

In the fall of 1982 the U.S. Centers for Disease Control and Intervention named the mysterious ailment acquired immunodeficiency syndrome: AIDS. For gay men it was a horror beyond comprehension. It had been less than fifteen years since Stonewall—when men first dared to be out without much fear of being locked up—and to many of us, looking good and having lots of sex defined being gay. AIDS depleted the body in a highly visible way as it contorted the mind, feeding the sublimated homophobia that was all too common for homosexual men in those years. You'd wonder: *Why is this happening to so many gay men? What are we being punished for? Is there something wrong with us?*

Then you'd shake your head and realize how terribly wrong it was to be thinking that way.

With the newly named but still mystifying and terrifying contagion of AIDS spreading uncontrollably, this was a treacherous time to be a gay man playing the field. I wanted to enjoy my newfound freedom but not at the risk of my life. No one yet knew what AIDS *was*, exactly—a "syndrome" by definition, though all that meant was that it was *something*, a condition of some kind. It was not until mid-1983 that researchers determined that AIDS appeared to be caused by some kind of virus. No one yet knew how it spread or why certain people or groups of people seemed to be more susceptible to it than others. Could it be airborne? Carried on clothing or drinking glasses or environmental surfaces like tabletops and the handgrips in subway cars? Or contracted through the exchange of bodily fluids? If so, which fluids? Saliva? Blood? Semen? Sweat?

At this point, having been successful as a gigging jazz musician and now running a recording studio of my own, I was fairly assured socially. I had no trouble talking to strange men, for the most part, and I was confident sexually, even though I tended to be attracted to men who were physically or emotionally unavailable—much like my father was to me, a not uncommon pattern for gay men. And as with many gay men, pornography became a part of my life once the VCR was invented. But like most of us, I was appropriately terrified of AIDS and not entirely sure how to function socially and sexually in the atmosphere of what was rapidly emerging as an epidemic. And yet even as I acted out my feelings with compulsive sex, as many of us did at the time, I read everything I could about the issue, which was being covered exhaustively but without undue panic or sensationalism in the *Advocate* and other gay publications. I followed the health recommendations as they were made, trying to be as responsible as I knew how to be. I mostly (but not always) had protected sex and never once took drugs intravenously. Thinking back on the time I had done heroin with Chet Baker, I was glad I had snorted and not shot up.

I began to hear of a few drug-using jazz musicians who passed away mysteriously. The fine pianist Albert Dailey, who played for years with Stan Getz and was one of the first guys to let me sit in on his gig when I was new to New York, shriveled up before our eyes and died—and rumors began to spread about the cause of his death. His was the earliest death that I knew of in the jazz community that was probably from AIDS due to drug use, and it was frightening. I saw men all around me growing ill and recognized the symptoms when I began to get them myself. Over the course of 1984 I felt progressively weaker and weirdly off-kilter, as if I was coming down with a flu that never fully arrived. I felt thirsty all the time. If I got up quickly to answer the phone, I'd feel a little woozy. My skin hurt when I shaved. I developed molluscum facial warts. I was losing weight. I just felt "off."

Early in 1984, just I was making plans to record my first album as a leader, I saw my doctor, a general practitioner named Stan Roman who happened to be gay and had quite a few gay patients. He had been dealing with men with AIDS since it had first surfaced in New York. He was attuned to the disease and could recognize its early effects as well as any doctor in practice at the time. Unfortunately for countless men, there was no reliable diagnostic test for AIDS until someone determined what to test *for*. It was not until April of the year before that a team of researchers at the

National Cancer Institute identified the retrovirus HTLV-III as the cause of AIDS.

Dr. Roman said, "Well, let's just monitor your T-cell count." Being a syndrome defined as a deficiency of the autoimmune system, AIDS was associated with a reduction in the number of T-cells in the bloodstream. As every gay man knew by this time, T-cells (sometimes referred to as CD4 cells) play a key role in fighting disease and could be measured by a blood test that was standard for chemotherapy patients and others with compromised immune systems. By the mid-1980s the science of immunology had become part of the standard vocabulary of gay life. In some cases, especially outside the major cities, patients knew more about the disease than their doctors by reading pre-Internet medical journals.

Scared but still driven in my career, I carried on my usual routine, making music and going out, feeling worse by the week. I tried to keep my calendar booked, figuring that if I had a gig a month or two down the road, I needed to stay alive to do it. Every four months I took a blood test for my T-cell count. With every test, my count dropped. The normal range is approximately 800 to 1,500 T-cells per cubic milliliter of blood. Before the end of 1984, my count had steadily sunk until it got to around 400. Dr. Roman reviewed the pattern of my deteriorating immune system and said, "Fred, this looks like AIDS."

This came as no surprise to me. I had felt in my bones for a couple of years that I probably had AIDS. My doctor's statement only moved me closer to the reality of it. I never knew exactly when and from whom I may have been infected—thus being spared the "if only I would have—or not have—done this with someone in particular" that would have been even more demoralizing. I may have been infected as early as the time I was living with Eric and he was sleeping around.

But what was in store for me now? Very little was known about the disease except that there was no cure and that it was ultimately fatal. You didn't die from the virus itself, but the immune system was so compromised by it that you were susceptible to a host of opportunistic infections that could carry you away. By the end of 1984 there were about 7,000 cases of AIDS reported in the United States and more than 5,500 deaths. The numbers would double the following year and double again the year after that. To be diagnosed with AIDS was a death sentence. I don't say that with self-pity or melodrama. This was the reality. AIDS was an unknown new disease, ravaging and lethal.

The men I knew with AIDS responded in varying ways. Eric, my former boyfriend, was diagnosed around the same time I was, and his reaction was one of cavalier fatalism: *If I'm dying, I may as well go out blazing. I'm going to make the most of the time I have.* For Eric, that meant an accelerated and compressed schedule of partying. I wouldn't begrudge him the privilege, and I found myself having the same kinds of feelings at times—*I'm on my way out, so fuck it all!* For me, though, the impulses toward resignation or recklessness were at odds with each other. After the initial numbness and denial passed, I began to feel a complicated mix of emotions and urges, some of them deeply dark, some oddly life-affirming and constructive. In an effort to do something positive, I resolved to make my first recorded statement as a bandleader—I didn't know how much time I had left.

I probably could have made my debut album earlier. After all, I had been a sideman on numerous dates and even had my own recording studio. But I had a certain amount of pride in wanting to be paid by a real record label to make the album. I wanted them to pay me and the side musicians, to cover the recording costs, and to have a plan and a budget for its release and promotion.

Having been a sideman on two Art Farmer albums for Concord, I figured I was in a position to ask them for a record deal, and they agreed to take me on. Though conservative in its roster, Concord did have a number of fine pianists on the label, and it would make sure the album got reviews, distribution in stores, and radio play. It was a big deal to me to feel "signed" to a real label.

I focused with an acute sense of purpose on making this album, a trio record. The classic trio format was favored by many of my piano heroes, and I was doing more and more trio playing at that time. I used bassist Marc Johnson, a musician just a couple of years older than me who had played in Bill Evans's last trio until Evans's death in 1980. Marc had a great harmonic sense and a contemporary-feeling approach to line that suited the musically grounded but forward-looking sound I wanted. For drums I used Joey Baron, an adventurous and experienced player. Joey is a highly creative musician with a keen sense of tone and texture as well as superb time. Marc and I had played duos at the Knickerbocker, and Joey, Marc, and I were also playing together backing the Belgian harmonica legend Toots Thielemans. We also did a few local trio gigs around New York City. We had good energy together, and it was a joy to make music with them. I produced the record at Classic Sound with the engineer Michael MacDonald at the soundboard. We did the recording live to two-track over two days of sessions in October 1984.

I called the album *Horizons*. I liked the word's evocation of both equilibrium and aspiration. I used the plural to suggest that multiple possibilities lie before us all—at a distance, perhaps, but in sight. For me, at that moment, the future was clearly uncertain. But I was just beginning as a recording artist. It was strange and disorienting to be starting, in a way, as I was facing the prospect that everything could be ending for me.

The selections on the album were tunes from all corners of the jazz world that I enjoyed playing: standards such as "My Heart Stood Still," the Rodgers and Hart ballad from the 1920s, which I refashioned as a bright, swinging number; "Moon and Sand," one of the treasures by Alec Wilder that I learned from the songbook he had given me at Bradley's; "The Star-Crossed Lovers," the lush Billy Strayhorn tune (officially credited jointly to Duke Ellington and Strayhorn but composed and initially recorded by Strayhorn), which Tommy Flanagan had taught me; and pieces from the contemporary jazz repertoire such as Herbie Hancock's sprightly "One Finger Snap" and Wayne Shorter's lovely "Miyako." The album closes with a bright, up-tempo composition I had written for the occasion, "Cloudless Sky." Though the repertoire was diverse, I deliberately selected a group of tunes that just felt right to do. I thought that the range of songs would let the public know who I was as an interpretive pianist and as an emerging bandleader. If a young visual artist paints a classic subject—a bowl of fruit, a landscape, or a nude—you can see where that artist is coming from. If all of the music would have been my own (not that I had enough strong original pieces at that point), it might have been more difficult for the listener to place me in the context in which I wanted to be seen. All of the selections were unified by

Me, age four,
with my brother,
Hank, just under
two years old

Me, age thirteen, and Hank, age eleven,
jamming at the family home

My high school
senior picture, 1973

With Hank and my dad, Henry, July 1976

Me with an unidentified man in Key West, 1986

My first publicity photo in New York, 1977

With Hank the night of
the Grammy® Awards,
NYC, 2004

With Hank and my mom,
Flo, at the Classical
Action: Fred Hersch &
Friends concert, Town
Hall, NYC, 1998

With Scott Morgan at our house in Pennsylvania, 2012

With my piano teacher Sophia Rosoff, NYC, 2003

With Scott at the Grammy® Awards, Los Angeles, 2015

In my loft, 2013

World premiere of *My Coma Dreams*, Alexander Kasser Theater,
Montclair State University, New Jersey, 2011

Listening to a playback at Systems Two Recording Studio, 1995

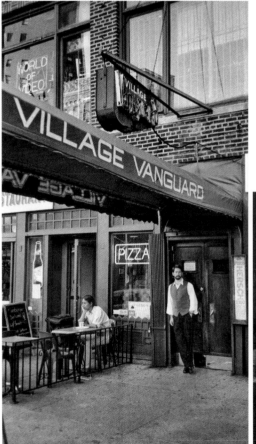

In front of the Village Vanguard, 1997

Composing at Veltin Studio,
the MacDowell Colony,
Peterborough, New Hampshire,
2000

Promo photo,
2003

Playing trio in Paris, 2016, with John Hébert, bass; and Eric McPherson, drums

Playing piano four-hands with Dr. Billy Taylor at Classical Action:
Fred Hersch & Friends

Playing solo at the Village Vanguard, 2005

a style that I hoped was becoming recognizable as my own. From the beginning of my recording career, I've wanted each album I made to have integrity and a natural progression from tune to tune. Sequencing an album (or a club or concert set) is like planning a menu—you need variety of tempo, key, and mood. You wouldn't serve a meal of all starches and no vegetables or protein.

Though we were recording in my own studio and I was playing my own Steinway, I was surprisingly nervous at first. I was also the producer for the album, so I was responsible for both the music and the sound, a lot to take on when you have never done an album as a leader. I recognize now that there is never a perfect time to make your first album—you have to jump into the water and let your experience guide you. You must believe that you will make many more and that this album is just one musical snapshot of where you are at that time, on those two days in the studio. But for me the second album was not a certainty, so everything became loaded—and on the first day I was frustrated by almost everything. I was feeling like I had to drive the musical bus myself, and I was thinking and judging rather than listening or feeling. But on the second day I was less anxious, able to allow the guys in the band to give me their musical support—I put one phrase after another in a relaxed way, and I had some fun doing it. There are flaws, but in the end I was able to make a record I was pleased with.

For the cover art, rather than the more obvious choice of a portrait of me (common for a first album), I selected a photograph of a rock formation jutting up from the ocean, with the horizon in the distance. It's a geological wonder. The rock looks like a clay sculpture rather than a natural object, and appears like a human bust in left profile. It doesn't mean anything literal to me; it's an object of mysterious beauty molded by nature—a weirdly compelling protrusion into an expanse of calm sea.

Horizons was released in 1985, the year I turned thirty. Shortly after the record came out, *Newsday* published the first full-length profile of me, written by jazz writer Stuart Troup. The piece was published with a nice big photo of me, beaming and looking stylish in a vest and a thin eighties tie. The headline read, "Fred Hersch's Time Has Come." It made me feel that all my hard work was beginning to pay off.

Horizons got good reviews, and not only in the jazz press. The critic for the *Chicago Tribune*, Larry Kart, called the record "a pleasant surprise." I don't remember having ever met him, and I had never played in Chicago with my own band. I wonder what he had been expecting!

I wasn't exactly surprised to see so many writers comparing me to Bill Evans. Though I didn't play but one tune that was associated with him, I was recording with the bassist in his final trio—and I was white. The comparisons were favorable (no shame there) but, in my mind, somewhat simpleminded and misguided. I had been equally influenced by numerous other pianists—Paul Bley, Ahmad Jamal, Monk, and Herbie Hancock, to name a few—and I thought that was discernible in my performances on *Horizons*. In the *Guardian*, the headline for a review of *Horizons* went so far as to say, "Thank Evans." I got this quite a bit early in my career from people who found that one of the things I could do was play a ballad with lyric sensitivity. This approach often made people think of Bill Evans, but that's where they stopped thinking. While I'd always admired Evans, as most jazz pianists do, I'd never sought to emulate him slavishly, and if you listened closely, you'd hear that we didn't actually sound that much alike (and we sound more and more different as the years have gone by). But all credit is due to Evans for making possible the conversational trio style by moving his left hand up toward the middle of the piano and adding voice leading to it, thereby giving the bass more of a chance to be an independent melodic and rhythmic voice and allowing the drums to add colors to the whole trio rather than just keep time.

As a matter of fact, the sound I had at the time of *Horizons* was not only much different from Evans's but it was somewhat different from my sound today. When I listen to the album now, I recognize myself—but I hear a younger version of me with a different, slightly pushier energy than I have now. I was simply trying too hard to make a masterpiece. But this *was* my first album, and I was naturally eager to prove myself. My approach to some of the tunes was harder-hitting than it is now. But as I continued to study with Sophia Rosoff, learned how to employ my whole body to produce a holistic sound, and settled into myself as a person, my two-handed style matured.

If I sound defensive on the subject of Bill Evans, it's partly because my individual identity as an artist is important to me, as it is with every jazz musician. Since Louis Armstrong first established jazz as a soloist's art in the 1920s, individuality of expression has been a primary value in the music. No jazz artist wants to sound like anyone else, though creative theft is part of how the music evolves and every player has discernible musical influences, which you will discover if you know where to look. I am always pleased when someone says, "I turned on the radio and it was in the middle of a piano solo and I knew it was you." To me, this is one of the highest compliments.

Another element in the Evans comparison, for me, was that Evans's playing was often described as beautiful, lyrical, elegant, or romantic. (The beautiful, round sound that I fell in love with from his early Village Vanguard recordings did change through the years as drug use, mostly cocaine, began to take its toll.) Those were fair descriptions, and I have always been interested in beauty and lyricism as a pianist and composer—though I never allow the rhythm to take a backseat. The problem for me was that all those terms had traditionally been associated with male homosexuality in a restrictive and demeaning way. It was one thing for a straight man such as Evans—or Chet Baker or Miles Davis—to be praised for playing beautifully. But for a gay man to be described that way, it was almost like saying, *Of course he plays beautifully—he's gay!*

The listening public did not yet know that I was gay, and that's part of the reason I was so uneasy with being associated with Evans and his school of lush romanticism. I didn't want to be pigeonholed. I had just about had my fill of leading a double life. From the day I had run to hide Eric's toothbrush before Stan Getz could see it, the folly of hiding my sexual identity had sunk in. Still, I hadn't determined how to come out to the jazz world, and I wanted to do it wisely, in my own way and at the right time.

This might be hard for a young gay person of the twenty-first century to understand. Today, in many cases, gay or transgender kids as early as middle school can tell their family, friends, and teachers about their sexual or gender identity, and a lot of people will just nod and say, "Okay." There are gay-straight alliances in high schools. As I write this, an openly gay man is serving as secretary of the army. Discrimination against transgender soldiers is prohibited in the military. The mid-1980s were a very different time, though, and the rise of AIDS only added to the stigma attached to homosexuality for some time. In the early years of the epidemic, hatemongers glommed onto AIDS as a sign that God was punishing homosexuals for their deviance. Some young gay men today have a hard time relating to what my generation lived through in the early days of the disease, caring for our sick and dying, angry as hell about the lack of treatment—and as a result, some are more cavalier about their sexual practices. The rate of infection in the United States has remained fairly constant in recent years despite all of the education out there about the dangers of HIV/AIDS. There is still no cure, but most people who are newly infected can take one or two pills a day and keep the virus at bay if they start treatment immediately after their diagnosis.

I was just about ready to come out to the jazz world as a bandleader and recording artist when I learned that I definitely had AIDS. In May 1986, the International Committee on the Taxonomy of Viruses announced that the cause of AIDS was HIV, human immunodeficiency virus. The first test to verify the presence of the virus in patients soon followed. That year I took the HIV test anonymously at the Community Health Center on Ninth Avenue in Chelsea. When I came back a week later, they confirmed that I was positive and asked if I wanted counseling. I declined. I had to work out a good way to handle it on my own. In the meantime, it was challenge enough to break the news of my illness to my family.

Though I had told my family at age nineteen that I was gay

and didn't get a negative reaction, I don't remember how or when I told each of my parents about my HIV status or what their reactions were. I do recall that they were both appropriately concerned for me. But I have a precise recollection of when I told my brother, who, after graduating from the Columbia School of Journalism, was living in New York and writing for *Sports Illustrated*. He has been an important part of my life both as a support and as a friend. He and I had grown very close, and I told him in person. Hank's response was so real, so genuinely connected, that I was able to cry for the first time since my diagnosis, knowing how much he felt for me. In 1986 there was an opening in the loft across the hall from me. I helped him get into the building. As I look back, I imagine that I was thinking, *If I get really sick, he will be there to take care of me.* But that turned out to be a long way away.

CHAPTER 9

OUT

My first album could be my last. I had no reason to feel any other way. Because I learned that I was living with HIV around the same time I started making my own records, my illness and my music were inextricably linked in my mind. There was a death cloud hanging over my head from the time of my first effort as a recording artist.

It is a truism of homosexual history in America that the gay male subculture was forced to grow up when the AIDS crisis developed. I saw this all around me and felt it myself. Suddenly, being gay was not only about having sex or enjoying the company of other men like you, it was about sickness and taking care of friends and lovers who were dying. The AIDS Coalition to Unleash Power (ACT UP) was formed, and many of us began to sound like medical students as we read up on the virus and its effects. We banded together to pressure the government to fund the development of antiretroviral medications and fast-track treatments for opportunistic infections that occurred as a result of having HIV. I was officially diagnosed as HIV positive; drugs to treat it were still years down the road. To be HIV positive was to be terminally ill—though by the Centers for Disease Control guidelines, you went from being positive to having AIDS if your T-cell count was below 200 or you had one of the infections associated with immune suppression. (At some points in my life I have had AIDS, at others I have been just HIV positive; it is a fluid diagnosis.)

Always career-oriented and serious about my work, I now made music with a fierce urgency. Time felt more precious than ever. Soon after I recorded *Horizons*, I made a duo record with the soprano saxophonist and composer Jane Ira Bloom, whom I had gotten to know through Charlie Haden. Jane, who is almost exactly my age, had come to New York the same year I did, after studying music at Yale. She stood out among musicians of our generation as a distinctive composer who made formally adventurous music that always had deep feeling and soulfulness. And we found that we had a lot in common. I have always loved playing with her, and I treasure what we've brought out in each other. We called the album *As One*. We recorded "Janeology," which I wrote in Jane's honor (an abstract take on the chord changes of Charlie Parker's "Confirmation"), and "A Child's Song," a tribute to Charlie Haden, who grew up in Missouri as part of the singing Haden Family. There has always been a folkish element to his playing, and I allude to that in this composition. I included it on the next trio album I made, with Charlie himself on bass and Joey Baron on drums. I named the album *Sarabande*, for a Bach-inspired composition of mine.

Bach has been part of my musical life for as long as I have been playing the piano. Although his music is superbly and rigorously crafted, a monument to one of the great minds of all time, his music is always lyrical and rhythmic, never sacrificing emotion. When I close my eyes and play his music, I feel myself stepping into his beautiful, timeless world—much as I try to do when I play jazz. My favorite Bach keyboard works are the six Partitas. They are larger-scale counterparts to his six French Suites and six English Suites; in fact, they are sometimes known as the German Suites. Of course, I love the *Well-Tempered Clavier*, the *Goldberg Variations*, and all the rest, but I prefer the Partitas because each movement is based on a dance rhythm. Many are characteristic dances of various countries—the allemande is German, the courante is French, and the sicilienne is Italian—and some, such as the gigue and the minuet, were popular court dances of the day. Because of these dance origins, the individual movements of each suite have a rhythmic liveliness that is infectious. The Partitas are virtuoso masterpieces of the baroque dance suite form for keyboard, and each contains an exquisite slow movement in three-quarter time called a sarabande. I decided to use this as the inspiration because I wanted to write a tune in three-four that didn't feel like a waltz.

I finished one album and started the next one, with another project or two brewing on the side. In 1989 I released three albums, each exploring its own musical territory. The clock was ticking, and I wanted to express myself in as many musical ways as possible, wanting to be remembered. *Short Stories* was a voice-and-piano duo recording with Janis Siegel, a founding member of the Manhattan Transfer who shared my affection for both jazz tunes by lyric-oriented composers such as Dave Frishberg and recent-vintage pop by literate singer-songwriters such as Julia Fordham and Todd Rundgren. (This was the last album recorded at Classic Sound, in 1988.) On *The French Collection*, produced by Mike Berniker and Ettore Stratta, I wrote chamber-jazz reconsiderations of eleven works by impressionist composers, including Debussy's Prelude from Suite *Bergamasque* and Ravel's Prelude from *Le Tombeau de Couperin*, with a trio and some all-star guest artists. The third album, *Heartsongs*, featured my working trio with bassist Michael Formanek and drummer Jeff Hirshfield. Along with arrangements of pieces by some of my favorite jazz composers there were five new tunes of my own. Two of these, "Heartsong" and "Lullabye," have become signature tunes—and are now widely sung with wonderful lyrics added by British vocalist-lyricist Norma Winstone.

I was beginning to hit my stride as a writer of jazz tunes, and my range of compositional expression was widening. I was working feverishly to express myself in as many ways as possible and to be recognized—and remembered—before it was too late. I was taking more and more chances on every level. And with the first selection on *Heartsongs*, George and Ira Gershwin's "The Man I Love," I winked in the direction of my gay identity. Other than loving playing the song, I selected it—and its title—to make a statement even though I didn't have a partner at that time and longed for one. After that, I decided, I would give up the winking. There would be no more innuendo.

In 1991 I began work on an album of original material for the

Chesky Record label, which I titled *Forward Motion* and saw very much as a statement of renewed purpose and new candor. I used a quintet with an unusual front line of tenor sax and 'cello and billed it as the Fred Hersch Group. With this project I sought to make clearer my musical identity as a composer and a pianist, as well as my identity as a gay man. Not knowing how much longer I would be around, I saw no reason to be in any kind of closet. Indeed, I would begin to reconcile my musical and personal selves in a public way. I was moving forward.

Of the fourteen tracks on *Forward Motion*, thirteen were my own compositions. The one exception was "Frevo," a deliciously exciting piece by the Brazilian guitarist/pianist/composer Egberto Gismonti, which I had heard him play on several recordings. Gismonti is one of the great musicians of our time. He manages to marry the rhythm and harmony of all the various strands of Brazilian music with a classical and jazz sensibility and has amazing virtuosity on two instruments that could not be more unlike each other. Two of my tunes on the album, "Tango Bittersweet" and ". . . departed" were directly inspired by the tragedy of the AIDS epidemic. The mournful "Tango"—a duet for piano and 'cello, played by Erik Friedlander—I conceived of as the music for the dance of death. And ". . . departed" was a heartfelt, yet understated, solo piano homage to those I knew who had died of AIDS.

Musically, I was making a proclamation of my identification with AIDS. After the release of *Forward Motion*, I began the process of coming out more personally. I knew that it was just a matter of time before I spoke publicly about my sexual identity and HIV status.

I was ready but nervous, fearful of coming off as publicity-hungry or self-pitying. But when I finally went ahead and revealed everything to the world, I was genuinely motivated by a desire to help others who were closeted about AIDS and being gay. I was also tired of the effort required to keep secrets. I was much less concerned about being ostracized by homophobes and those scared of AIDS, despite the warnings from gay friends. People were saying, "You really shouldn't do this. You're going to kill your career. Jazz is a club for macho guys. Nobody's going to book you for next season, because they think you're going to be dead by then." And I easily might have been.

I thought, *If I'm going to die, that's all the more reason to come out now.* I was haunted by a regret I had about Sam Jones.

My debt to Sam was immeasurable. He was not only one of the greatest bass players in the history of jazz, he was my mentor and my friend. Playing with him gave me credibility and got me started in New York. Sam died in 1981, and I had never told him I was gay—though he probably surmised it. He trusted me and put his reputation on the line for me, and I was living a lie with him. I never showed him the respect he deserved by telling him who I was. I never told Bradley Cunningham before he died, either. Before I died myself, I was going to make sure people knew me for who I was.

I was out about everything to my family and close friends but not to the world. I had given it a lot of thought, that's for sure, but had always been afraid that straight musicians might not understand and that the music—and my reputation—would suffer as a result. I don't know how much sense this makes, but that is what I thought: When people are playing jazz music, creating something new and unique together spontaneously, it's extraordinarily intimate. When you're in a band, you fall in love with other musicians in a way. If you're a pianist, you may have found the perfect bass player, finally, or the drummer of your dreams. Musicians get musical crushes on one another. Then you get to know that player personally and musically, and you realize, well, maybe you're not so compatible after all; or one of you changes over time. What happens is a lot like what goes on in any personal relationship.

I play at a fairly high level of intensity and emotional engagement. With this in mind, I thought the musicians I was playing with might misconstrue that with me as a kind of come-on. I was genuinely concerned about this. I didn't care so much if they disapproved of my sexual orientation. I just didn't want any misunderstanding to get in the way of the music. I didn't want anything to undermine the musical intimacy that I count on and that I need to fully express myself.

At various times, certain straight jazz musicians who knew I was gay would say things like, "It's okay that you're gay. Just don't hit on me," and I would think (or sometimes say to them), *I don't need your permission. You think you're being open-minded and magnanimous here, but, in fact you're not—and don't flatter yourself!*

My fear for the music had kept me closeted. As time passed, though, I realized it would be better for the music, as well as for me, to come out.

There was another jazz pianist, an African American man just a few years older than me, who was also gay but never came out. Musicians suspected he was gay, though he never talked about it. I can't even remember exactly how I knew. But I knew—and eventually we came out to each other. We were able to fess up that each one of us was not the other's favorite piano player but that we did have this one thing in common. This pianist died in his fifties in the early twenty-first century. Because he never chose to come out, I'm not going to out him here.

To my ears, his music sounded somewhat constricted and forced. It didn't feel natural and organic. And I thought that in his playing he was putting on an act, playing the way he thought his audience would expect a straight piano player to play. This is not to say that if he had let down his guard, he would have suddenly sounded like Liberace. I don't know *how* he would have sounded if he had come out. But I have a feeling that he would have sounded different—more comfortable, more relaxed, more at home in his own skin. There was a quality of artifice in his music that must have been a burden to sustain. I believe his music suffered because he wasn't honest—and I feel that as I became more honest with the world, my music evolved into a more personal and relaxed form of expression.

The pianist I'm describing was far from an isolated case. I didn't want to out anyone or pressure other people to come forward as gay if they didn't want to or weren't ready. I knew how hard it was. It took years and the immutable force of AIDS to stir me to come out myself. I understood the pressures gay jazz musicians faced in a creative sphere that was dominated by straight males, a world closely associated with so-called heteronormative values. Historically, the rhetoric of jazz was rife with the tropes of straight machismo: "cutting contests" of pseudo-pugilistic musical competition to prove your prowess. With no mission to smoke people out, I thought my precedent, if it went well, might make things easier for others.

In 1992 I took my first major step as an emerging AIDS activist, and it seemed karmically right for this to happen in Cincinnati.

That February I was the featured artist in a concert to benefit AIDS Volunteers of Cincinnati (AVOC), a community-based service organization founded in 1983 after the first known death by AIDS reported in the city. Grass-roots groups such as AVOC, run without government funding, were critical to patient care in the days before institutional support for AIDS was well established, and AVOC was early among them. The concert, held at the First Unitarian Church of Cincinnati, was sold out and covered prominently in the regional media. I selected the performers and the format, wanting to make a musical statement of where I was at that time as well as doing something challenging and raising some much needed funds. One of the reasons I got connected with AVOC was that my father was quietly serving on its board. I give him a lot of credit for standing up, giving his time and insight, and helping so many people and numerous worthy causes for many years—as he does even in his nineties.

The other musicians were four members of the string section of the Cincinnati Symphony who named themselves the Bartlett String Quartet for the concert. We played a Mozart piano quartet, a Beethoven trio, and a few reconsiderations of classical pieces I had arranged for my *French Collection* album. I arranged Monk's "I Mean You" for the five of us. And I played one original tune acutely attuned to the occasion, ". . . departed." I was a bit nervous—it was the first big coming-out concert I gave, acknowledging my HIV status, and I was playing some difficult music as well. As something of a local-boy-made-good, I thought I could come home and put a public face on the disease for people in Cincinnati who might think, *Oh, it's too bad about AIDS. But that doesn't have very much to do with us. It couldn't happen to anyone from here.*

The *Cincinnati Enquirer* published a story about me and the concert on the front page of its arts section with a huge photo of me at the piano, and the *American Israelite* ran a similar piece, mentioning my HIV status matter-of-factly and describing me in oversize type as "a 1973 graduate of Walnut Hills High School and piano student of the late Jeanne Kirstein." A Hersch other than my father had finally made "Jews in the News."

It was meaningful that both of my parents attended the concert—along with my grandmother Ella. They were many years divorced now, fortunately for each of them—especially my mother, who had been dutifully fulfilling her role as a prominent lawyer's wife without much emotional reward. Not long after they formally divorced in 1976, my father remarried a dynamic woman in their social circle, Gloria Fabe. By the time of the concert, my mother was also in a very happy second marriage, with an intelligent and kind attorney, Harry Hoffheimer.

As I came out more easily about being gay, I found myself speaking to others about the price of keeping that personal closet locked. Gary Burton, the innovative vibraphonist, heard about what I was doing, coming out. Divorced and living in Boston, he was playing with Marc Johnson, the bassist who had recorded with me, and he told Marc, somewhat cryptically, that he was *very interested* in my situation. Marc gave him my phone number, and Gary called me out of the blue. We didn't know each other, though of course I was very aware of his prominent stature in the jazz world. He started the conversation in his characteristically direct manner and said, "Fred, this is Gary Burton, and I think I'm gay."

I said, "How does it feel to be talking about it?"

"It feels pretty great," he said. It wasn't long after that that Gary decided for sure that he was gay and came out in an interview in the *Advocate*.

Gary was a household name in jazz, and he could come out without sacrificing his reputation or his concert calendar. But there were others for whom this decision was much more fraught. There was a younger gay jazz musician in Texas named Dave Catney. He had come up slowly in and around Houston, playing lounge piano and small jazz venues, taking requests, and singing a tune sometimes. He had spent some time in New York studying with some heavyweight jazz pianists, and those in the know were aware of his considerable talent. Dave played beautifully and began developing a personal style in the nineties, around the time he turned thirty. He recorded two subtle, lyrical trio albums, and later a first-class solo record. On his debut, *First Flight*, he did a slow, somber version of "Put on a Happy Face" that teased out all the poignancy in the act of putting on a good front in the face of adversity. It could have been his leitmotif.

Dave had AIDS but had never really come out to his parents. In the early nineties I got to know him through his booking me at a small club in Houston where he was the artistic director, and we eventually became good friends. (Though not right away—the first time I played at the club he was in the hospital for CMV retinitis, a viral infection that affects the eyesight, more common in the early days of AIDS.) Despite being very thin, he was warm and boyish, good-looking, smart, and seriously talented—a total package with all the potential for success were it not for his health.

Playing small clubs and the occasional jazz festival and recording for a minor local label, Dave never made a lot of money and was struggling mightily to pay for his medical treatment. He had no health insurance and couldn't actually afford to go to the hospital. But he was so beloved by the doctors and the hospital staff that they treated him anyway and just buried the cost of his numerous stays and medications in their accounting. As he got sicker and sicker, he and I grew closer. By late 1993 and into early '94, we were talking on the phone weekly. Over about six months, I talked him through what turned out to be the end of his life.

Dave had always assumed that if he fell on hard times, his parents would help him. But he was afraid to tell them what was really going on. They were obstinately intolerant—both homophobic and AIDS-phobic.

I told him, "Look, in your own self-interest, you need to come out, because you never know if your family will be there when the chips are down. Just save your own ass. You'll be surprised that certain friends will really stand up, and some people in your family may be there for you. But some people won't, for whatever reasons. So you have to learn who's on your side, because if you really get sick, you have to know who you can count on."

I said, "Dave, you need help, and they're your parents. You don't have a lot of options. You're dying of AIDS, and you haven't even told them directly. And if, God forbid, you pass away, you'll go without them ever really having known you. That would be a tragedy for all of you. At the very least, you need to be honest with them, just to have some closure one way or the other."

Just a few days before he died, in August 1994, from his hospital bed, Dave mustered the strength to call his father, and he told me about the conversation when it was over. Dave said, "Dad, there's something I've got to talk to you about."

His father said, "Dave, I told you, we're not going to discuss your lifestyle choice."

And Dave simply said, "Bye, Dad. I love you."

Dave died at age thirty-three, owing hundreds of thousands of dollars in medical expenses, with no life insurance to cover any of it or pay for his funeral. His parents never laid out a cent—but they did spend a couple of thousand dollars to embalm him for a rosary service, despite his written wish to be cremated. His memorial celebration took place in the grand ballroom of the Wyndham Warwick Hotel in Houston. The room was packed; there was a gospel choir singing and every musician in town was there. But his father didn't show up, and his mother came in disguise, sitting in the back wearing oversize sunglasses and a wig.

I wanted Dave to benefit from what I learned from coming out. As a person and an artist, you have to be who you are. And to be honest with yourself, you need to be honest with other people.

When I started talking about my sexual identity and HIV status in interviews, the process was more liberating than I had expected it to be. I felt different—more complete. As I explained in interviews at that time, it takes a lot of energy to stay in the closet, any kind of closet. And I think now, looking back, that until *Forward Motion* I had been in a bit of a musical closet as well. Once everything was laid bare, I felt this tremendous surge of confidence, of energy, to do and say whatever I wanted. I became more relaxed as a person, even as my health was deteriorating, by coming out about who I was and what I was dealing with. I didn't think making music could become any more important to me. But it did.

CHAPTER 10

DANCING IN THE DARK

n the mid-1980s and early '90s, there was an explosive resurgence of interest in jazz, much of it attributed to and focused on a group of musicians the press was calling "the Young Lions." Like many social and aesthetic trends, this one was a phenomenon that journalists not only observed and identified but also helped construct and sustain. The jazz repertory movement, which I brought up earlier in the context of Gunther Schuller and my experience at the New England Conservatory, dovetailed neatly with the conservative atmosphere of the Reagan era. There was a vogue for entertainers such as singer-pianist Michael Feinstein, whose cabaret-style renditions of both well-known and obscure standards harkened back to the pre-rock entertainers of the fifties and sixties.

The simultaneous emergence of the CD format, a new delivery

system for recorded music that turned the album market into a replacement market, provided record companies with a rationale for promoting their back catalogs—product that cost practically nothing to repackage and was therefore fantastically profitable. All this came together in a way that focused the attention of the jazz world on music made by masters of the past—or newcomers who brought the past masters to mind. Many of the so-called Young Lions were, broadly speaking, musicians who brought fresh faces to old ideas.

Always serious-minded and superbly gifted as a jazz and classical trumpeter, Wynton Marsalis was anointed as the de facto leader of this group, and he took to his prominence with fervor and skill, playing a key role in establishing Jazz at Lincoln Center, an institution that conferred formal status to jazz as an art equal in stature to symphonic music, opera, and ballet. I first met Wynton when he was still at Juilliard and had begun playing with Art Blakey and the Jazz Messengers in New York. He came to Fat Tuesday's one night to hear Art Farmer when I was working with Art—whom he justifiably admired. Between sets, Wynton and I talked for a few minutes at the bar, and he struck me as a smart and charming guy who cared deeply about music. I've never had a problem with Wynton as a person or as a musician, and I think that he is a fantastic educator and a fine ambassador for the music. What I'm not so fond of is the aesthetic of musical traditionalism and conservatism that Wynton is associated with.

I believe that Wynton subscribes to the theory that the essence of jazz is best exemplified by Louis Armstrong and, through extension, Duke Ellington.

My take on jazz history, which follows here, is not original.

I believe that the three great revolutionaries in jazz were Louis Armstrong, in the twenties (the first great solo virtuoso; inventor of scat singing; way ahead of his time harmonically); Charlie Parker and the beboppers, including Monk, Bud Powell, and Dizzy Gillespie, in the forties (jazz as art music; as listening music, not dance music; fast and complex compositions played with astounding technique); and Ornette Coleman, in the late fifties and early sixties (harmonic progressions are not always played literally; improvise melodically and create your own structure as you go). There have been many major figures in the music who have moved it forward in important ways, but these three giants marked the beginnings of new eras and were perhaps the most influential from where we sit today.

Thanks largely to the hype surrounding this craze for new talent, all the classic jazz record labels became active again. Verve and Blue Note Records were revived. Atlantic, RCA, and Warner Records reconstituted their jazz divisions and went on a signing frenzy, with everyone competing to snatch up the youngest of the Young Lions. Looks were important, and even clothing designers and hairstylists were credited in CD packages. These musicians were marketed like pop stars, even though the jazz record market was small.

After years of working on my craft, playing and learning, studying and maturing, I was beginning to hit my creative stride in the early nineties, and I was pushing forty years old. Leonine or not, I was not quite young anymore—nor was I yet an old master. I didn't have matinee-idol looks or great hair, and I wasn't a super-flashy player. I didn't qualify for classification as a member of the voguish new-jazz herd on many levels.

By now I was well accustomed to not fitting in. Strangely, it didn't feel odd at all to watch much less seasoned (and, in a few cases, less skilled or less creative) musicians getting signed to major labels. Some of them were huge talents and have sustained long and successful careers; others have long since disappeared. But a few of these musicians who got these label contracts had been my students, and that hit me hard. I thought, *Why am I being passed over?* Again, I wanted to be a member of a club whose entrance seemed closed off to me.

As a result, I bounced around a bit within the industry. At Concord Jazz, the label that had released *Horizons*, the marketing people had never quite known what to make of me. On a roster with Mel Tormé and Rosemary Clooney I was an outlier. I had to go elsewhere with my second record, *Sarabande*, which was released by Sunnyside Records, a highly independent-minded label run by the French impresario François Zalacain, who made a policy of not signing artists to multi-record contracts. The trio album I recorded next, *E.T.C.*, was issued by an Italian label, Red Records. The following year Sunnyside recorded a trio CD, *Heartsongs*. After that I decided to record an album of Bill Evans music, *Evanessence*, primarily to hush up the critics and show that I admired Evans's music but had my own viewpoint on it.

I was fully coming into my own as both a pianist and composer. Though Chesky Records tried to market the Fred Hersch Group as a hip, "downtown" ensemble and we played big concerts in New York at Town Hall and the Bottom Line, *Forward Motion* didn't sell terribly well. Chesky was not exactly clamoring for me to do another record. In the midst of a big boom in jazz, my music wasn't booming in accord. I didn't look or sound like a young

Herbie Hancock, Chick Corea, or McCoy Tyner, and I didn't play like them either. Although critics were responding well to my music and giving me great press, I wasn't breaking through to the jazz audience in a significant way. I was unsuccessful in getting interest from a reputable agent or manager.

I was reminded of a story I once heard about Duke Ellington. He was recording for Columbia Records in the late fifties and early sixties and created a series of unqualified masterpieces, including the *Live at Newport* album with "Diminuendo and Crescendo in Blue," which I studied in the back room of the Family Owl in Cincinnati, and the "Shakespeare suite" he composed with Strayhorn, *Such Sweet Thunder*. In the midst of this string of creative triumphs, the head of Columbia, Goddard Lieberson, told Ellington he was dropping him from the label. Duke said, "Why?"

Lieberson said, "You're not selling records."

And Duke said, "I'm sorry—I thought it was my job to make music and your job to sell records."

Forty years later, the records Duke Ellington made for Columbia were still selling well, and Ellington was Wynton Marsalis's role model. The Ellingtonian aesthetic of jazz classicism, the living jazz legends who survived—and the sixties Miles Davis Quintet model—so dominated the jazz record business that it was hard for those who made a different kind of music to get a foothold or to be widely heard.

The Chesky label was run by two brothers, David and Norman Chesky. David, a Juilliard-trained pianist/composer himself and around my age, did a lot of the hands-on work with the musicians. After *Forward Motion* had been out for a little while, he told me, in so many words, that I should be talking to other labels. I said to him, "Look—I'm not doing so great here. The fact of the matter is, I don't know how much longer I have on the planet. I just want to record. You don't have to pay me anything, just cover the band's fees and the recording costs. Please let me make another album for you."

Being a very decent guy, Dave said, "Okay," and I went into the studio with my working trio: Drew Gress on bass and Tom Rainey on drums. We had been playing together for a year or two, gigging around, traveling some, appearing in such clubs as Visiones, a venue for mid-career artists in the Village, getting used to one another over time and beginning to gel nicely as a group. This was the first trio I had that was truly my band. We were devoted to working with one another.

In contrast to *Forward Motion*, this album had no original compositions. I didn't have any time to write new material, so we just recorded tunes we had been playing that I liked, our takes on standards from the Great American Songbook: "So in Love" by Cole Porter, "I Fall in Love Too Easily" by Jule Styne and Sammy Cahn. The record is named for an evocative song by Howard Dietz and Arthur Schwartz, "Dancing in the Dark." The title had a double meaning—I was truly in the dark, dancing as fast as I knew how, and not sure of what would befall me. We made the tunes ours. After all, it can be as creative an endeavor to play someone else's compositions as it is to play something you wrote. Louis Armstrong played a lot of music with other people's names on the copyrights, and he turned every song into a work of original expression by the force of his interpretive imagination. Coleman Hawkins didn't write a great deal. Nor did Miles Davis.

But even when I play my own pieces, I have to learn them just the way I have to learn a Monk tune or a standard. I have to internalize them. I have to memorize them. I have to work with them. I have to find just the right tempo. I have to fine-tune them so I can play them with fluency. I have to interpret my own music just as I would anything else. A tune doesn't have to be a so-called original to have originality.

We recorded the eleven tracks on *Dancing in the Dark* over two days of sessions in December 1992. Chesky had it pressed and packaged for release in the spring of 1993, and thought well enough of it to submit it for consideration for a Grammy Award. I didn't think much about it, figuring the Grammys was another exclusive club that wouldn't have me as a member. When the nominations for 1993 releases were announced in December, I was stunned to see that I had been nominated for Best Jazz Instrumental Performance, Individual or Group, for *Dancing in the Dark*.

The awards were presented at that time on a schedule that alternated between New York and Los Angeles. Fortunately for my travel budget, the 1994 ceremony was held in New York, at the historic Radio City Music Hall. To celebrate, Hank, his wife, Sharon, and I had a fancy dinner in SoHo; she had just lost her older sister to colon cancer, and I got her a hard-to-get ticket to the ceremony and the after party to cheer her up. I invited a new friend of mine, David Hajdu, to join us.

David and I had recently bonded over the music of Billy Strayhorn, which I had been playing often since my early days at Bradley's. I was doing a trio date once and slipped for a moment, absent-mindedly introducing "The Star-Crossed Lovers" as a composition by Duke Ellington. During the break David came up to me, introduced himself as a writer working on a biography of Strayhorn, and gently corrected me. Ever since then, we've been close friends and occasional songwriting collaborators.

The Grammy in my category that year went to my old boss Joe Henderson for his album *So Near, So Far*—a tribute to Miles Davis. It was the second album Joe had made for Verve since the label had been revived. The first was *Lush Life*, another tribute to a past master, Strayhorn, which also won Joe a Grammy. The awards were timely honors for a retrospective time. I never expected to win but was weirdly, irrationally disappointed.

I thought about Joe, who had been playing at the highest level since the late 1950s and didn't win a Grammy until 1992, near the end of his life. (Of course, dozens of remarkable jazz albums are released each year that are not even nominated.) I knew he had worked hard and steadily for decades and was absolutely revered by all astute jazz musicians. I recognized the wisdom in patience—not just in the way Joe built those incredible long solos at the Village Vanguard but in sticking it out and doing things resolutely his own way. I was grateful for the peer recognition, and it dawned on me that by simply being my musical self, playing the way I play without trying to "get over," and letting go in general, good things might come. It would just take time, the one resource I knew I could never count on.

CHAPTER 11

ACTING OUT AND ACTIVISM

I t is not always easy to think or act rationally when you have a
debilitating disease that no one fully understands.

Three years after my diagnosis, in 1989, the first drug approved by the FDA for the treatment of HIV/AIDS became
available, and I went on it. It was a retroviral repressor called
azidothymidine (or zidovudine), which had been developed as
a cancer treatment in the 1960s, when new research had linked
cancer to retroviruses in birds. After the drug failed to have
much application outside the avian population, drug companies
shelved it until research proved that AIDS was caused by a retrovirus. Azidothymidine was marketed under the name Retrovir,
though everybody called it AZT. There was intense debate in
the gay community about whether or not to go on the drug, with
some even denying that HIV was the cause of AIDS, but I was so

desperate for any treatment with some promise that I crossed my fingers and went ahead.

AZT was, in some cases, effective at slowing the progression of HIV, though it failed to stop it entirely. (Eventually the drug was administered in combination with other medications as part of an antiretroviral therapy regimen that became known as the "triple cocktail." But this development was seven or eight years down the road.) The side effects were rough: weight loss, stomach pain, and sleeplessness, not to mention potential risks to the cardiovascular system. Before long, AZT, which had been invented as a cancer treatment, was found to be a possible carcinogen; and initially it was prescribed in doses that were way too high—some people even died as a result. At the new, lower dose I was on, AZT somewhat slowed the replication of my HIV. But it kicked my ass.

I was sick from the effects of the virus and sick from the treatment, both debilitated and rejuvenated, driven by a new sense of purpose, and more than a bit confused. I'd wake up light-headed and aching, put something in my stomach so I could take my first pill for the day, try to get up the energy to sit at the piano and play or compose, then often end up lying down on my couch and closing my eyes, exhausted and afraid.

During my first years with the illness, I did some smart and constructive things. But I also did some stupid and destructive things. It was a rocky, dark time in many ways—there was still no cure, and people were dropping all around me. The papers reported the deaths of famous people who passed away from the effects of AIDS: Rock Hudson, whose startling decay and death helped destigmatize AIDS to millions of people who hadn't even known he was gay; Freddie Mercury, from the pop-rock band

Queen; Liberace. But there were also the unpublicized deaths of un-famous AIDS casualties every day. I lost a lot of gay friends and acquaintances. The world lost an entire generation of supremely creative individuals: visual artists, dancers, musicians, and writers. I was scared each day to read the *New York Times'* obituary section—or the one in the local gay newspaper—which chronicled the deaths of men in their thirties and forties from pneumonia or heart attacks, hardly normal for men that age. They no doubt died from the effects of AIDS, their death notices written in code. It was dispiriting and destabilizing. I didn't know what to think or how to feel or what to do with myself sometimes, and I acted out in ways I'm hardly proud of now.

My sexually compulsive activities escalated. My addiction to pornography became more consuming. I went out to bars and picked up strangers, just for the sex, went home with them or brought them to my loft, and never thought about them again. The next night I'd go looking for someone new. Eager to hook up, I dated men I would be ashamed to be seen with now, just for the sexual connection.

I always told the guys I was HIV positive and always practiced safe sex, of course. I was being obsessive but not reckless. I felt somehow like I needed to have sex as much as possible, to numb myself, even though by that time it wasn't any fun and I actually had enough insight to know that this behavior was just a way to get away from myself. But I couldn't stop. I was using the only coping mechanism I knew to act out my justified anxiety about getting sick—just as I was deluding myself that I was actually looking for love.

Being a musician, I worked at night. So I couldn't always count on doing nighttime pickups. I mined the personal ads. Toward the end of my addiction, I even hired call boys a few times. In a state of delusion that is probably not atypical among customers of skilled sex professionals, I started thinking that one rent boy and I had a special thing going on. I believed he was truly attracted to me and wanted to see me again for reasons unrelated to the nice payment he always made sure to get in advance. I thought about him even when I was playing music. He took up *way* too much of my brain space. In 1999 I was on a long solo tour of the United Kingdom and I was obsessed with him the whole time. After a month of this self-torture I decided that I had had enough and that paying for sex didn't square with my values; in fact, it made me feel disgusted. And given the endless supply of men out there, this type of acting out could only escalate; it was dangerous to me on every level. This was the proverbial bottom that eventually led to my recovery from sexual compulsion.

As I sensed myself slipping into an ever-darkening hole of addiction, I hoped that my longtime psychotherapist would be there for me. I had been seeing him at least twice a week since 1980. Unfortunately, this Freudian-oriented gay man with a nice office and impressive credentials was extremely destructive in his own ways, though they were so subtle that it took me almost two decades to recognize them. Over time I realized he was taking advantage of my insecurity and had begun to control my life. Instead of helping me with clear-eyed insight and useful counsel, he was increasingly dismissive, belittling, and manipulative. He was narcissistic and, toward the end, verbally and psychologically abusive.

For years he had done much more damage to me than good. He fostered my low self-esteem and became completely directive about *everything*. He had to approve of my love interests, how I read the newspaper, and what I was doing as a musician—not that he actually cared to learn anything about my music. If he was filing his nails while I was talking to him and I intimated that I wanted him to pay closer attention, he would remark in a condescending manner, "You're not being very interesting." He took phone calls in the middle of sessions and, without my consent, mentioned things that I had said in private sessions to the gay men's therapy group that he ran once a week—with me sitting in the group and having no choice in the matter. Therapy is supposed to be a safe space, but his version was anything but safe. He deluded himself into thinking that he was practicing a new and improved form of psychotherapy, but he was using his position of power to indulge his outrageous grandiosity.

At my own initiative, I eventually enrolled in a 12-step program to confront my sexual compulsion, and it was invaluable in helping me to see my behavior as out of control and self-destructive— and giving me support and concrete tools to help me stop. Though entering that first meeting and saying, "Hi, I'm Fred, and I am sexually compulsive" to a roomful of strangers was difficult, I knew from my past coming-out experiences that I needed to be brutally honest and out of this new closet if I was going to get better. No more secrets. (In a wild twist, at my first meeting I recognized one of the men in the couple that I had seen strolling around together on the Grinnell campus so many years before.)

Over about two years of hard work, following the guidelines of the program, I was able to see my compulsion with growing clarity and to contain it. I got a sponsor and learned to sponsor other men struggling as hard as I was in the grip of this addiction.

My work on my issues in the program also enabled me to recognize the harm my therapist was doing to me. Terminating with him—once I was solidly in recovery—was akin to a battered wife leaving a batterer. He had me in such knots that it was one of the hardest things I've ever done. After twenty years of psychological entrapment, I reached a point where I simply could not take his belittlement and manipulation anymore. I fired him and I never saw him again.

SINCE I first came out as gay and HIV positive, I've said many times that I never wanted to be the gay jazz poster boy. I've always wanted to be thought of first and foremost as a person—just a person, not one defined by his sexual orientation or his gender or his ethnicity. Then I'm a jazz musician, specifically a pianist and a composer. After that I'm a jazz musician who happens to be gay. And after that, I'm a jazz musician who happens to be gay and HIV positive. Those are the file folders nested on the computer desktop—this is how I would, ideally, like the world to see me. My thinking is this: I don't want to be defined by any one classification or by my disease—I don't want to be limited as a musician or as a man. Also, I don't want anyone ever to think I have exploited my sexual orientation or my health status for the benefit of my career.

At various times circumstances have prompted me to organize the files in that folder of my selves in particular ways. For many years, the reality of being a person living with AIDS felt like an enormous slab of prime rib completely covering a dinner plate, leaving no room for any side dishes. I took many medications that had terrible side effects I couldn't ignore: weight loss, depression, facial wasting, lipodystrophy and lipoatrophy (loss of and disfiguring movement of body fat), lack of salivation that made eating almost impossible. When I first came out, I moved my sexual orientation to the top of the pile. It was important at the time, and in addition to the emotional and creative benefits to me, I thought I might be able to help others by my example. I soon realized that I could leverage my growing visibility as a public advocate for gay consciousness and HIV/AIDS awareness. I found myself becoming what I call an "accidental activist." Over the decades, I have embraced that mission as a vital part of my life's work.

In New York my first high-profile involvement in a project to benefit AIDS research and treatment came to fruition in the summer of 1992, when I contributed a song to the AIDS Quilt Songbook, a project organized by the lyric baritone William Parker, who was gravely ill with AIDS. He was widely known as a champion and interpreter of new American art songs as well as the core European classical vocal repertoire. He had a creamy voice and great diction and was a superb musician. When I heard about the project, I got in touch with him immediately to ask if I could participate, but he told me that there were already too many composers involved. When I told him right then that I had AIDS (as I knew he did) and about my sense of urgency, he agreed to include me.

I wrote both the music and the text for a melancholy piece I titled "blues for an imaginary valentine," and I performed it with baritone William Sharp singing in the AIDS Quilt Songbook concert at Alice Tully Hall in Lincoln Center, a program that included works composed for the occasion by Ned Rorem, William

Bolcom, John Harbison, and more than a dozen others. It was the first of many times that I would be included in projects featuring numerous composers from the classical world either writing variations on one theme or interpreting and arranging music of another composer. It was also my first lyric song, and I wanted to express myself in a different and more direct way than I had in my instrumental compositions that had been inspired by the health crisis. So I wrote the lyric from the perspective of a bereft lover who can't believe that his partner died before him—he thought he would pass away first.

It was a wrenchingly emotional concert, with Parker near death but clearly exhilarated by the extraordinary demonstration of generosity, unity, and creativity in the hall. A recording of the songbook material was scheduled for the following day, at the National Academy of Arts and Letters, but Parker was too debilitated by having performed in the concert to take part in it. Out of respect for him, the three pieces Parker had sung the previous evening were not included in the recording. Eight months later, in the spring of 1993, Parker died.

Over the course of the early nineties, I grew more and more engaged—and visible—as an AIDS activist. Later in 1992 I produced what may have been the first AIDS benefit concert in the jazz community, to take place on a Sunday afternoon at the famed Village Gate. I planned the event myself, got the venue to donate the use of the club, and gathered some well-known performers who played for free. But I didn't have many media connections and had never promoted a concert, so I was unable to get the word out to draw a large crowd or raise much money. This would change when I met Charles Hamlen through record producer David Chesky.

Charlie, one of my closest friends then and now, was by that time well established as a manager of top-tier classical concert artists. Tall, with owlish glasses and a white beard, he is warm and easygoing but methodical and irresistibly persuasive. Charlie cofounded one of the leading concert-artist management firms in the late 1970s, sold it to the powerhouse International Management Group (IMG), and continued working at IMG with enormous success. He handled many of the biggest names in the classical world: Joshua Bell, Itzhak Perlman, André Watts, the Emerson String Quartet, and Leila Josefowicz, among others. Charlie's partner, Carlos Flor, had died of AIDS in 1988. Taking stock, Charlie weaned himself from IMG and set up a new organization with the mission of mobilizing the classical music community to benefit AIDS services and education. He called it Classical Action: Performing Arts Against AIDS. After a few years as an independent organization, Classical Action became a program under the auspices of Broadway Cares/Equity Fights AIDS, one of the earliest performing arts initiatives to raise money to directly help those dealing with AIDS.

Though I wasn't known as a classical musician, it has been a consistent passion in my life. And though Charlie didn't know much about the jazz world, we both loved music and had enough in common to prompt a friendship. I liked Charlie immediately and was impressed that he had walked away from such a powerful, lucrative job to do something he found more meaningful. It turned out that Charlie was open to expanding the reach of Classical Action beyond the realm of formal music. One of the ventures he launched was a series of house concerts, for which musicians he had come to know through IMG would donate their talent, and ticket buyers would pay a healthy price to hear an intimate performance by someone such as Renée Fleming in someone's fabulous living room. Other artists he knew would donate a percentage of their concert fees; this artist donation was prominently mentioned in the concert program, and often the presenters would match the amount donated by the performers. All the money went to Classical Action.

After my initial events for AVOC and at the Village Gate, I wanted to do something as well but was hardly in a position to write a big check. Inspired by the AIDS Quilt Songbook, I decided to produce a jazz album with a roster of artists appropriate to the cause with the proceeds going to Classical Action. I sat down and made a list of all my famous musician friends, studio owners, engineers, and others I thought I could count on, and I started making phone calls. I asked everyone to take part without payment, and nobody hesitated. For the repertoire, I thought ruminative or bittersweet pieces—ballads—would be fitting. (And I wasn't sure that hard-hitting jazz would have as much resonance in the gay community.) The brilliant and idiosyncratic jazz singer Mark Murphy, who was gay (though not out) and had lost his longtime partner to AIDS, sang a devastating one-take duet rendition with me of Harold Arlen and "Yip" Harburg's "Last Night When We Were Young," which we named the record for. When you think of "Last Night" in the context of AIDS, it takes on a whole new meaning. Mark's interpretation summed up the project beautifully.

Nearly a dozen other artists, straight and gay—George Shearing,

Janis Siegel, Toots Thielemans, Gary Burton, the saxophonist Phil Woods, among others—contributed tracks. Jane Ira Bloom and I did a medley built around "In the Wee Small Hours of the Morning," which we made the opening track—setting the "after hours" mood. Andy Bey, a deeply soulful jazz singer who is gay (but was still in the closet at the time of this recording), did a sensitive reading of Kern and Hammerstein's "Nobody Else but Me." Dave Catney, in a duet with the Houston-based singer Sandra Dudley, performed a poignant original of Dave's "Little Prayer," taped in Houston in what would be the last recording of his lifetime. And with my trio I played "Somewhere," the Bernstein-Sondheim ballad of yearning from *West Side Story*. We used a touchingly sweet black-and-white photograph—taken by master photographer Lee Friedlander of his two toddlers ('cellist Erik and his little sister, Anna) innocently embracing in a tender dance, which he donated for the cover art. David Hajdu wrote the liner notes. It came together organically, session by session, over about a month, and I was thrilled by all of the music and by the generosity of everyone involved. The jazz community had united to raise funds for the health crisis in a visible and artistic way.

Originally, I had hoped to have the album picked up and marketed by a major label that would then distribute the profits to Classical Action and other worthy AIDS causes. I thought I would have no problem at all placing it given the level of talent involved and the high quality of the performances. But no one would take it. A number of labels said, "We love it—it's a beautiful record with great artists, and it's a great concept. But if we're going to do something like this, we'd rather do it in-house with our own artists." Of course, none of the labels I talked to actually did that.

All of the artists had put heart and soul into this album, and I was offering the labels something world-class that was ready to release—for nothing. And they wouldn't run with it.

After numerous rejections, I couldn't wait any longer to get this record out into the world. So I called Charlie and said, "I guess we're going into the record business!" The Chesky brothers donated manufacturing and graphic design, and Classical Action made the record available by phone orders. Dial (800) 321-AIDS, and read us your credit card number. No Internet, no "one-click"—just an 800 number—and we brought in more than $150,000 for Classical Action, all profit for the organization.

My publicist at the time, Helene Greece, did amazing pro bono work for the project, and the media response to it was overwhelming. Other than the choreographer Bill T. Jones, who had lost his partner, Arnie Zane, a few years previously, no prominent and active performing artist was revealing that he had AIDS—so there was a great deal of interest in my story. I knew I was coming out about it all for the right reasons, and though it took a lot of energy, I saw this process as an opportunity to make a difference, to put a face on something that, frankly, people were scared of. Over the course of the next few months I did interviews with *Newsweek, Entertainment Weekly,* CNN, *CBS Sunday Morning, Billboard,* the *Advocate,* various newspapers, and the jazz magazines, speaking candidly about my history as a semi-secretly gay man in jazz and the larger issue of AIDS consciousness. It was an exhausting process, as my health was tenuous at the time, but I felt that these media opportunities had been handed to me and that it was in my best interest—and that of everyone else in both the jazz and gay worlds—for me to put myself out there, speaking forthrightly about AIDS and the price of being in a closet of any kind. Most people were amazingly supportive—though one jerk of a jazz critic told me, "Yeah, Fred, this AIDS thing will be great for your career." As if having a deadly disease is good for business!

With all the press, I found myself front and center as an AIDS activist. In an interview for the *Los Angeles Times* I told the writer Dan Heckman, "Very few of the gay jazz musicians I know are out. But there's a longer list than you might think, and nine out of ten are still in the closet. So I decided it was time for somebody to break the mold a bit."

Still, it has always seemed to me that effective activism doesn't actually need to be so visible. There's an activism that comes from just being who you are—setting an example and making a statement, minute by minute, in your daily life. If you actively live life as an open human being, that's a kind of activism.

I was fortunate to get to know Tom Stoddard, the influential attorney and gay-rights advocate, who directed the Lambda Legal Defense and Education Fund in the late eighties and early nineties. Tom was the principal author of a landmark act of municipal legislation: the 1986 gay-rights bill, which for the first time protected homosexuals from discrimination in housing, employment, and public accommodations in New York City. Tom was easygoing and unintimidating but brilliant and unrelenting on matters of principle. He put a cheery—and cheering—face on the gay-rights movement. In the summer of 1996, less than a year before he died of AIDS, Tom was the grand marshal of the Gay and Lesbian Pride March in New York. As the march began, the clouds grew dark and it started to rain. Tom found the pool of reporters covering the event and told them, with a smile, "The rain is not a metaphor! The future of the movement is full of sun!" He understood the power of symbolism.

Tom was a master of the political system—Ed Koch, the New York mayor who signed the gay and lesbian rights bill into law, called him "extraordinary" and the legislation "perfect." Tom also understood that human progress begins on the personal level. He was a big believer in private action. We talked about this quite a bit, and we agreed that much of the most important activism takes place in the workplace, in the lunchroom, in the gym, and at family gatherings—in day-to-day life. If you're straight and you meet someone who is out at your job, at a party, or as your neighbor, and get to know the person and become friends, and then one day there's a ballot initiative to deny rights for gay people, you won't think of gay rights as "special rights." You'll recognize them as human rights—and you'll know deep down that the gay people you know should have the same protections and advantages as everybody else. In the twenty-first century this way of thinking is pretty standard. But in the 1990s it was groundbreaking.

As Tom once said, "We have to change the way people think one by one, and then they'll change the way they act. But we need to be out to make that happen." History has proven him right.

I had learned from experience that telling is the best policy, in combination with *showing* that the whole world won't go to hell if there's a gay person on the assembly line or in the judge's chambers—or at the piano in a jazz club. In fact, the world may be a little richer for it.

Activism can take a great range of forms, as I saw many times in the early days of the AIDS crisis. I was in and out of St. Vincent's, the Catholic hospital on Seventh and Greenwich Avenues in the

West Village, half a block north of the Vanguard. St. Vincent's was the first medical center in New York City to have an AIDS ward, and it was a busy one. If you walked past St. Vincent's in the late eighties, you'd often see a black town car parked in front, with a driver alone in the front seat. He'd likely be waiting for a woman named Judith Peabody.

Judy was a celebrated socialite from the Kennedy era, a doyenne of old-money Upper East Side society. Her husband came from the family that founded the Kidder, Peabody investment firm, and one of his uncles was an Episcopal bishop. She dressed strictly in Chanel and Bill Blass, custom made for her. Her appearance was striking: white hair perfectly sculpted into a lacquered mane. Rouged cheeks, scarlet lipstick.

In the early 1980s, Judy and her friends noticed that men in the support system for high society—designers and stylists and florists and hairdressers—were dying. Judy learned about AIDS. Driven by the sense of social responsibility that was once considered part of being a woman of privilege, Judy volunteered for the Gay Men's Health Crisis, working as a "care partner" at St. Vincent's. She would walk down the halls in her spike heels, major jewelry, and designer clothing, and she'd see that a nurse had left an AIDS patient's food on a tray in the hallway. There were people, even nurses, who were afraid to get too close to people with AIDS.

Judy would find the nurse and say, "Excuse me, John seems not to have gotten his dinner yet. Could you kindly bring it in to him? *Right now.* I'll go with you." If she didn't get results, she'd go to the nurses' station and find the person in charge. She'd say, "Excuse me, my name is Judith Peabody, and my husband, Samuel

Peabody, is on the board of this hospital. You need to get John fed, immediately."

Her friends would say to her, "Judy, why don't you dress a little more comfortably if you're going be working in an AIDS ward and carrying trays around?" She would say, "When people see me, they expect Judy Peabody. They will get Judy Peabody."

She donated a lot of money to the Gay Men's Health Crisis, and she made sure that friends contributed substantial sums as well. But it was her hard work in the wards that made the deepest impression. She was no checkbook activist. She *lived* her activism. And she looked sensational doing it. I was grateful to and had intense admiration for Judy, Charlie, and others who were actively engaged in helping the cause, walking the walk—taking personal risks and putting the greater good first.

CHAPTER 12

NONESUCH

There are moments in the act of playing jazz when everything comes together. It's hard for me to explain, because I don't entirely understand it. Maybe nobody does. You're on the bandstand one night, and you know the same things you knew an hour earlier—how the tunes go, how harmony and counterpoint work, how to sit on the stool and how to breathe, how to listen and respond to your bandmates as you play. And yet something's different. Everything *works*, and you're soaring along in the slipstream of a mysterious force. Most people would probably think of this as the moment of inspiration. As I learned in Latin class at Walnut Hills High, the derivation of that term is *spiritus*, which referred originally to breath or wind. One could think of the breath of God, if one is so inclined, or the wind as a phenomenon of nature. Either way, it's something invisible, ungraspable, outside your power. And the more you try to achieve this state, the less likely it is to happen—you have to be relaxed and present enough to allow it to occur.

The same kind of thing can happen in the course of a musical career. Just as there are moments in a performance when things mysteriously come together, there can be periods in an artist's creative lifetime when everything suddenly connects.

For me, all the pieces started falling into place in the mid-1990s. After practically begging Chesky Records to let me do a second album, I got the Grammy nomination for *Dancing in the Dark*, and Chesky was happy to have me do another record for them. I made a no-gimmicks album to showcase my working band and called it, simply, *The Fred Hersch Trio Plays*. It featured my spin on tunes by my favorite jazz composers. I had become a solid enough club and concert performer to attract the attention of a good booking agency, SRO Artists. After a time, my point person there, Alison Loerke, went out to form her own agency, and I went with her. But after two years she decided to concentrate on booking world music acts and not jazz artists. So I persuaded Robert Rund, a youngish agent at IMG as well as a composer and arranger of choral music, to manage me when he left the agency for another position that allowed him to take outside work. Though he was solidly in the classical world and didn't know that much about the jazz sphere, Rund, a low-key, bespectacled, warm, and musically astute guy, liked that I didn't fit the standard jazz mold, and he was keen on strategic planning. He was enthusiastic, uncorrupted by the business of music, and was an avid supporter of my music.

In 1995 I released four albums on three labels: Sunnyside, Enja, and Verése Sarabande. One was a solo-piano record of the music of Johnny Mandel, a master whose association with movie music and reputation as an arranger for singers probably kept him from being thought of as the first-class writer of jazz tunes that he was. I had met Mandel in passing a couple of times in Los Angeles, and I let him know I was doing a whole album of his music. He sent me some lead sheets including a piece that had never been recorded before—a beautiful, moody tune called "Moon Song." I titled the record for Mandel's bittersweet minor-key ballad "I Never Told You." In the same year I also made an album with my working trio and two guest soloists, the tenor saxophonist Rich Perry and the trumpeter Dave Douglas, called *Point in Time*, which featured a tune I wrote in memory of Dave Catney and his joyful spirit, "Cat's Paws." I made a second album with Janis Siegel, *Slow Hot Wind*, continuing our exploration of multiple traditions in jazz and pop. And I made a different sort of vocal album of standards with the experimental singer Jay Clayton, whom I had known for several years and admired greatly. Jay, who is ten years older than me, had been an integral part of the jazz loft scene in New York during the 1960s, and she embodies the experimental loft sensibility. She had worked with avant-gardists such as Steve Reich and Muhal Richard Abrams and has a gift for free, nonverbal vocal improvisation. Singing like an instrument— much like a jazz horn player—she utilizes wordless sounds and extended techniques that are unique to the human voice. She's a fearless improviser, but she can also dig into a lyric and sing with superb interpretive sensitivity and spontaneity.

I loved working with both Janis and Jay—so different from each other. I have been lucky enough to work over the course of my career with many great singers from every sphere of the music world. In fact, I've always had as much in common with singers as I've had with the wonderful jazz instrumentalists I've played with. From my days in the boys' choir in Cincinnati, I've always enjoyed singing. Historians say the voice was almost certainly the first musical instrument, and it is self-evidently the most human, produced in the body itself. We draw breath from our lungs, give it shape with our mouths, and produce music. The breath, after all, was the original inspiration for the very idea of inspiration. I've sung for pleasure my whole life but have never considered singing professionally—mostly because my voice just isn't good enough but also to avoid the stereotype of the gay man singing and playing piano. (I could never erase the memory of singing, in my T-shirt, at that Upper East Side gay bar.) Still, when I'm at the keyboard, I tend to think in vocal terms. The melodies I improvise have the flow of vocal lines, sentences in music. Some writers have said that I "sing" on the piano, and that's not a bad way to describe my music—or at least some of it. Any great jazz singer who improvises abstract, nonverbal sounds is clearly working much the same way.

When Janis or Jay is singing the words to a song, we're working much the same way, too. For *Slow Hot Wind*, I came up with a new arrangement of "For No One," the Paul McCartney tune from the Beatles' album *Revolver*. The Beatles' original recording sounds a bit too cheerful if you look closely at the dark lyric, a pained cry at the breakup of a relationship. I reharmonized it and added a few beats here and there, and we slowed it *way* down. Janis sang it with great subtlety and attention to the lyric. When she sang, "In her eyes, you see nothing," she got across the meaning of the language better than McCartney himself on the Beatles record. Over the years since Janis and I recorded the tune, I've continued to play the arrangement as an instrumental piece—sometimes with my trio, sometimes on solo piano—and I think of the words as I'm playing as much as I would if I were singing them.

There's a story that has circulated among jazz musicians for decades. I've heard it mostly attributed to Lester Young, the lyrical tenor saxophonist for the Count Basie band and frequent collaborator with Billie Holliday. As the story goes, Young is in a recording session, in the middle of a solo, when he suddenly stops. The producer hits the talk-back button and says, "What happened? Is something wrong?" And then Lester says, "Oh, sorry—I forgot the words."

I can't count the times when I've applied the lesson of that anecdote while teaching jazz piano. A student will play a standard for me, and there will be no question of the student's skill—or lack thereof. But there will be something missing in the playing. It will be disconnected from the content of the music—more about showing off what the student can do than expressing the meaning of the song.

I once heard a student play "It Never Entered My Mind" by Rodgers and Hart. The song has a simple diatonic melody (made out of the pitches of the major scale) and a devastating lyric by the repressed, gay, and alcoholic Larry Hart. The student's performance was middle-of-the-road—and, more important, he seemed to be missing a point of view in his interpretation. I said to the student, "What's the tune *about*?" He was flummoxed. He had never thought about that.

So I got out the original sheet music and asked him to read the lyrics to me. He said, "Now I get it. It's sad. It's all about loneliness and disappointment."

I made him play the tune again. It was like he was playing a different piece of music. He made an emotional connection. He was putting across a feeling—a specific feeling—instead of just playing the notes as they appear in a book of lead sheets for jazz musicians.

With four releases I was proud of and with a new manager, things really were coming together for me. And then, in a moment, I suddenly found myself on the next level. At the time, I was just about to sign an exclusive deal with the small German label Enja Records, which had just released *Point in Time.* The contract was literally on my desk when my phone rang one day and it was Bob Hurwitz, the head of Nonesuch Records, asking if I could come up to his office as soon as possible to discuss my recording for his label. It was a prank-call moment, too good to be true, but it was real.

Nonesuch was (and is) one of the most prestigious record companies in the world. It wasn't a jazz label like Blue Note or Verve, but it had a famously eclectic roster of artists, including some of the most respected living composers and performers of the day. It had a reputation for taking what was essentially noncommercial music—the Buena Vista Social Club, the Bulgarian Women's State Chorus, the obscure Polish composer Henryk Górecki's Third Symphony, Cape Verdean morna singer Cesária Évora— and selling millions of copies of it.

As a child of the sixties, I had grown up buying Nonesuch albums when the label was first establishing itself as a low-budget outlet for baroque, contemporary, and ragtime—music for refined but quirky, vaguely nerdish tastes. As I noted earlier, Cecil Lytle, my professor and mentor at Grinnell, had recorded for Nonesuch.

The label was one of the first to present Moog synthesizer music, and it recorded new works by the avant-gardists George Crumb and Elliott Carter as well as important music by American icono-clasts Charles Ives and Conlon Nancarrow. I owned dozens of Nonesuch records, and now it looked like I might get to *make* a Nonesuch record.

Bob had taken charge of the company in 1984, when it was floundering a bit, and he turned it into the major force in music that it had become by the 1990s. He had a huge reputation, so when he said that someone had handed him my Johnny Mandel solo album and, after hearing my version of "Emily," he had im-mediately picked up the phone to call me—well, I was floored.

When I hung up the phone, having agreed to meet Bob later that day, I was exhilarated and gratified and a little numb from the conjoined feelings of pride, self-doubt, and nervousness that come when you suddenly have something you've always hoped for. A few hours later Bob was regaling me with stories of his friend-ships with Philip Glass, Steve Reich, John Adams, and the Kronos Quartet. I was duly impressed and flattered. We talked a bit about me and my music and what I might do for Nonesuch. Bob seemed particularly interested in my ability as an interpreter of other com-posers' music. He said nice things and smart things about my taste in material, my approach to harmony, and my piano sound. He said he'd love to hear me do an entire album of the work of one composer like I had done with Johnny Mandel.

I thought immediately of Billy Strayhorn, and not simply be-cause he was a gay jazz musician. For several years I had been helping David Hajdu with his long-in-the-works but still unfin-ished Strayhorn biography. David had uncovered a significant number of little-known or entirely unknown Strayhorn compositions, and he brought them to me for musicological help. We would sit together on the piano bench in my loft and study Strayhorn's original pencil scores, including the music for some rarities such as "Ballad for Very Tired and Very Sad Lotus Eaters" and "Lament for an Orchid."

I chose twelve Strayhorn compositions, from tunes I had learned from Tommy Flanagan and Jimmy Rowles to some of the pieces David brought to me, and arranged them in a variety of musical settings: trio, solo piano, voice and piano (with Andy Bey singing on "Something to Live For"), and piano duet (with the concert pianist Nurit Tilles) on a transcription of "Tonk," which Strayhorn and Ellington had recorded with four hands at one piano.

When we were ready to record, Nonesuch was in the midst of a two-week "lockout" for the big tracking room at the Hit Factory, one of the largest and most deluxe studios in New York. A superb nine-foot Steinway was in residence. For the album, and for the first time since my days in London with Berniker, I was able to include three tracks with a large string orchestra playing my arrangements. Working with a big record-company budget for the first time in my life, I enjoyed the freedom to use some instrumental colors that I hadn't been able to employ before. It was a treat to have the machinery of a major label available to me.

We called the album *Passion Flower*, in reference both to the Strayhorn ballad of that title and to Strayhorn as a composer of deep and colorful passions who referred to flowers in many of his tunes' names, such as "A Flower Is a Lovesome Thing" and "Lotus Blossom." Inevitably, I suppose, quite a few music writers took the album as a statement of solidarity with the best-known openly gay composer in jazz history. My intention was certainly not to make a "gay record." But I definitely related to Strayhorn on several levels. I admired the harmonic sophistication, the maturity, and the melodic beauty of his music, and I enjoyed his sense of fun. He was a quadruple threat: a great composer of jazz tunes, a first-rate jazz pianist, a remarkable songwriter (music and lyrics), and one of the all-time great arrangers for jazz orchestra. I imagined that if Billy Strayhorn were still around, he and I would probably get along pretty well. We'd have a lot to talk about, and I bet we'd have some laughs—and more than a cocktail or two.

Two weeks before *Passion Flower* was due for release, in January 1996, I got the news that I had been nominated for my second Grammy Award, once again in the category of Best Jazz Instrumental Performance, for my Johnny Mandel album. Strangely, this nomination felt more gratifying than the earlier one. I had been delighted the first time, of course, but took it as a kind of fluke—like, *This is a great thing to have just once in your life.* The second time it felt like more of a validation—like, *Oh, I guess people are really paying attention to what I'm doing!* It felt bigger, even though I didn't win the final award.

Prodded by Bob Hurwitz, I made three consecutive tributes to other composers in my first three years with Nonesuch. Following the Strayhorn project, I recorded an album of songs by Rodgers and Hammerstein on solo piano, followed by a record of music by Thelonious Monk, also solo. The idea of both these projects was to position me as an interpretive pianist, rather than a composer or bandleader. As Bob said to me at the time, "The solo recital is the test of a great pianist. Glenn Gould didn't use a trio. We don't make straight-ahead jazz albums like Blue Note or Verve. And besides, I have John Adams on the roster, and who composes better than that?" Though I have intense admiration for John Adams as one of the greatest living composers, this comment didn't exactly thrill me. I thought I was writing some pretty good music too, even if it was not opera or symphonic work. But I also loved the challenge of creatively interpreting music, so I trusted Bob's vision for me.

I knew there were hazards in taking on Rodgers and Hammerstein, phenomenally successful Broadway composers whose collaborations were not as popular with jazz musicians as the songs Rodgers wrote with Hart. After all, their names are practically shorthand for mainstream middlebrow taste. But I think that point of view is a narrow one that ignores the richness and the beauty of the scores Rodgers wrote for all those hit musicals: *South Pacific, Carousel, The King and I*, and the rest. Hammerstein's words are part of the vocabulary of twentieth-century America: "Some enchanted evening . . . ," "The hills are alive . . ." It's almost impossible to hear or even think of Rodgers and Hammerstein songs without focusing on the words. The challenge for me on this project was to honor the lyrical meaning of the songs, as I always try to do, while teasing out the greatness in the music itself *and* bringing ideas of my own to the table. Interpreting Rodgers and Hammerstein songs wasn't the simple task it may have seemed at first glance. It was a tricky balancing act to work with songs that are so iconic.

Whenever I do an album of one composer's music, I go into heavy research mode. I try to get my hands on everything the composer wrote, on separate lead sheets and in compilation books. I play through *everything* and don't limit myself or choose the play-list too quickly. I don't say, "I could *never* record that tune," as it may work in the context of the rest of the disc. The more obscure the composition, the more faithful I am to it, but if something is very familiar, I assume that the listener wants to hear *my* take on it, and so I can stretch it out or totally rearrange it. But I have to find a way *in*to the tune, a signature that I can put on it—and most important, I have to find a deep connection to it, through the words (if there are any) and the music itself, that will allow me to be myself while still respecting the song.

Sometimes my take on a standard changes over the years. Cole Porter's "So in Love" from *Kiss Me, Kate* is a tune that I have recorded three times. On *Dancing in the Dark*, it took shape as a floating up-tempo swing number. On *Night & the Music* the trio still played it briskly but we broke it up with meter changes for different sections. Then when the multi-disc *Songs Without Words* was planned to have a disc wholly devoted to Cole Porter, I took another look at it, this time getting deeper into the lyrics. In the musical itself, the main characters sing it with a lot of bravado, trying to woo each other. But when I looked deeply at the second line of the lyric, "When I'm close to you, dear," I reconsidered it as a *very* slow ballad in three-quarter time and used the mental image of two lovers lying next to each other in bed, pillow to pillow, intimately confessing how deeply they feel about each other. It is tender, not blusterous—and that is the version that I play today in concert. The words gave me the clues that led me to this interpretation.

After recording Rodgers and Hammerstein, it was important for me to return to the jazz repertoire. So I turned, naturally, to the music of Thelonious Monk. I also wanted to do something that freed me from lyrics at that point, to show that yes, of course I know what I'm doing with American popular song, but I can do a few other things, too. I was starting to get put in the standard-player bin, and I didn't want to be stuck there. Monk's music is all rhythm, unique (and sometimes challenging) harmony, and melodic motive—often with a healthy dose of humor. I may have been one of the first, if not the first, to be either brave or crazy enough to tackle Monk as a solo pianist.

Thelonious Monk has always had a special place in my heart. Today I never play a concert or a set in a club without including a Monk tune, almost always as the closing number. The fact is that Monk occupies a special place in the history of jazz and in the history of American music as a whole. A brilliantly offbeat, cryptically fascinating person with a profoundly unconventional approach to the piano, he was one of the all-time greatest composers of short-form jazz pieces. His career began in the days of the great stride pianists such as James P. Johnson, Earl "Fatha" Hines, and Willie "the Lion" Smith in the 1930s, and it lasted into the 1970s. Monk absorbed the stride influence firsthand, and he played stride in a very idiosyncratic way in his solo work. Ellington was perhaps Monk's greatest influence as a pianist; this branch of the jazz piano tree had its beginnings in the playing of the stupendously imaginative Hines. Monk was on the scene at Minton's Playhouse in Harlem for the birth of bebop in the early 1940s, and he in turn was a major influence on Charlie Parker, Dizzy Gillespie, and Bud Powell.

Monk's music was never far from the blues. He wrote a number of tunes that could be thought of as twelve-bar blues but are unconventionally sophisticated compositionally, including "Ba-lue

Bolivar Ba-lues-are" (great title) and "Straight, No Chaser." He could work one idea through a tune better than anyone else. His blues "Misterioso" is built entirely of major and minor sixths. "Blue Monk" consists of mostly half and whole steps. He used rhythmic and chromatic displacement, turned motives upside down and backward, and it's said that he spent years perfecting some of his compositions. His often angular tunes—with their profound use of space, harmony, rhythm, and motivic development—are compositionally tight and *always* have his musical DNA in them. His music is unceasingly fascinating and inspiring to perform. He wrote literally dozens of masterpieces: "Evidence," "Crepuscule with Nellie," "I Mean You," "'Round Midnight," "Four in One," "Bye-Ya," "Brilliant Corners," "Ruby My Dear," and more. Yet he composed fewer than eighty tunes in his life. The entirety of Monk's output as a composer fits into one book of just over one hundred pages. I've written more songs than Monk in a shorter lifetime. But I've never written anything that comes close to Monk.

Among the qualities that align Monk with the great composers in any genre is his ability to write music that has a certain sense of inevitability about it. You couldn't change one note without diminishing the tune's effect. You could say the same of Bach.

Monk is one of those jazz artists who tempt imitation. Miles Davis is another one. A trumpet player can use a mute and play softly and simply and use a few devices trumpeters all know and sound like an imitation of Miles Davis. There are Monkisms, too—his dissonance and unexpected accents—that any good pianist can duplicate. But they're not what gives his music its depth. To play his music in a meaningful way, you need to internalize it fully and work from inside the tunes. You need to study it, play it, *live* with it, maybe put it away for a while and come back to it. So much is going on inside these short pinnacles of jazz composition. All the most interesting things aren't on the surface—they're not the Monkisms—they're deep in the compositions themselves.

While Monk's music may seem simple at times, a careful examination reveals its sophistication. It's worth taking a close look at one of his tunes, the deceptive little thirty-two-bar gem "Evidence." (The title is reported to be a product of Monk's inimitable sense of logic. The tune is based on the chord changes to "Just You, Just Me." In Monk's reckoning, if you had "Just You, Just Me," you then get "Just Us"—and to have "Justice" you need "Evidence." Fantastic!) The melody Monk composed to the tune's fairly conventional harmony is sparse but fascinating. It sounds almost like a twelve-tone row in the A section, a sequence of major and minor thirds that are rhythmically displaced and encircle the basic harmony in unorthodox ways; he places the consonant pitches on strong beats, where one might expect them, and sometimes he puts the dissonant pitches on strong beats, landing hard on the dissonance. The B section is a displaced chromatic scale that ascends in half steps on offbeats until the final pitch is a totally unexpected whole step. The effect of all this, rhythmically, is like the sound of a drunken tap dance.

I originally planned not to include "'Round Midnight" on the album, because it's so well known it's practically a cliché. Then I realized I could use it as a statement of the *idea* of Thelonious Monk, and I bracketed the album with it in two different interpretations. All of Monk's material presents the same kind of challenge. It's so distinctively his own that it's hard for anyone to do the music justice and make an original contribution to the material.

There's an idiosyncratic spirit in Monk's tunes, a kind of impish wisdom. You feel compelled to either fight it or give in to it—you have to humbly *interpret* it (from the written score rather than from his recordings), not *imitate* it. When I play Monk's music, I find different things in it every time, and I love it.

On the surface, Monk and I couldn't be less alike—we are two generations apart and are of different races and backgrounds, and our piano sounds are not remotely the same. Yet each of us values space in the music, has a devotion to the beat, and loves to improvise specifically off of the elements in the composition itself. At the end of a long set of music (and usually after I have played a ballad), to play my version of a Monk tune is to have *serious fun*—and it is totally freeing. By forcing me to have a different take on his musical language and enter his world on my own terms, I somehow connect to it and feel more *myself* playing his music than I do playing anything other than something I have composed.

MY first three albums for Nonesuch, all interpretations of music by other composers, were well received critically. Still, I picked up an unspoken feeling of something other than full-throttle enthusiasm from Bob. I was making the records Bob wanted me to make, yet I had the sense that he wanted something from me that he wasn't getting. This left me feeling insecure and a little nervous. I was certainly working hard for the label. In addition to the songbook albums, I played and arranged on two albums on which Nonesuch's star soprano, Dawn Upshaw, sang standards. The label also released a duo album of standards and jazz classics I made with the wonderful guitarist Bill Frisell, appropriately titled *Songs We Know,* as well as the recording of a solo recital I gave at the New England Conservatory, called *Let Yourself Go: Live at Jordan Hall.* Although the recording was done for archival purposes and hadn't been recorded specifically for release, Bob and I were so pleased with the performance that Nonesuch issued it. But after four years of recording for Nonesuch, I could tell Bob Hurwitz was getting impatient with me.

At the same time, I wasn't sure that Nonesuch was bringing out everything I had in me, either. I felt constricted by Bob's limited view of me as a solo interpreter of others' music, to the point where he was unwilling to record my working trio: "That's what Blue Note does, not Nonesuch," he'd say. And after *Forward Motion* I didn't want to give up on composing, which was an important aspect of my musical persona. Frisell had released numerous albums on Nonesuch featuring his original music, so I surmised that Bob didn't take me seriously as a writer. I was grateful, of course, for all the opportunities he was giving me, but since the beginning I had never been able to shake the feeling that Bob and I weren't on an even playing field as recording artist to label chief. I felt sometimes like the chorus girl in the back who is made into a star by an impresario who doesn't see the real her.

In the summer of 2000, a few months after the release of *Let Yourself Go,* Bob called a meeting with me in his office at the new Nonesuch headquarters in Rockefeller Plaza in Manhattan. The location made apparent that we'd be having a serious discussion, not trading thoughts over a meal. Bob told me he was frustrated that my last few releases had not had the "impact" he had hoped to see—though the albums must have sold at least well enough for him to continue to honor my multi-record exclusive contract. The diplomatic framing of his feelings as frustration—rather than disappointment—cast him as my ally, rather than my overseer, and I found some comfort in that. Bob said, surprisingly, "Let's give them something they can't ignore"—a "big statement," meaning a multi-disc set.

It was not at all clear whom he meant by "them" and what, in his mind, constituted "impact." I had gotten consistently strong reviews, with the minor whimper of dissent that every musician who's in the arena will get once in a while. Maybe he wanted another Grammy nomination for me? But I took the challenge Bob set before me as a great opportunity. We jointly—then and there—decided to make a four-CD set, showcasing me both as a composer and as an interpretive pianist. I'm not sure if he had a project of this scope in mind before the meeting, but I was nonetheless excited about the prospect.

I called the project *Songs Without Words*, after the first disc in the set, which was a collection of original music for piano mostly written specifically for this project. Though I had composed quite a bit of music by this point, I had, strangely, not written much for one of my favorite formats, solo piano. Most times, but not always, when I compose a piece, I just *write*, not knowing in which format the music will end up: trio, duo, quintet, or solo. I try to stay out of the way, letting the music take me where it wants to go. There are some tunes that I play only with a quintet (which I call the Trio +2) and others that work best for the trio. But I had seldom composed specifically for solo piano, and I looked forward to the challenge.

The heart of that opening disc was a six-movement suite inspired by the six-part Bach Partitas I've always loved. (The title was an overt nod to Mendelssohn's well-known suites, also called

"Songs Without Words," each of which was also a set of six works for piano.) In addition to the new compositions, I included four tunes I had already written, including "Child's Song," "Heartsong," and "Sarabande," because they seemed to fit—they have something lyrical and pianistic about them. I wanted this first disc to be solo piano in my own musical language: jazz at its core but with other elements (classical and Brazilian most prominently) in the mix. I wanted each piece to lead nicely into the next and for it all to come together in the end as a statement of my approach to composing for the piano. I tried to avoid concerning myself with how "jazzy" a statement I was making. I wanted only to say something that was meaningful and true for me and that conveyed my lifelong love for the piano.

The second album in the set was a collection of tunes by some of my favorite jazz composers: Wayne Shorter's "Fall," a lesser-known Monk number called "Work," a superb ballad by the underappreciated London-based trumpet and flügelhorn player Kenny Wheeler, "Winter Sweet," which I had played with Kenny himself in England; two of Charles Mingus's tributes to composers *he* admired, "Duke Ellington's Song of Love" and "Jump Monk," combined; and six others. The third and fourth albums I recorded for the set were each dedicated to a single composer: one, Cole Porter; the other, Antonio Carlos Jobim. Almost all of the performances were solo piano, though broken up occasionally by a few duets, trios, and quintets with varying combinations of guest musicians.

In literal terms, the project ended up being too big for Bob Hurwitz—and, I admit, for me. We opted not to include the Jobim set, deciding that to release just three volumes would actually make the project stronger. I described the three discs in the set as representing "the three basic food groups" of my musical diet: original compositions, jazz works with rhythm at their center, and songs with intelligent lyrics at their heart. I sought to communicate something of myself through all three bodies of work, in my own musical language.

The critical response to *Songs Without Words* was overwhelming. Among the many rave reviews, Fernando Gonzalez, in the *Washington Post*, wrote: "*Songs Without Words* might be the one three-CD set, this or any year, that leaves you asking for more. Talent combined with this much intelligence has its rewards." There were major feature articles about me—and about the boxed set—in the *New York Times* and in *Keyboard* magazine. I was excited that our idea of making a big statement was finding resonance in places that mattered to both of us, and felt proud of the work I had done on every level—the recorded sound, my approach to the repertoire, and above all, just being myself in the music. My confidence was high, and for the right reasons.

But if *Songs Without Words* left listeners like the *Washington Post* critic asking for more, Bob Hurwitz was not among them. I had been itching to record my working trio, but Bob wasn't interested. In 2001 the small Palmetto Records label gave me an opportunity to record it live at the Village Vanguard. I wanted to make a straight-up jazz record, and Bob just said, "Take the opportunity." It was a surprisingly natural evolution from one label to another—and finally I had total control about what I was going to record and with whom. I don't in any way regret my time with Nonesuch—Bob and I made some memorable records together, and being on a major label opened some important new doors for me. But we were both ready to move on.

CHAPTER 13

A WISH

At the beginning of every year, my manager, Robert Rund, and I would make something we called the BAWL, our "big-ass wish list." It was a dream litany of career aspirations—venues and cities I wanted to play in, projects I hoped to do. I'd let my imagination run free, not concerning myself with matters of feasibility.

In January 2002, the first year after my contract with Nonesuch had lapsed, I told Robert that one thing I would love to try someday was the writing of a big piece, a long-form work of some sort, using the poetry of Walt Whitman. Ever since I had studied Whitman at the New England Conservatory, I had a special affection for his *Leaves of Grass*. I was taken by the vivid beauty of the language, its intrinsic musicality, and Whitman's celebration of the connectedness of humankind and the natural world—as well as the glory Whitman took in male union. Since the wishes on the list I made with Robert were of the big-ass variety, I had a vague conception of the scale of a hypothetical Whitman project, but no ideas about its potential form. Then, a few months into 2002, Robert called me and said he had secured three performances of the piece in the spring of 2003. He had successfully sold and committed me to performing a huge piece I had yet to compose.

The time felt right for me to try this. After the terrorist attacks of September 11, 2001, I found solace in Whitman's view of life. By this time, I had been involved in a school of Buddhist practice for a couple of years, and I thought Whitman, at his most transcendental, was essentially Buddhist in his attention to self-awareness, acceptance, and love of nature.

What I practice is called insight (or *vipassana*) meditation, which is a widely practiced version of Buddhism in the United States, and I consider it an important part of who I am.

I wouldn't describe myself as religious in the Jewish sense— although I jokingly refer to myself as a "Jew-Bhu." Insight meditation, for me, is grounded in reality and humanity. You meditate by sitting on a cushion or walking back and forth, paying close and gentle attention to your breath (for me, usually first thing in the morning), carrying that awareness during the rest of the day and learning how life occurs as a series of present moments. The more you are aware of each moment, the more alert you are to how you react to situations, how you affect other people, and how other people and events affect you. It is not about "emptying your mind," as the mind's job is to think—it's about slowing down enough to see the mind as it is and to gain insight into how it works and what its tendencies are. During some sittings, I can remain largely free of planning, grasping, and avoiding—and other days I have "monkey mind," filled with internal chatter. But I try to be present in a nonjudgmental way with whatever is going on.

When I began my practice around 1999, it struck me immediately that, in a way, I had been meditating my whole life but on a piano bench instead of a *zafu*. My focus was on making sound in rhythm, and when I had a lapse of concentration in performance, I would just concentrate on the simplicity of the tactile relationship between my body and the piano keyboard, the same way that coming back to the body quieted discursive thoughts during my seated meditation.

As often as I can, I attend weeklong silent retreats at the Insight Meditation Society in Barre, Massachusetts—these are highly inspiring and grounding. Self-observation becomes more acute, though it is not easy to be with yourself and what can arise in complete quietude for so long when you are slowed *way* down and totally free from the distractions of modern life. It is a gift to myself to take this personal time out of my schedule—it provides fuel for my spiritual engine.

Whitman, in his poem "Song of Myself" in *Leaves of Grass*, seemed connected with this school of thought. He began with the self and celebrated living, but he also saw the self as intrinsically, interdependently connected to other people and the world. Whitman spoke to me in a number of ways. On the level of the ideas, I connected to his love of nature and his recognition of the primacy of the present moment. I related to the way he used language, too. The long, free-form, kinetic phrases of most of the poetry in *Leaves of Grass* felt improvised. In fact, Whitman revised *Leaves of Grass* frequently, as if he were starting fresh in each version, like a jazz musician rerecording a tune many times over the course of a long career.

Initially published in 1855, a hundred years before I was a born, *Leaves of Grass* was a perennial work in progress—or a series of works that varied in character and grew exponentially over more than three decades, until Whitman's death at age seventy-two in 1892. The first edition, something of a vanity project published by Whitman himself, included a dozen poems on 95 pages. The second edition, published fourteen months later, contained 32 poems. Over the next four years Whitman achieved full bloom as a writer (and as a person, owing in part to a visit to New Orleans that inspired the "Calamus" poems, concerned with male union), and he expanded *Leaves of Grass* to 156 poems, including revisions and new orderings of the earlier ones into thematic clusters. Whitman devoted most of the rest of his years to recasting and reshaping the work. By the last of the nine versions Whitman put together, the so-called Deathbed Edition of 1892, *Leaves of Grass* presented more than 400 poems on more than 600 pages. The Complete Deathbed Edition is the one I bought and started marking up with notes after Robert Rund plopped that deadline into my lap.

I also read up on Whitman's life and work as a prose writer, and was not surprised to find that he had been a public champion of homegrown American sounds and "black music" in particular. He worked for a while as a newspaper music critic in Brooklyn, using his forum to argue in favor of newly emerging modes of American folk music over forms of Western music then considered more respectable. He praised what he called "heart music" (earthy, informal, American) over "art music" (refined, formal,

European). I was certainly sympathetic to his way of thinking, though I'd never thought of the heart and art as mutually exclusive. The more deeply you tap the heart as a musician, the better your art, in my view. Like innumerable readers of *Leaves of Grass* over the years, I found the passion that permeates the work electrifying; and like many other gay men, I was knocked out by the vivid evocation of what Whitman called "manly attachment," in the "Calamus" poems:

> We two boys together clinging,
> One the other never leaving . . .
> Arm'd and fearless—eating, drinking, sleeping, loving,
> No law less than ourselves owning . . .

Whitman, however, was also an opera lover, and he thought of *Leaves of Grass* as indebted to the "emotions, raptures, and uplifts" of his musical experiences. "But not for opera," he said, "I could never have written *Leaves of Grass*." Though virtually all of *Leaves of Grass* has no rhyme scheme, if one looks closely, its internal rhythm makes it hospitable to a musical setting. At the same time, the monumental scale and stature of the work made the task of adapting it to music terribly daunting.

In the summer of 2002 I brought my copy of *Leaves of Grass*, all 628 pages of it, to a residency at the Banff Center for the Arts in Calgary. I had applied to Banff citing *Leaves* as my work in progress, though I had not yet made very much progress on it. I also applied for a Guggenheim Memorial Fellowship to buy me some time to write, and found out a little later in 2003 that I had been awarded one—a major vote of confidence in the project.

Alone in my studio after I arrived, I picked up my copy of *Leaves of Grass* and started marking poems and parts of poems that I thought might work well set to music, just using my gut reactions. I had begun the process.

I had already spent two (and would ultimately spend eight) fruitful and, in some ways, life-changing residencies at the MacDowell Colony, an artists' retreat in Peterborough, New Hampshire. I was honored and exhilarated to find my first application accepted in 2000, since in those days there were few, if any, jazz composers awarded residencies there. Much jazz composition (think of Monk) doesn't look nearly as impressive on the page as a string quartet or an orchestral piece does—the performance is what really makes it work, and the recording of the piece is more important than the score.

When I arrived at MacDowell—a hundred-year-old campus of pristine rustic cottages, evergreen woods, and rolling fields on some 450 acres—I was swept away by the bucolic serenity and history of the place. There's a wall of wooden "tombstones" in each studio where people who have done past residencies signed their names. I looked over the signatures, and there was Aaron Copland. There was Thornton Wilder. DuBose Heyward. Leonard Bernstein. I thought, *What in the hell am I doing here? How did I fake my way in? How long can it be till they catch on to me?*

I was taken over by the pressure to produce a masterpiece. I had been given the gift of free time in this dreamlike environment, and I felt a tremendous responsibility to use the time well. It was paralyzing, and that first week I was overwhelmed. I procrastinated, reading novels and napping during the day. At the group dinner for the residents one night, I was seated next to Jane

Brox, a respected nonfiction writer, essayist, and poet, and I told her I wasn't getting much work done, and I was feeling guilty for being so unproductive. She told me to stop punishing myself and enjoy the experience of being at MacDowell. This time was for me, and I was free to use it in any way that suited me. Lots of people leave MacDowell refreshed and then start working, Jane said. That made me feel a lot better and loosened me up, and I quickly became super-motivated and productive.

For more than six months, beginning in MacDowell and then back in New York, I focused entirely on the text selection for my *Leaves of Grass* piece, knowing instinctively that if I got the text right, the music would come. I went through my copy of the Deathbed Edition, typing and then cutting out every piece of text that I had marked up for consideration. I laid the pieces out on the floor of my studio and shuffled them around, setting possible sequences and weeding some out. I worked by gut, with no concern—yet—for how the pieces could fit together. For no reason other than that they just didn't speak so loudly to me, I passed over some of the best-known poems in *Leaves of Grass*, such as "When Lilacs Last in the Dooryard Bloom'd" and "O Captain! My Captain!" and I used none of the many poems about the Civil War or New York in the nineteenth century. I was more drawn to the poems with grand sentiments than the ones firmly grounded in time and place. I wanted to use his magical words to convey big thoughts and feelings in a way that I never could. And I was not afraid of using only a part of a longer poem (or even, in some cases, just the title) if that was what spoke to me.

Having never written a long-form work with words and music before, I asked for some advice from the composer Bob Aldridge, a fellow graduate of the New England Conservatory who was about my age. He had composed multiple concert-length pieces and had at this point been working for several years on an opera based on *Elmer Gantry*, the Sinclair Lewis novel. Bob suggested I contact his collaborator, Herschel Garfein, who had written the libretto for *Elmer Gantry* and was a respected composer in his own right. Herschel had grown up with the performing arts; his mother was the actor Carroll Baker, his father the film and stage director Jack Garfein. He was highly knowledgeable and skilled but wore his competence lightly.

I knew that there was a better order to be made of the texts that I loved, but I had been staring at them for so long, I was beginning to lose perspective. Herschel helped me by organizing them in way that moved obliquely from the universal to the particular in a dramatic arc. While Whitman had begun *Leaves of Grass* with the sixty-page poem "Song of Myself," I knew I wanted to start, after an overture, with what I was envisioning as an invocation, "Song of the Universal," then go right into my idiosyncratic selections from "Song of Myself." We divided the piece into two parts, with the finale a setting of a four-line poem written late in his career, "After the Dazzle of Day." There's a structure, but it's not rigid or schematic—and it is a work of art, not an academic work, and as such I felt free to use the words in any way I wished. I wanted to retain a sense of the freedom, the element of the unexpected, that's an essential part of Whitman's poetry. I didn't care if the finished piece fit neatly into any established category. I didn't set out to write an opera or an operetta or an oratorio or a work of musical theater. I wanted the piece to be what it would be. I figured the best way to be true to Walt Whitman was to be true to myself.

And yet back at MacDowell in January 2003, with the premiere looming that March, I still needed to make huge strides on the music, but I was once again feeling overwhelmed and a little paralyzed. I had to snap out of it, to shake myself up. So I tried something I'd never done before: I sang each poem over and over, using the poem's internal rhythm to tease out natural-sounding melodic shapes or find a groove that fit. Once I found that rhythm, the music appeared almost instantly. I wrote the piece in about four weeks, leaving myself February to do the orchestrations, hand-copying the parts in pencil just in time for the March premiere.

In the end, the project had become a fully scored, evening-long continuous program of songs and instrumental works for two voices, one male and one female, and a chamber ensemble of eight pieces: piano, trumpet, trombone, two woodwinds (tenor sax, and alto sax doubling on clarinet and bass clarinet), 'cello, bass, and drums. It's largely formal, in that every note (except for solos) was written out—with a pencil on staff paper, the way I have always written; and it relates to jazz, in that the instrumentation is associated with jazz and all the musicians I used were badass jazz players. There's not that much improvisation in the piece, only modest-length solos that feature each player, with the notable exception of a piece called "The Mystic Trumpeter," which has space for free improvisation for trumpet and voice. Whitman's words were all-important, and the ensemble took a backseat to the vocalists.

That meant the singers would have to be just the right people. I knew I wanted to use lyrically astute jazz singers and not classical singers, for whom vowel sounds are often more important than the words and their meaning. I wanted to be sure the words would be *heard* and experienced by the listener, which meant finding vocalists attuned to the value of great diction and who were capable of singing with emotional sincerity.

For the male singer, there was no question that it would be Kurt Elling—I wrote the male part with Kurt in mind. I had known him since the mid-1990s, when he was still living in Chicago. Kurt had studied most of the great poets, and he could quote many of them from memory. His readiness to do so in casual conversation spoke of his bravura as well as his intellect. Both were of value in taking on Whitman. Not every singer could stand at a microphone and sing, "I celebrate myself, and sing myself," the opening words of Whitman's "Song of Myself." The singer had to mean that in his bones, and Kurt Elling did. I don't intend that as a backhanded compliment. Kurt's self-confidence was well earned. I knew he would appreciate Whitman's language—and he is a superb musician. Kurt had written a good deal of poetry himself, much of it in the form of vocalese lyrics crafted to the music of improvised jazz solos.

Not long after I started working on *Leaves of Grass*, I realized there was an awful lot of male energy in it. I wanted a female counterbalance. For a female singer, I engaged Norma Winstone and, again, wrote the music with her in mind. Norma, who lives near London and is not as well known in the United States as she should be, is a uniquely wonderful jazz singer with a pure voice, great instincts, and impeccable diction. Like Kurt, she is also a superb lyricist attuned to the art of poetry. (She has since written lyrics to many of my tunes, including delicately plaintive words for my ballad "Valentine," which, in its lyric version, we retitled "A Wish.") As a singer, Norma exuded womanly warmth that was just right for the project.

Norma came to the States for the March 2003 tour of performances of *Leaves of Grass* that Robert Rund had set up. We premiered it at Western Michigan University in Kalamazoo and ultimately performed it at the Spoleto Festival in South Carolina and at performing arts centers and universities in Washington, DC, and New Jersey. Inevitably, Norma had to go back home, so for both the recording of *Leaves and Grass* and its 2005 CD release tour, including a sold-out premiere in New York, at the new Zankel Hall in Carnegie Hall, Kate McGarry took over from Norma. Kate, though just emerging in the jazz scene, had already released two wonderful albums, and I was a big fan. Steeped in Irish and folk music as well as jazz, she sang with an earthy sensibility, like Norma, but with a rootsy American feeling that was ideally suited to Walt Whitman. On the album of *Leaves of Grass* that we recorded for Palmetto, the first voice you hear is Kate's, singing with ringing clarity:

Come, said the Muse,
Sing me a song no poet has yet chanted
Sing me the Universal.

The universal grows out of the particulars in Whitman's poetry and ultimately transcends them.

At Carnegie, when I heard Kate's pure, tender voice singing music I had composed, I was moved almost to tears, overcome with joy and affirmed in my decision to follow my instincts with this project from the beginning. As to the broader response, I need not have worried, as it was almost completely positive. Among the many heartening reviews of the work, the *Washington Post* said that *Leaves of Grass* was "an eloquently orchestrated celebration of Walt Whitman's poetry, vision and, above all else, humanity." My intention was to serve Whitman's language with music so that the listener hears his words in a new way. At least that was my hope, my big-ass wish.

CHAPTER 14

SCOTT

I go to jazz clubs on most weekend nights, but usually to work. Though I try, my schedule doesn't allow me to go out as a listener as much as I would like. It was a rare experience for me to be at New York's Birdland on the evening of Saturday, April 13, 2002, to hear Janis Siegel singing with the pianist Eric Reed and his trio. I went with a friend—someone I had met in the recovery program I had joined to deal with my sexual compulsion. This iteration of the renowned bebop haunt of the postwar Fifty-Second Street scene had opened just a few years earlier, on West Forty-Fourth Street in the theater district. Unlike the original Birdland, this one was roomy and designed in the style of a ritzy nightspot in a vintage Hollywood musical. There were tables on an elevated level to one side of the stage, and that's where my friend and I were seated.

At one point in the show, Janis was about to sing the standard "I Remember You" in a medley with Kenny Wheeler's "Who Are You?" She introduced the arrangement as mine and pointed me out in the audience, saying some nice things about our friendship and collaboration. I smiled and waved.

When the show was over, a man came over to my table and knelt down alongside me, so we were eye to eye. He was a well-put-together guy with blond hair, boy-next-door looks, and a radiant smile. He said, "Excuse me, Mr. Hersch. I have your records with Janis and a couple of your own albums, and I just want to say that I really dig your music."

I said, "Thanks for saying that," and we locked eyes for a moment. When we shook hands, there was a bit more warmth than the situation called for. He went back to his table, and I thought, *Something a little unusual just happened.*

On my way out of the club I spotted him, made it a point to walk by his table, where he was sitting with another guy, said good night, and put my hand on his shoulder.

A couple of days later I got an e-mail through my website, and the sender introduced himself as Scott Morgan, the guy from Birdland. He said he was interested in buying a copy of the book of sheet music of my original tunes that I was offering through the site. He could have purchased it directly without e-mailing me, of course. And I could have sold him the book without engaging him, as I did, with questions about his musical background and experience. He sent back a longish note saying that he was a jazz lover and had studied music seriously before making a career in technology. I was *definitely* more interested. After a few exchanges like this, I asked him out to dinner via e-mail. I wrote, with characteristic forthrightness, "Yes, I do mean a date."

We went to a place called Anita's on Broadway and Broome Street, which had opened just a few months earlier. He had come straight from his job at Microsoft, where he was working in senior management, and was dressed smartly in "business casual." I wore shorts and one of my many vintage shirts from the 1950s. We both looked pretty sharp. I brought up my HIV status almost immediately, in fairness to him, and he said he had read about it in both the gay and jazz press and understood the situation before he'd agreed to the date. He told me he was not HIV positive but understood AIDS and its risks.

Jazz doesn't have a large audience, so proportionately there are not that many gay jazz fans. Most of them are into singers and not instrumental jazz, but Scott's knowledge struck me as pretty deep. He impressed me with his knowledge of an obscure singer named Nancy King, who is one of my all-time favorites but has had a barely visible career. And he knew a good bit about my music, too. He told me he had my album *Forward Motion* and said, "It was cool how you used the chord progression of Charlie Parker's 'Confirmation' in your tune 'Janeology.'" He had great taste and good ears, and I was seriously digging him. When the check came, I offered to pay and said he could cover the next one.

After a couple more nice dinner dates in the following weeks, Scott said he'd like to make a meal for me and invited me to his house in Verona, New Jersey, a short bus ride from midtown Manhattan. I asked, "Should I bring a toothbrush?" and he said, "Yes." Scott cooked up an impressive dinner of Mediterranean red mackerel, with perfectly prepared homemade crème brûlée for dessert. This would be the first of hundreds of meals that Scott would cook for the two of us over the ensuing years, but he never made crème brûlée again until I dogged him about it many years later. He knew how to impress me in all the right ways.

I had been in some longish relationships since Eric, but for one reason or another they had not worked out; my sexual issues were responsible for ending some of them. But after two years in recovery, supported by a committed meditation practice, I felt wide open to this sweet, gentle man who seemed different from any of the others for reasons that would become apparent (and more and more attractive) as I got to know him.

Scott and I had a great many things in common: our love of music; our interest in culture more broadly; our progressive political orientation. Though he worked in digital coding and then in senior management for Electronic Data Systems, and later at Microsoft, he had studied music in college, earning a BFA in musical theater from Florida State University. He could play piano well enough to accompany himself with some hip chords and was a genuinely gifted singer. He had a warm, appealing vocal quality and sang with feeling and sensitivity to the words. Over the years since we've met, I've encouraged him and coached him from time to time in jazz singing, to help channel his considerable talent. In 2016 he released a well-received jazz vocal CD, *Songs of Life*—naturally I was the pianist, arranger, and producer, and we had a ball doing it.

Almost seven years younger than me, he grew up as part of a close-knit, athletic, and outdoorsy family in Sarasota, Florida. When he was a child, Sarasota was not as overdeveloped with condos as it is now. There were wetlands and sandy beaches and lots of open spaces. Venice, just down the road from Sarasota, has for decades been the winter home base for the Ringling Bros. and Barnum & Bailey Circus. All the animals, including the elephants, lived off-season on a ranch there, and the performers trained and practiced in Venice. Scott had joined the Sailor Circus in first grade—it was a youth circus staffed by many of the Ringling performers. He learned how to fly on the trapeze, how to tumble and walk tightrope, and how to ride a unicycle. As an adult, he kept up his circus skills for the exercise and the fun.

His childhood experience and mine, in Cincinnati, could hardly have been more different. On our first date, I asked him to be my guest for a show I was playing at the Vanguard in two weeks, but he said he couldn't—he was going hiking in the Pyrenees with his parents. Thinking of my own disastrous family vacations, I thought, *This guy is either really well adjusted or he has not cut the cord with his family.* Thankfully, it turned out to be the former. Scott felt closely connected to both his mother, who worked as a special education teacher, and his father, a corporate executive who retired in early middle age so he could travel, enjoy outdoor sports, and hike. Both of his parents, now in their eighties, run competitively. Not long after Scott and I met, when Scott was forty-one and his father was sixty-eight, the two of them scaled Mount Kilimanjaro together.

Scott was raised in the southern way, with good manners and a deferential attitude toward his elders—you called people "sir" and "ma'am." He knew when to speak and when not to speak, and he could handle himself with grace and charm in any situation. I learned a lot just by watching him with people. My parents were somewhat southerners, and I grew up on the cusp of the South, but I'm a little more intense than Scott. And after four decades of living in Manhattan, I tend to say what's on my mind. It's not that I have no self-control—I can function socially as a responsible human being. I'm just inclined to be up-front about my feelings and my thoughts. That's how I'm wired, and that wiring works for me as a jazz musician. I need to trust my gut instincts and feel comfortable putting them out there. When I have the notion to play something, I play it, and I don't apologize for it. I work the same way offstage, too, generally speaking.

If Scott and I were at a party and I was having a bad time, I might say to him, "This sucks—let's get out of here." He'd say, "Oh, I don't think it's so bad. But I understand how you feel. Let's just hang out for a little while longer, so we don't offend anyone, and then we can leave quietly." We worked well as a team and complemented each other. He was certainly good for me—and I was pretty sure I was just as good for him.

When I met Scott, he had a female Rottweiler—a sweet, older rescue dog named Barkley whom he was deeply attached to and whom I loved the moment I met her. One of the main reasons he lived in Verona was so Barkley could have a backyard to run around in. Scott and I had been together for about a year, going back and forth to each other's places, when Barkley was diagnosed with bone cancer and she had to be put down. With no more need for the yard, Scott sold the house and moved into my loft.

Living with Scott, like everything involving Scott, was a pleasure from the start. I found him to be generally easygoing, and in many ways he was more mature than I am, despite my being older. He was stable and patient where I was quicker to get angry and frustrated. (He's helped me out more times than I can count when I have been in IT hell.) He had a solid sense of himself and his place in the world and cared deeply for those who didn't have a voice. He solved his own problems, as a rule, but if he needed me, he knew that I would be there to talk things over or just to listen to him. And he would prove again and again that he was very good at taking care of me.

We became best friends who like to be around each other but don't need to be connected every second of the day. When we can't be together, just thinking about him brightens my spirits. Scott has a great, subtle sense of humor. He's not a jokester, but he's very playful—affectionate and endearing nicknames are bestowed upon me regularly. Monogamy has been something we agreed on from the start, and it has been easy with him despite my years of wanderlust. We have been through a lot together, and our love is deep and strong.

I'm not everybody's idea of a perfect partner, I know. I'm a touring musician who's traveling often for weeks at a time, and I'm not always available emotionally when I'm home or in composing mode. Often I come back from a road trip to do my laundry, dig out my in-box, and pay bills, then I repack and head out a day or two later. We have had to learn to manage these swift entrances and exits.

I've never worked nine to five, and I can't leave my work at the office. I can be preoccupied—and as time has gone by, my career and the music business take up more of my time. My office is in a corner of our loft, and I teach and rehearse there as well. I may be in the kitchen, hanging out with Scott, and suddenly get an idea for a tune. When that happens, my downtime is over. I'm at the piano, trying to make the most of that moment of inspiration. (I have to admit that these days it's increasingly difficult for me to get to the piano in a non-distracted way—too often I succumb to the compulsive lure of e-mail and the Internet.)

It takes a special kind of person to put up with someone like me, but Scott has always been up for the challenge. If I'm working on a big project, it consumes me for days and sometimes weeks at a time. The work takes up all my brain space, and there's not much left of me for anything or anyone else. Sometimes, I admit, I get too lost in myself, for the sake of my work, and Scott is not afraid to call me on it. He'll say, gently but firmly, "You know, Fred, there *are* two of us here. I don't want to be ignored," and I'll wake up and realize, *I'd better get out of my bubble for a while.*

Our relationship, more than fifteen years old as of this writing, is one of the best things that has ever happened to me. Scott is, by all definitions, a reasonable adult. I never thought I would have such a person for a partner—and one who is smart, sexy, committed, and fun to be around. I didn't think I was worthy of that. For most of my life since adolescence, I was attracted to men who didn't treat me particularly well, because deep down I didn't think I was worthy of much better. I thought of myself as inadequate or defective, and I hooked up with people who reinforced that. Scott has been a gift to me I never thought I deserved.

ONCE Barkley left us, the house in Verona sold at a great price, leaving Scott with a windfall that he, with his good business sense and generous income from Microsoft, wanted to reinvest in other property.

After I closed Classic Sound in 1988, I was justifiably worried about my health—which had been tenuous. My romantic fantasy in the years right after I was diagnosed was to have a second home outside the city, especially as I didn't know how much time I had left. With what money I had from the sale of all the audio gear, in 1989 I bought a small house near a lake outside the town of Milford, Pennsylvania, and put a serviceable baby grand Yamaha piano in the living room. After I realized I had to take absolutely every gig, no matter how demeaning, to keep up with the expenses of maintaining the house, I sold it in 1993. But I remained fond of the area. It's peaceful and woodsy—a refuge from New York City but only about two hours' drive away, making it ideal for a weekend retreat. In 2003, after the sale of his house went through, Scott and I shopped around in that area for homes but couldn't find anything with a living room big enough for the seven-foot Steinway that I wanted to move from our SoHo loft. So we decided to build.

We found a secluded and affordable plot of land on the side of a hill in an area that real-estate agents were spinning as the Delaware Highlands but which everyone else considered the northern end of the Poconos—though the nearest hotel with a heart-shaped bathtub was at least forty-five minutes away. Working with a stock bi-level design, modified by an architect and built by a local contractor, we had a lovely 1,700-square-foot house built. It had an open plan, like a loft, for the primary space, as well as several gracious rooms on two levels. A forest of hickory and red oak surrounded the house. We constructed a huge deck running the length of the back of the house, and with the house being on the hill, you feel like you are living up in a tree house—especially in the summer when the trees are lush and full.

We filled out the house with some new furniture (I am the one with the decorating gene) as well as some nice pieces that Scott had in storage from his Verona house, including a Stickley dining room set, and we decorated it with artwork and objects each of us had collected over the years—a photograph of a street scene in Calcutta by the fine-art photographer Rosalind Fox Solomon; whimsical animal wood carvings by the Santa Fe artist Miguel Rodriguez; visual works by artists I had met at MacDowell; an acrylic portrait of Barkley that Scott had commissioned . . .

The first night we slept in the barely furnished house together, in October, it was spookily quiet and so dark outside that we could hardly see our hands in front of our faces. We were taking a bath by candlelight, giddily drinking a bottle of champagne (vintage, and a gift from Charlie) and wondering *how the hell* we had pulled this off—we were so thrilled. When I went to the house our first summer there and sat on the sofa or the deck, looking out at the trees, I felt happy and calm. I could barely believe how fortunate I was to have this beautiful home and the great partner who made it possible. Today when I go for a walk along the gravel road that leads to the house or for a lap swim in the community pool, or when I sit at the piano, looking out at the view of the treetops and hills, soaking in the sounds of the woodpeckers and hummingbirds while Scott is singing in the downstairs bedroom, I'll think, *Is this really happening? It feels like a dream, a fantastic one.* I am one lucky man.

IT takes a fairly high degree of commitment for two people to build a house together. In the world of my parents, engagement and marriage would generally come before the house. At the time Scott and I got together, however, matrimonial traditions and benefits were still restricted to straight couples. Bill Clinton had blithely signed the so-called Defense of Marriage Act, which legally defined marriage as "a legal union between one man and one woman," redundantly defining a "spouse" as "a person of the opposite sex." When our house in Pennsylvania was being built, in 2003, the landmark decision that led the Massachusetts Supreme Court to legalize same-sex marriage in the state had not yet been made. Legalization in New York State would not come until June 2011, followed by the great U.S. Supreme Court decision legalizing gay marriage in June 2013.

Ten years before that ruling, in 2003, Scott and I took the next step. While the house was under construction, we went on a short vacation to Saint Croix. We were staying in a fantastic Thai-style wooden guesthouse on the enormous estate of close friends. On a perfect moonlit night, sitting in a Jacuzzi after dinner (I am not making this up), it just felt like the perfect moment to ask Scott to marry me. I used those words, meaning that in the depth of my heart I was proposing a lifetime commitment. I didn't give a shit if gay marriage was legal or illegal. I knew Scott and I loved each other, and I wanted us to be together for the rest of our lives. I was in a good place emotionally after my time in recovery. All the hard work I had done on myself had brought me to a place where I was able to feel deeply and simply that he was *the one*. I saw this gorgeous, emotionally available man in front of me, and I asked him to marry me without hesitating or second-guessing myself.

On October 3, 2004, a picture-perfect autumn day about two and a half years after we met, Scott and I had a commitment ceremony in a homey restaurant called the Kitchen Club on Prince and Mott Streets, where SoHo intersects with Little Italy. We worked out an arrangement with the owner, a visual artist from the Netherlands who had started the restaurant for her friends and maintained a neighborhood atmosphere in the midst of SoHo's accelerated gentrification. Charlie Hamlen, the head of Classical Action, whom we thought of as the living embodiment of moral authority, officiated.

Scott and I both wore suits, and everyone else wore what they wanted. Our parents, our siblings, and their families were there, and Hank's children, Max and Eva, presented the rings. Scott had written his vows in advance and read them. I, extraordinarily for me, also used a prepared text, instead of improvising. I didn't want to take any chance of not getting this right.

Scott said, in part, "Commitment—the commitment to share your path with another person—is about the single biggest conscious choice that I think two people can make. This is a life-changing, life-affirming choice, and I'm privileged to be making it with Fred. Today, I feel very lucky to be here, with Fred, and whether it is part of some plan by a higher power, God, Allah, Yahweh—however you experience that which can't really be explained with words or whether it was just the confluence of random events—I am grateful. And I have to say a huge *thank you* to Janis Siegel for singing at Birdland two and a half years ago." Janis was there, beaming.

There were just twenty immediate family members and two dozen close friends in attendance. Kate McGarry sang "A Wish," music by me and words by Norma Winstone, moving almost everybody to tears. We chose texts to be read by selected friends and family, including Whitman's poem "When I Heard at the Close of the Day." Hearing those powerful words read aloud, standing next to Scott, brimming with love, I had never been happier in my life. My long personal journey was entering a new and promising phase. As icing on the wedding cake, we got our picture prominently placed in that Sunday's *New York Times* Style section. We were as married as we could be.

CHAPTER 15

MADNESS

Among the more treacherous myths about illness is the delusion that sick people can will themselves into wellness. If you just stay positive and pretend nothing's wrong, by this way of thinking, you can push your way through whatever ailment afflicts you. There is indisputably some truth and real value to the idea that a good attitude is helpful. At the very least, positive thinking can make day-to-day life with a disease significantly more bearable. The danger lies in the proposition that human beings have absolute control over disease. We do not, and those who suffer terribly from an illness or die from it are not weaker or lesser people than those who recover and survive. The suffering of some people is not all their own fault any more than the wellness of others is all their own doing.

For the first seven years of the new century, I felt as if AIDS and I had come to an uneasy truce. I had, at one point or another, taken every one of the fifteen major drugs that had been devised to treat the virus. By the mid-nineties, antiretroviral "cocktail" therapy, which combined three classes of medications (including the new protease inhibitors), had replaced the monotherapy that been prescribed to early AIDS patients, with limited success. My T-cell count was low but fairly stable, and my viral load, a measure of the efficacy of my immune system, fluctuated between acceptable and alarming. I was still far from the point of having an undetectable viral load, the holy grail of HIV treatment. I was on what was becoming known as "salvage therapy," experimenting with new drugs as they came on the market, looking for a combination that would effectively suppress the virus.

Many of the treatments carried serious, sometimes horrible and debilitating side effects. I was visibly, dangerously underweight. I suffered incontinence and developed medication-related diabetes, requiring additional treatment with insulin. One of the drugs I took for a while, a fusion inhibitor, had to be injected with a powerful CO_2 gun in the ever-shrinking areas of my body where I could find a few cells of fat, and the drug itself had psychological side effects, including depression. My health was unstable but seemed to have reached a tolerable level of instability.

I settled into a routine of pill taking that would continue to this day. Every morning I would go into the kitchen and take out a large plastic bin that held about two dozen pill bottles. I would sit at the table and make two piles: morning pills (fourteen) and dinner pills (nine). I would put them in small, clear, sealable plastic jewelry bags, to have them in my pocket at mealtimes. In addition to all these, I would take three before breakfast, one other pill before dinner, and six pills at bedtime for a total of thirty-three per day. Before bed, and before a heavy meal, I would inject my insulin.

For many years I was relatively fortunate as an AIDS patient for having spent so little time in the hospital. Back when I was recording for Nonesuch, I had been admitted to St. Vincent's for out-of-control diabetes. But that was treated quickly, and I was discharged in just a week. A few years later I was hospitalized, again at St. Vincent's, for MRSA, a multiple-resistant staph infection that had taken form during a solo tour of Europe. The infection ate a hole in my back the size of a quarter but was treatable with potent intravenous antibiotics, and I was once again released in a week's time.

By 2007, I felt like AIDS was something I might well be able to live with. The year started out beautifully. I had been working since 2006 on a major new project, a staged song cycle on the theme of photography called *Rooms of Light*. I was writing it with the fine American poet Mary Jo Salter, whom I had met during one of my residencies at MacDowell. Lincoln Center had recently decided to reposition its American Songbook Series, expanding its programming beyond the Tin Pan Alley canon to present works by contemporary songwriters, and I was invited to perform an evening of my songs in a concert that January. I featured seven selections from *Rooms of Light*, some excerpts from *Leaves of Grass*, and a few of the tunes of mine that Norma Winstone had set to lyrics. There were four vocalists—Kate McGarry and Peter Eldridge from the jazz world, and Michael Winther and Jessica Molaskey, who were music-theater singers. I did the musical direction, wrote the arrangements, and played piano with a six-piece mixed ensemble. I took this event as a significant acknowledgment of my emergence as a writer of songs as well as instrumental works, and I was enormously gratified by that.

Over the course of the year, I pushed myself hard. I went to Saint Louis for a staging of *Leaves of Grass* at the exquisite, historic Sheldon Concert Hall. A week later I flew to London for a duo show with my harmonica pal Toots Thielemans at Barbican Hall, coming back in time to do an American round of club dates to support my latest trio CD, *Night & the Music*. The trio now had the imaginative young Nasheet Waits on drums, along with Drew Gress on bass. I also recorded a night of duo performances at the Jazz Standard with the Portland-based jazz singer Nancy King, who is one of the purest in-the-moment performers I have ever known. (I had the recording done without Nancy's knowledge at the time, so as not to spook her, not that she's easily spooked.) The Maxjazz label released it, and it was nominated for a Grammy for Best Jazz Vocal Album, overdue recognition for an artist who has long deserved much more.

When summer came, I prepared for a recording of my collected concert works to be recorded at the Sosnoff Theater at Bard College's Fisher Center in Upstate New York. The program, released by the classical label Naxos the following year, consisted of all the fully notated music for solo piano and chamber groups I had done to date. The centerpiece of the album was the twenty-five-minute piece "24 Variations on a Bach Chorale," which I had composed at MacDowell in 2002. The composition is built on the famous theme Bach had used in his Saint Matthew Passion, which I had first heard as a teenager in an adaptation with lyrics by the folk singer Tom Glazer, called "Because All Men Are Brothers," and recorded by Peter, Paul and Mary. After the events of September 11, 2001, the powerful, timeless melody and its universal spiritual quality inspired me to write my own set of variations.

When fall came, my schedule grew heavier still. I pushed and pushed and pushed some more, flying around the country and all over Europe. For the eighth year, I did a three-day residency at Western Michigan University in Kalamazoo, conducting master classes and workshops and giving concerts. Immediately after that I flew off to Europe with my trio, which now had the superb bassist John Hébert along with Waits. It was a battering tour of twelve concerts in fourteen days in icy weather: Amsterdam one night, Paris the next, Dublin the night after that, and so on. Then I flew to Japan and gave a series of three solo concerts.

I started to feel pretty awful. I had little energy and almost no appetite. I was having trouble salivating. On the road, I couldn't even eat a sandwich—the bread was too dry for me to swallow. It was hard to find food that I could get down, even though I had to eat *something* for breakfast and dinner to go along with my pills. But I lost a lot of weight fast and got down to about 115 pounds, 20 pounds less than usual for me then; my debilitating incontinence grew worse, accelerating my weight loss. I forced myself through it. Through all my years with HIV, I had always made a point of keeping my calendar fully booked. After all, if I had a gig six months down the road, I would have to stay alive to make it. Now I was managing to keep the bookings but at the cost of my health. I was feeling the limits of the force of my will.

When I came back from the European tour in early December, I felt absolutely beaten up, and I looked like hell—I could see it in Scott's eyes when he first laid eyes on me. I was haggard and gaunt, with brittle, straw stalks for hair. With Scott's encouragement, I went to see my doctor, Michael Liguori, and he said, "Well, there's something we can try. Let's do a strategic therapeutic interruption." This was an experiment that some doctors were attempting with AIDS patients at the time. It was sometimes called a "drug holiday," whereby patients went off all of their antiretroviral drugs for a short, controlled period. The term could only be taken ironically, since the experience was anything but a day at the beach.

In clinical studies at that point, the results were inconclusive. In some cases, patients experienced a reduction of their viral load and a bump in their T cells when the drug interruption was over and treatment was restored. In other cases, the virus reverted to a wild state when it wasn't under attack by the antiretroviral drugs, and treatment was not always effective when it resumed. I felt so awful that I was willing to try almost anything, and I didn't have a lot of options. So I went along with the strategic interruption in the hope it would restore my appetite, help me put some weight back on, and generally revive me.

With Christmas approaching, Scott and I went to our house in Pennsylvania. We have always enjoyed having a little yuletide respite together. (Growing up, our family lit the Hanukkah lights and had a Christmas tree.) If I was going on a drug holiday, I thought it might as well be festive.

About ten days after I had stopped my HIV meds, I started to behave strangely. Alone in the house with Scott, I felt oddly caged. I had a hard time communicating. I would say, "Honey, I'm feeling . . ." or "Let's . . ." or "Can we . . . ?" and not be able to finish the sentence. I often couldn't remember what I had been talking about a few seconds earlier. I couldn't form words coherently. I didn't know why I was so confused, and I didn't fully realize how confused I was.

We stayed in the house through Christmas and into the last week of December, and my behavior grew increasingly erratic and volatile. I spent most of my time lying on the living room couch, avoiding talking to Scott. When we opened Christmas presents from various friends and members of my family, I was irrationally outraged by some of the gifts. "Look at this scarf—what a piece of shit!" I hated the color of the new towels Scott had thoughtfully bought for our bathroom. I got weirder and weirder, and I kept feeling that there were things I wanted to say to Scott but couldn't say. The darkness inside me was unspeakable, literally, and foreign to me, given how well Scott and I generally communicated and how much I loved him. I felt increasingly like I was faking at everything, and I thought Scott would see through me and leave me. I was withdrawing and becoming paranoid.

Scott was confused and worried for me but tried not to let me know how scared he was. Fortunately, he knew what to do: He betrayed nothing, and was very good at disguising his fear, to keep me calm. By New Year's Eve day, he was so afraid for me that he called Dr. Liguori. They talked—Scott told him briefly what was going on—but he was mostly listening to Michael and nodding. I listened from across the room but didn't say anything. After a few minutes, Scott handed me the phone. Michael said, "Fred, how do you feel?"

I said, "Uh . . . uh . . . uh . . ." He asked a few more questions, and I couldn't give him anything like intelligible answers.

Michael said calmly, "Can you put Scott back on the phone?"

Scott nodded and looked at me while Michael talked for a few minutes. He hung up and said without hesitation, "We're driving back to New York. We're going to the hospital."

I didn't fight him. In fact, I think I was probably relieved on some level. I could sense that there was something very wrong and that I needed help. We canceled our New Year's Eve dinner with Pennsylvania friends and left in midafternoon.

Over our holiday break we had been watching my brother Hank's dog, a beautiful border collie named Homer, so on the way back to New York we had to return him to Montclair, New Jersey, where Hank was living with his wife and their two children. Scott arranged for Hank to meet us in a parking lot off the highway, to save time getting me into the city. I sat in the car and watched, hunched down in the backseat, trying to act invisible, as Scott brought Homer over to Hank and they talked for a minute. I remember seeing Hank just looking my way from time to time and nodding. I thought, *Aaah . . . this is going beautifully. I'm fooling them all. My plan is working!* Somehow I was convinced that I was playacting and pulling an elaborate trick on everybody. My behavior had quickly gone from morose and uncommunicative to quasi-hopeful to full-bore delusional paranoia.

When we got to the emergency room at St. Vincent's Hospital, I was seated on a bed in a curtained-off area, with Scott sitting alongside me. A doctor came in and gave me a standard psychological evaluation: "What's the date and the day of the week today? Count to ten, forward and backward. Who is the president of the United States?" I answered all the questions quickly, laughing inside at the fact that I was fooling Scott and the doctor into thinking I wasn't going mad.

I was given a blood test, and it showed that my T-cell count had plummeted to the double digits and my viral load had soared into the millions. Prior to the break in my drug regimen, in the more than twenty years that I had been living with HIV, my viral load had gotten as low as around 50,000—meaning there were 50,000 copies of the virus in one milliliter of my blood. The virus was always present at a certain level but somewhat under control. Now the virus was taking over my body and my mind. During the few weeks I had been going without drugs, the virus had multiplied at an exponential rate and spread beyond the bloodstream into the central nervous system, crossing the blood-brain barrier. It was literally poisoning my brain.

The hospital staff allowed me to go home briefly to pick up some personal things, and I packed as if I were heading off on vacation, stuffing multiple changes of clothes into a big suitcase. I even brought a book to read in my leisure, William Faulkner's *As I Lay Dying*, which I chose with no ironic intention. I was admitted to the St. Vincent's AIDS ward, where I spent the next eleven days in a state of twilight consciousness, sometimes referred to as a semicoma.

My mother came in from Cincinnati the next day, and I remember being annoyed by her presence. I wouldn't talk to her. I would whisper random incoherent thoughts to Hank, who visited often, but was cold to Scott. The nurses in the AIDS ward, who had no doubt seen this kind of behavior many times before, kept a firm grip on me. When I refused to shower or shave, they forced my hand. I had no appetite, but they made me eat. Afterward, I would defecate on my bed, unable or unwilling to get up to use the bathroom. I just lay there for days, balled up inside my un-abating madness.

In an extraordinary stroke of good fortune, two important new antiretroviral drugs had just become available that month—Selzentry and Isentress—and I was put on them, along with a potent antipsychotic drug called Zyprexa. Since the fall of 2007, I had also been taking yet another new antiretroviral drug, Intel-ence, under the "compassionate use" guidelines that permitted experimentation by willing patients, as I was eager to try anything to get better. So I was taking three new ARV drugs at the same time. The combination of medications was effective enough for me to be discharged on January 11, 2008. If I saw you that day and you asked me how long I had been in the hospital, I wouldn't have known what to say. *Two days? Two weeks?* I had no idea.

I went home with Scott to our loft. My viral load had begun to drop, thanks to the new drugs, but the HIV was still rampant in my brain, and the antipsychotic drugs were not enough to coun-teract it. The diagnostic term for my condition was AIDS-related dementia. Put less clinically, I was crazy.

At the time Scott was in the last term of study for his master of public administration degree at New York University's Wagner School. He stayed home with me as much as he could, but he had to go to classes, do our grocery shopping, and handle everything else necessary to keep our life intact. When he came home, he never knew which Fred he would find—the insatiably needy one, the cruelly icy one, or an unpredictably weird new one. It was all he could do to contain his frustration with me, even as he knew I wasn't responsible for my own behavior. My manager, Robert

Rund, cleared my calendar, while I curled up on the couch for nearly two months, refusing to see anyone, because in my mind everyone was conspiring against me. The only person I consistently wanted to see was Hank, whose presence had a way of calming me. I had almost no contact with my parents.

I believed I had the power to control time. Watching TV, I thought I could manipulate the content of the shows with my mind. I walked around the halls of our building naked. I had suicidal thoughts—if I'd had the strength, I would have opened the window in the back hallway and jumped out. I let my hair and my beard grow long and unbrushed. I looked like a homeless person. I deleted all my e-mails in the middle of the night. I thought someone was going to come and take away my piano and sue me for breach of contract.

If I ventured outside the loft, it was in a state of manic delusion. I thought there was a plot against me in the local supermarket. If I announced one day, "I am only going to eat Cheerios from now on," Scott did what one should do when dealing with someone who is psychotic: He just agreed with me, since there was no point in trying to make me see reason. When the few friends I allowed to see me came over, I lay on the couch, thinking, *They're all lying to me.*

In my rare moments of near lucidity, I could sense what was going on with me. I remembered having seen it before in friends with AIDS, including my first partner, Eric. He had moved back to San Francisco in the early nineties, where he became the manager of a gay bar, the Edge, in the Castro district. He drank even more heavily, had lots of sex, and didn't bother to take his AIDS meds with any consistency. The last time I had seen him socially he was loud, belligerent, and irrational—no doubt suffering from AIDS-related dementia. He died in 2005, lying alone in his bed, refusing all treatment, slipping away. The same thing happened to a gay neighbor on my floor in SoHo, Chris. After he fell into madness, he moved back to Idaho, where he died in the care of his family. At their end of their lives, right before they passed, both of them looked and acted exactly as I looked and acted now. Dementia was the canary in the HIV/AIDS coal mine. I knew I couldn't have long to live now. As strange as that was to face, the way I felt about it was stranger yet. I was so crazed and unhappy, I wanted to die.

CHAPTER 16

COMA

S cott watched over me in the loft, keeping me under control with his warm presence and calming voice, trying his best not to send me spinning out of control. I watched TV listlessly, read snippets of magazines and the *New York Times*, dozed off, and paced around the loft with no desire to play the piano. I had no energy. Every now and then I'd blurt out something nasty or semi-rational or groan. Looking back on this period now, I can remember most of it well, strangely, despite being powerless in my own skin at the time. After a while, the periods of extreme behavior came less and less often, and the stretches of near normalcy grew longer and longer. The doctors told Scott and me that the combination of the antiviral and antipsychotic drugs was working in my favor, and I would get better by the day. I began to believe this as my energy and appetite started coming back. In time, my death wish was supplanted by gratitude that I was still alive, and I got itchy to get back to making music.

Over the course of February and March 2008 my condition improved dramatically. I recovered my weight and was back at around 130 pounds, about right for me in those days. It wasn't until the end of March or thereabouts that my head was fully cleared and my energy returned to something close to normal. I was becoming myself again. In late March I managed to conduct an intense one-week professional training workshop for twelve young musicians administered through the Weill Institute at Carnegie Hall. Though I had originally been scheduled to run this alone, I wasn't *that* well yet, and Carnegie helped me out by hiring a few additional colleagues to manage the students. Around that time I went to see Dr. Liguori for a checkup, and he said, "Fred, you're a very lucky man. You are a Lazarus patient. You have virtually risen from the dead."

Later that spring, I found myself working at almost my usual pace once more, though I was still not up to going on the road. Ruminating on my good fortune, I got to thinking about my past and how I had become the musician and the man I was. I thought about the artists and others who had most influenced or inspired me. I had procrastinated on a commission from Jed Wheeler at Peak Performances at Montclair State University in New Jersey to write an evening-length work for jazz trio. With the deadline looming, in just a few weeks I composed twelve new tunes—in twelve different keys—in homage to people I have found inspirational, building on my established practice of writing dedication pieces. I wrote tunes for the composers Antonio Carlos Jobim and Egberto Gismonti, the pianists George Shearing and Jimmy

Rowles, the composer and saxophonist Ornette Coleman, the renowned ballerina (and muse to George Balanchine) Suzanne Farrell, the Vietnamese Buddhist monk and peace activist Thich Nhat Hanh, and others. The resultant piece made its premiere in early May.

Also that spring, mysteriously, I felt freed up to express myself in new ways—pushing ahead with the memory of my escape from death actually receding faster than I expected. Two weeks earlier I had introduced a whole new group concept called the Pocket Orchestra: a quartet of piano, trumpet, voice, and percussion. I invited the sensational young Australian vocalist Jo Lawry, who could sing anything with precision, agility, and sensitivity. (Since the days when we first worked together, Jo has emerged as an admired singer-songwriter, in addition to becoming world famous as the sole female backup singer in Sting's touring band.) I wrote new arrangements of pieces I had composed for other configurations of instruments, such as "Free Flying," my dedication to Gismonti, and "Child's Song," my tribute to Charlie Haden, with nonverbal, instrumental-style parts for Jo. Ralph Alessi played trumpet to round out the ensemble.

We played two nights of sets at the Jazz Standard, recording them off the soundboard for posterity, with plans to go into the studio to record a proper album of the material. After the shows Jo Lawry and I listened to the live recording in my loft, and she broke into tears. "It's *you*," she said. "Welcome back!" I ended up canceling the studio plans and released the live recording. Despite a few technical flaws, it seemed to capture something precious.

Bob Hurwitz of Nonesuch generously gave me the rights to release the master recording of *Fred Hersch Plays Jobim*, the fourth, unreleased album recorded for the multi-disc set *Songs Without Words*. Sunnyside Records released it that summer. I was proud of this project but still a bit unsure of how far I would come back physically and musically. So I wanted to get this out to show I was not done yet.

I took a string of bookings of myriad kinds—among them, a date with my trio and Kurt Elling at a small but nicely curated jazz festival in wine country in Healdsburg, California, and a concert in Cincinnati to celebrate an important local deejay, Oscar Treadwell, who had died a couple of years earlier. (Jazz musicians' appreciation for Treadwell was such that Charlie Parker composed a piece in his honor, "An Oscar for Treadwell.") The pianist Bill Charlap had taken over from his mentor Dick Hyman as director of the Jazz in July series at the 92nd Street Y in Manhattan, and asked me to participate in a tribute to George Shearing, who had recently been awarded an Order of the British Empire and was enjoying a flurry of late-life appreciation.

When I returned from the California trip, in early June, I felt a little blah, like I might have caught a bug on the plane, as many people do after sharing germs in a pressurized cabin for hours. Over the next few days I felt significantly worse—I was listless and achy, and I'd started to run a fever. I thought, *Oh, shit—now I've come down with the flu.* On the third or fourth day of feeling progressively debilitated, I called Dr. Liguori, found that he was on vacation, and went in to see the physician on call. He told me it looked like it might be pneumonia and said to rest for a couple of days and call him if it didn't improve. At that point he'd have a chest X-ray taken.

That Monday night, June 9, I was alone in the loft—Scott was out hearing some music—and felt terrible. I was feverish, weak, and afraid to be alone. I called Scott, who was hanging out with some friends after the show, and asked him to come home as soon as possible. He returned soon and made me some tea. We decided to call the doctor first thing the following day and arrange to have that chest X-ray taken.

The next morning I took a cool bath to try to get some relief from the fever. I lay there for some time, depleted. As the water drained, I put my hands on the side of tub and tried to get up but found that I couldn't lift my own weight. In horror, I called to Scott for help. Coming into the bathroom, he saw me struggling and said, "Fred, you need to tell me if you're exaggerating in the slightest and being melodramatic, or if you really can't get out by yourself."

I said, "No, I really can't get out of the tub."

Scott lifted me, shivering and weak, out of the bathtub. What happened after that—in the days, weeks, and months that followed—is a blur of fleeting impressions and sensations, hazy memories, and dream images. Nearly everything I now know about the events in my life from that day, Tuesday, June 10, 2008, to the end of that summer, I know from Scott relaying the details to me sometime after the fact.

As he later told me, I was limp and delirious, breathing heavily. Though Scott was surely terrified himself, he calmly dressed me and somehow got me down to the street and into a taxi. In a few minutes' time, we were at St. Vincent's Hospital. Scott told the person doing intake in the ER that I had HIV/AIDS and was having trouble breathing. A clamp was slipped onto my finger to read my pulse and blood-oxygen level, and the numbers were bad.

My blood-oxygen level was 70 percent, whereas 98–99 percent is normal. I was immediately put into a bed in the emergency room, and people started working on me.

Scott stood by, trying to take in what was happening. Someone said my breathing was failing and I would need intubation. As one doctor and a nurse were preparing to insert the tube, others were hooking me up to equipment, taking readings, and doing lots of other things—fast. Scott was told my blood pressure had fallen through the floor and my kidneys were failing. I was in septic shock.

In the intensive care unit, the physician on duty was Dr. Mark Astiz. (The regular intensive care unit at St. Vincent's was full to capacity, as it often was, so I was moved into the surgical ICU.) Dr. Astiz told Scott I was in critical condition and made utterly clear that it could hardly be more serious. He said, "The next forty-eight to seventy-two hours will determine if he survives." Scott was numb, overwhelmed. Less than an hour had passed since we arrived at the hospital.

Scott called my mother from the ER and told her to get on the next flight from Cincinnati to New York, and he called Hank's house and told Sharon, Hank's wife, to reach Hank at work and tell him to come to St. Vincent's. Hank came right away from his office at *Sports Illustrated,* where he was working as a senior editor. When he finally was able to see me, he was convinced that this was the end. My mother was there by nightfall—she knew full well how dangerous sepsis is, and she was rightfully fearful for my life. Scott also called my father, who flew in a day later from Healdsburg, California, where he had been living since his retirement from his legal practice. My immediate family had gathered for what they thought would be the last time they would see me alive.

On Thursday morning Dr. Astiz told Scott that my condition was still critical—and not improving. I needed to be put on life support—a respirator for my breathing, as well as kidney dialysis. Scott asked for a frank assessment of my prospects for coming through this, and Dr. Astiz told him things could go either way.

Already under heavy sedation, I would need to be medicated into a comatose state in order to have any chance of survival. In an induced coma, my body would be functioning at the lowest possible level, buying time for my compromised immune system to fight the pneumonia.

After ten days or so in a coma, my condition was getting no worse, though not better. My father went back to California, and my mother stayed for a couple of weeks with Scott at our loft, both of them spending all day by my side in the ICU.

After an initial breakdown in the ER when I was first admitted to St. Vincent's, Scott shifted into his management mode. It was the best way he knew to deal with such a crisis. What this meant was waiting patiently every day for the doctors to do their morning rounds so he could get an update; forging relationships with the ICU nurses to obtain unfettered access to me during visiting hours and beyond; keeping the insurance company at bay; and managing the countless calls and e-mails coming in from friends and family inquiring about my condition. This way of dealing with the devastating circumstances was simply a natural reaction for Scott; it kept him too occupied to fix on the worst possibilities.

One of the hardest days for Scott and my mother was the day

that the doctors informed them that it was necessary to surgically insert a feeding tube, an act that carried with it associations of patients in comas for months or longer, people who were never again the same, if they lived at all. Around the same time, the doctors told Scott that I would need a tracheotomy, to minimize the chance of developing a new infection or incurring damage to my vocal cords from the intubation. The surgery was done in the ICU, with Scott's consent. But my right vocal cord had been damaged—irreparably paralyzed by the plastic tube that had been resting against it for too many days. I still had one functioning vocal cord, but without the second cord for it to vibrate against, I could not speak—or swallow. The problem was academic at this point, anyway. I couldn't speak or eat in a coma, with or without functioning vocal cords.

As I learned much later, I was on the brink of death for weeks and comatose for almost two months. By a fortunate fluke of timing, Scott had just finished graduate school when I was hospitalized, and he was free for the summer. He was available to be at the hospital, watching over my care and acting as my advocate, the whole time. He arrived early every morning, around eight o'clock, and got a briefing from the staff on duty. If I had sheet scars, he could tell that I hadn't been moved enough during the night and he would let the nurses know about it squarely and firmly. He was constantly massaging my hands in the hope that I would one day use them again to play the piano. If permission was needed for a surgical procedure, such as the tracheotomy, Scott had medical power of attorney, and he would evaluate the situation and make the decision. He was letting certain people know that I was seriously ill and not able to see visitors, but even among those closest to me, many did not know I was in a coma, on life support, and under kidney dialysis.

Scott let Robert Rund know that I would not be able to perform at the Cincinnati concert or the Jazz in July show in honor of George Shearing. Announcements said that I had withdrawn "due to illness." Inevitably, many people connected my HIV status with the cancellations and my increasingly apparent absence from the New York jazz scene. I couldn't have blamed them. In the early days of AIDS, a particular strain of pneumonia, *Pneumocystis carinii* (PCP), was closely associated with the disease and cited often as the final cause of death. However, what I had contracted was pneumococcal pneumonia, a different and unrelated strain. My case actually had nothing whatsoever to do with my having HIV. I just happened to come down with an acutely virulent strain of pneumonia, one of eighty or so variants of the disease known to medical science at the time. I was near death from pneumonia, but not dying from anything related to AIDS.

Day after day, week after week, Scott watched me attentively, with no improvement in my condition. The ritual of going to the hospital, making his own rounds to gather as much information as possible, ensuring that information was being shared among the nurses, the ICU doctors, and the specialists, was his survival mechanism. In the face the dark tyrannies of disease, the innumerable unknowables, and the obtuse arcana of medical science, he found solace in his daily routine. It gave him a sense of purpose and value in a sphere where feelings of powerlessness can be overwhelming.

I remember reading once that virtually all of the world's religions, from ancient paganism to Islam and Buddhism, are rooted as much in ritual as in systems of belief. Through the repetition of routine, especially social routine, human beings find comfort and hope. I know something along those lines takes place in the making of jazz. The rituals of the bandstand and the recording studio put the musicians in a place where they feel sufficiently secure in the high-risk business of collective improvisation. I think Scott's hospital routine had the same kind of function for him, with stakes considerably higher than anything I would ever face as a musician.

My temperature would not settle down to normal; every week or so it would spike to 102 or 103, and the doctors didn't know why. They told Scott I had "fevers of unknown origin." I also developed a secondary pneumonia, *Klebsiella*, a deadly strain that can strike people in a deeply compromised state. My prospects were grim, and I was oblivious to it all, lying comatose. Scott was adamant that no one other than my immediate family was to see me while I was in the ICU hooked up to machines. He struggled to hold on to the memory of how my face used to look, while what he saw seemed more and more like a skull.

I had been in a coma for about a month and was still in the ICU when Scott asked Dr. Astiz when he expected to see some change in my status. "In a case like this," Dr. Astiz said, looking down at me, "good things happen slowly." Turning to face Scott, he added, "But bad things happen fast."

THOUGH I was comatose, I wasn't brain-dead. My mind was somehow functional, and my senses were intact but in a state drastically restricted and distorted by medication. I was knocked out by the drug propofol—and later methadone—to keep me from standing up in my bed or pulling out my tubes. In fact, toward the end of the coma, I was strapped to my bed for a short period.

I was living in my own world, having dream experiences that were possibly connected to what my body was going through in the real world. A number of my coma dreams—and nightmares— were so vivid and memorable that I will never forget them. Though I rarely remember my dreams well, recalling perhaps just one or two details in the morning, I remembered these precisely. There is no knowing exactly when the events took form in my mind during my long period of unconsciousness. For all I know, the totality of these fantasies could have come to me in a blink of twenty seconds a moment before I began to reenter consciousness. Eventually, about a month after I came out of the coma, I was able to type up my recollection of the dreams in the words below.

THE KNITTERS

I am in a foreign country that for some reason I identify as Wales, although I have never been to Wales. I am looking down from an elevation at a table around which are seated six to eight women in traditional attire that reminds me of Amish garb—dark woolen dresses, aprons, and white caps. There are candles burning, and the room smells of honey and wax. The women are using nubby brown wool and are talking to one another as in a quilting circle. I cannot hear what they're saying. At the point when a knitter has produced a foot or two of fabric, the ends of her knitting metamorphose into a small, beautiful brown goose. The bird swoops out of the knitting, flies up to the rafters, and disappears. Then the knitter starts again. More and more birds are created in this fashion. The atmosphere is serene.

THE NIGHTMARE OF THE VAN

I am strapped into the backseat of a panel van, the only person in the van—the driver's seat is empty. I am restrained by both seat belts and rope. I cannot speak, though I try to do so; my mouth is covered with duct tape. A man keeps coming to me and yelling through the window that I have to pay a fee to be released, but I can't speak and can't reach my wallet. I am struggling and terrified. The scene is loud and chaotic, and there are bright lights and sirens interspersed with patches of darkness. Men in uniforms seem to be running the operation. It is a parking lot in hell.

BRUSSELS

I am in the foyer of a beautiful concert hall, one almost like a church, in Belgium. I have been flown there to do a special musical collaboration with a Belgian woman in her fifties who is somewhat motherly. She plays a hybrid instrument that sounds sometimes like a viola and sometimes like a lute. I want to rehearse and keep asking to see the music, but she keeps telling me to trust her—everything will be all right. We chat with people in the foyer. Everything is super-relaxed. When the woman and I finally play together, the music is simple and emotionally powerful.

THE BOY

I am lying on a high bed, one higher than a hospital bed. I can hear adults speaking in the other room. There are several children running about the room I'm in, and one little boy in particular is very attentive. He gives me my medicine even though he has no idea what he is giving me or how to administer it. I keep telling him not to get near me, because I am contagious, but he pays no attention, and I am too weak to argue with him. He has big green eyes and is the essence of sweetness.

THE DREAM OF MONK

I am in a small cage, just five feet by five feet. I can neither stand straight up nor lie flat—I have to crouch or be in a fetal position. In the next cage over is Thelonious Monk. His cage is just slightly larger than mine. A man bursts into the room, turns on bright lights, gives us each a piece of music manuscript paper and a pencil—and challenges us to write a tune. The first one who finishes is the one who gets released. I frantically write as fast as I can. I look over—and Monk is taking his time, while smiling beatifically and enigmatically.

THE NIGHTMARE OF THE AIRPLANE

I am lying in a full-size bed in the first-class section of a plane, accompanied by Scott. There are Asian flight attendants in colorful outfits. From my bed, I watch sushi chefs and a floor show of a couple dancing an erotic tango. Cocktails are served. I drink and eat and immediately start to vomit and develop a high fever. Scott begins to argue with someone, saying that we are not being treated well and that I am seriously ill. I am taken off the plane and put on another one, where there is another full-size bed. The flight attendants are dressed like waiters in an upper-class restaurant of the Victorian era. The food is luxurious. I eat and slip again into a high fever.

THE JAZZ CLUB/DINER IN THE WOODS

I have been hired to play the piano for a nervous female singer. She is certain this gig will be her "big break" and is having the show recorded. Everything is dark as we unload the instruments and recording equipment from the van to the door of the club, which is somewhere deep in the woods. We go inside and find that the place is a diner with rows of liquor bottles behind the counter. The owner/bartender barely looks at us, and that sends the singer spiraling into deeper nervousness. A few of her family members are the only people in the audience, and I am playing a cheesy electronic keyboard. I am extremely uncomfortable.

THE ORB

Scott's face appears in front of me inside a glowing orb, much like the wizard in the great room of the palace in *The Wizard of Oz*. He is smiling to me with his whole being and is glowing and radiant with love. He says, "Come to me—I love you" repeatedly. I slowly walk toward him.

I was in a coma for more than six weeks before my temperature stabilized and the doctors decided to try seeing if I could be weaned off life support and sedation. Scott was there, watching carefully, anxiously. The first step was to remove the respirator briefly, to see if I could breathe at all on my own. I took one breath successfully and was put back on the respirator. Over several days' time I was taken off the respirator for longer increments. Eventually, I was able to take ten breaths on my own before being put back on the respirator.

The regimen of sedatives was reduced by tiny amounts each day, and I slowly began to rouse. For some reason, when this happened, the nurses in ICU would become uneasy and increase the sedatives again to knock me back out, much to Scott's dismay. He told me, much later, that this was really the only time during my coma that he challenged the hospital staff emphatically. "Give him a chance," he said. "He can do this."

It took more than a week of slow, steady extraction from life support and reduction of the sedatives for me to gain a semblance of consciousness again. I remember distinctly seeing Scott's face in early August for the first time since he had pulled me out of the tub in June. My head was still cloudy, with sedatives still in my bloodstream, but I recognized him and could see that I was in the hospital. (In my dream world, it was Scott's loving face inside the pulsing orb that brought me out of the coma and back to life.) I tried to talk and couldn't, and didn't know why.

As I was slowly becoming more and more conscious, it sank in to me that I was not able to communicate. I thought I was talking, but no sound was coming out. Once I began to get my bearings, Scott gently gave me the bare facts: I had been near death and in a coma, and it would take some time for me to regain my faculties. He didn't tell me how long I had been under.

During a few miserable days just out of the ICU, in a chilly step-down unit, I found myself so weak I couldn't move a pillow, unable to speak to get anyone's attention. I received my first few visitors, some of whom kept their composure with me but broke down in tears with Scott after they left the room. Then I was moved into a regular single hospital room. We discovered I had a thick layer of crusted gunk in my mouth from breathing with my mouth open and not ingesting anything orally for so long. The hospital staff and Scott struggled to figure out a way for me to communicate, with no success. They put a pencil in my hand and tried to get me to write, but I was too weak to grip it. They brought in a letter board with the alphabet printed on a grid, so I could point to letters and spell words, but I didn't have the strength to hold up my arm and point. The occupational therapist handed me my flip phone, and I just stared at it, not knowing how to open it. I attempted to stand for the first time and fell immediately into the physical therapist's arms at the edge of the bed, like a baby who has not yet learned to walk.

Though it was hardly my most immediate priority, the big question lay in the recesses of my mind: If I didn't have the capacity to lift a finger to point, how could I possibly play the piano again? Scott, sensing the depth of my fears, slept on a cot next to me in my room, so I wouldn't have to be alone at night.

Once I was fully conscious and off the respirator and in my own room for two days, the hospital assigned me to a pair of "patient advocates." This was the Orwellian title for advocates for the insurance companies, whose actual job was to get me out of the hospital as soon as possible. On Friday, August 8, they told Scott they had "great news" and had "found a room" for me in a city-run rehabilitation facility for people with AIDS called Rivington House, on the Lower East Side. Scott raised hell, imploring the doctors to intercede and buy me more time. I was given two extra days and told I would be moving into rehab on Monday.

I was taken to Rivington House on a stretcher by ambulance. My head was slumped over from muscle atrophy, and my beard and hair had grown long and straggly. I weighed less than one hundred pounds. I could take in sustenance, in liquid form, only through the feeding tube that had been surgically inserted into my stomach. Since working vocal cords are necessary for swallowing and I had no gag reflex, a sip of water could go right into my lungs, causing me to aspirate and perhaps develop another pneumonia. All of my antiretroviral, psychotropic, and prophylactic drugs had to be ground up by the nurses and administered to me through the G-tube. I didn't have the strength to sit up in a chair. My hands and feet were grotesquely swollen, and I was physically uncoordinated. I was forbidden to get out of my bed on my own, because if I was to fall, I could easily break a hip, I was so frail.

Scott told a few of my closest friends that they could visit me, and David Hajdu came on my second day at Rivington House. He checked in at the front desk, got my room number, went to the room, saw me, and went back to the desk to report that he had been given the wrong room number. "There's an old man in the room you sent me to," he said. "I would like to see Fred Hersch."

Told that the man he saw was Fred Hersch, David went back to my room, took another look, and bolted out of the rehab center before I could see how shocked and distressed he was. He didn't muster the strength to come back till the next day, and never told me about the aborted visit until we were working on this book together.

Hank, as always busy with his job and family, made time to see me almost every day, even if just for a short visit, boosting my spirits with his kind demeanor. And Scott sat with me all day at Rivington House, helping me in every way possible, doing oral care, massaging my swollen hands and fingers. Over time, he explained—in broad terms, still sparing some of the details—what I had gone through during the past few months. I still had no idea how long I had been in the hospital. This came out a few weeks later, when Scott asked me if I wanted to watch some TV and, being a tennis fan, I suggested putting on Wimbledon, which had concluded more than a month earlier. That's when Scott laid out the whole timeline for me.

After I had been at Rivington House a couple of weeks, I asked Scott to wheel me down to the first floor, because I knew there was a piano in the chapel there. Scott tried to talk me out of it, but I insisted. Sitting in the wheelchair at the piano, I tried to play "Body and Soul," a tune I had played hundreds of times over the years. My fingers could barely move, and I couldn't remember the chords to the bridge. I don't know what I was expecting, but I was shattered to confront the vast distance between my entire history as a person and the reality of what I had become.

I was profoundly shaken, deeply vulnerable, in desperate need of Scott and despondent when he wasn't there. When I thought about how radically everything I knew had changed, I would burst into tears. At the same time I realized ever more clearly how close I had come to death and how lucky I was to be alive.

To say that is a cliché, I know. Yes, yes, of course—a confrontation with death brings home the preciousness of life. Everybody knows that. But there was nothing the least bit hackneyed in how I felt. It was the newest, brightest, shining, most surprising, most uplifting feeling I had ever had. I was *alive*, and I felt the gift of life in a way I had never conceived of before. When I was suffering from dementia the previous year, I had wanted to die. Now I was determined to get my life back as it had been before.

I could not eat or drink. I could barely move. But I was *alive*. It was a gift, for sure—and perhaps even one I didn't deserve. But I was not about to give it up now.

CHAPTER 17

BETTER

'm not going to retrace every step of my recovery here, and I don't want to give myself too much credit for what turned out over time to be an extraordinary recovery. It was more daunting and more taxing than anything I had ever attempted. I had superb medical care, expert physical therapy, and a partner whose devotion to my well-being was and remains unsurpassed. I also worked my fucking ass off, obsessed with getting better. All that came together, and as the weeks and months passed, my condition improved dramatically. In fact, in certain ways I ended up better than ever. The experience of living in a coma and coming out of it was absolutely transformative to me. The coma was the B.C./A.D. point of delineation in my history as a man and as a musician.

Like many patients at inpatient rehab facilities, I was pushed out of Rivington House too early. Scott fought doggedly to keep me under the facility's care for as long as possible, and he bought me a precious week by escalating my case to the state insurance board. Still, by the insurance company's standards, I qualified as healthy enough to be discharged when I could walk thirty feet. So I was shooed out of Rivington House on Friday, September 5, 2008. At that point, I had successfully walked for thirty feet—but only with a person on each side of me, guiding me, braced to support me if I wobbled or catch me if I fell.

Unfortunately, Scott's summer reprieve from professional responsibilities was now over. Since earning his graduate degree at NYU, he had been hired to be the deputy director, the second in command, of TAG (Treatment Action Group), an important not-for-profit organization dedicated to globally expanding access to treatment and providing advocacy for those dealing with HIV/AIDS, tuberculosis, and hepatitis C. It was a big job, managing the daily operations of a non-profit with global reach. He was scheduled to start work the week I came home from rehab. I would be on my own when he was at work, with help during the day from Marie, a sweet and attentive private nurse's aide we hired to stay with me during my first two weeks back in the loft. She was there mostly to be sure that I didn't fall—I was so fragile I could have easily broken a hip—and to accompany me to my physical therapy appointments.

I was still on the feeding tube, virtually unable to speak, and I wouldn't come off of the G-tube until February 2009, when, after exhaustive swallow therapy three times a week, I was deemed ready to take in liquids and soft food orally for the first time since June 2008. Swallow therapy was one of the most difficult and frustrating of all the rehab challenges I faced. It involved months of tedious oral contortions, often with tongue depressors, trying to build small muscles in my mouth and throat that I had never been aware of and couldn't even begin to feel. I wasn't able to sit down for a meal until well into the following year, but I longed for food constantly. Not only did I miss tasting food; I realized how important mealtimes and coffee or drinks with friends are in shaping our days.

When I came home from Rivington House, I was walking with a cane—I flat-out refused to use a walker. I didn't even like the cane, but I wasn't able to stand upright without it yet. After the first week home, I wouldn't touch it. I was determined to walk on my own.

During the first days of my rehab at Rivington House, I had been in a wheelchair, and it was a sign of progress at that point to be able to stand upright at all. My first day in the rehab facility's exercise room, I caught a glimpse of a stick-thin, decrepit, slope-backed old patient with a wild mane of hair, also using a walker, on the other side of the room. When I turned my head and noticed that he turned his head at the same time, I realized the wall of the room was mirrored. I vowed then and there that no one would see me the way I had just seen myself.

Once home, I received physical therapy five days a week at an outpatient facility just up the street from our home in SoHo. The superb therapist, Vinita, did hands-on work with me, and I would also do exercises on my own to strengthen my gait and improve my balance. My left side was so badly compromised that I could barely hold my left arm above my waist.

After my demoralizing experience trying to play the piano at Rivington House, I was wary for at least a week before attempting it again at home. I did better than I had at the rehab center, but I was no Fred Hersch.

Before long, I was able to use my hands to a limited extent, tap-tapping a few words on my computer keyboard. But then, in October, just about a month after I had come home, I came down with pneumonia again. I had to be hospitalized once more and was given five units of blood. Fortunately, I was put on a breathing mask (called CPAP, for "continuous positive airway pressure") instead of being in-tubated again. St. Vincent's, as ever putting the welfare of its patients above its bottom line, hired a twenty-four-hour "sitter" to keep me from pulling off the mask. I was in for less than a week. This time I couldn't believe how lucky I was not to be in septic shock.

Though I still had only one working vocal cord, I was able to talk in a hoarse and weak whisper. I could communicate with any-one leaning *very* close to me. But I was unable to use the phone with any reliability—forget verbal menu-tree prompts—and would have to write my destination on a slip of paper to give to taxi driv-ers on the way to my swallow therapy, since they couldn't hear me through the partition.

On the Saturday after my release from St. Vincent's following the second pneumonia, I was feeling strangely energetic. Scott and I went for a little walk around the Village. It was a clear, warm autumn day. When we got back to the loft, Scott took a catnap and I sat down at my computer. I looked up the calendar at Smalls, a cozy little fifty-seat basement club a few blocks south of the Village Vanguard, and I saw that there was a blank spot on the schedule for the seven-thirty set the following Monday, October 13. Nervously, I tapped out a quick e-mail to one of the club's own-ers, Spike Wilner, to see if I could have that slot. Spike presumed I wouldn't be asking if I weren't up to playing, and gave me the date. I e-mailed John Hébert and Richie Barshay, inviting them to join me; both got right back to me and said they could. Neither of them asked anything about my ability to play the set. I wasn't sure how I would do myself, but I wanted to try—in a low-key and supportive atmosphere such as Smalls.

When Scott woke up from his nap, he came over, gave me a kiss, and asked me how I was doing. I whispered, "Honey, I just booked myself a trio gig at Smalls on Monday night."

Scott looked more than a little concerned. But all he said was "Oh . . . well . . . *okay!*"

My mother was still in town after my bout in the ICU, and I think both she and Scott were more nervous about my return to playing than I was. They were worried that if my performance was unsuccessful, it would be too big a blow to me. I did feel pretty lousy that Monday, apprehensive about playing in public again. But I was eager to do it and get the first time over with. My mom was recovering from a partial knee-replacement surgery, and I successfully distracted myself from my anxiety by worrying about how she would get down the narrow steps of the club.

As I've mentioned, I am a longtime tennis fan. I love the reactive, improvisatory nature of the sport. And like a jazz solo or set, it's not over until the last point is played. You can have a bad patch and still win the match, just as Joe Henderson could slog his way through a tune and wind up at a point of deep inventiveness. As I struggled to recover from the coma, I thought about Monica Seles, the great Hungarian-Yugoslavian tennis champion, who was the top player in the world when she was stabbed between the shoulders on the tennis court by a crazed fan of her chief rival, the German champ Steffi Graf, in the early nineties. The wound from the stabbing healed within a few weeks. But Seles was so shaken psychologically that she didn't return to the game for two years. She became depressed and suffered from both isolation and food addiction. When she finally played again, her renowned killer instinct was gone, and she would never really recover it.

I knew I was limited physically, and my memory was shaky. I could play with only a fraction of the dexterity, force, and speed that I had had before the coma. I didn't have the piano technique I had before.

I was not terribly concerned about that, though, because I have never thought of music primarily in technical terms. I've always valued feeling and sound over raw chops, and the one thing I could still do—in fact, do better than ever now—was *feel*. I had just come home from a long, rough trip to the brink of the Other Side. I had a perspective on living that I could never have imagined before, and I was feeling everything more deeply than I had ever felt.

At 7:20 P.M. I made my way gingerly down the steps of Smalls, holding tight to the railing, with Scott, who was nervous about getting both me and my mom safely downstairs. Word had gotten around quickly that I would be playing, and the club was stocked to capacity with musicians, friends from our building, some colleagues from my various artist residencies, a few music-business people. At 7:30 I walked slowly and cautiously from the back of the room to the piano, determined not to use a cane, and the house burst into warm applause. I silently nodded thanks and pointed to acknowledge my bandmates. As I sat on the bench and looked down at the keyboard, I could see the bulge from my feeding tube protruding under my shirt. For the first time, my fondness for loose-fitting, untucked vintage sport shirts was serving a practical purpose, covering the tube like a hospital gown.

I started with "Days Gone By," a medium-tempo original tune I feel very comfortable with. As always, I found myself in my own musical world, eyes shut, playing, connecting, listening, reacting. The feeling was utterly familiar and at the same time much different from anything I had experienced before—or since. Some things were working surprisingly well, other things were just outside my reach. But I felt strangely serene about it all, playing as if I had nothing to lose.

The set was recorded for the Smalls archive, and I listened to it for the first time in years while I was writing this book. I can hear that the playing is a bit unfocused, tenuous at points, and the tempo of this first tune (and, for that matter, most of the songs in the set) is awfully slow. But I sound like *me*. When I finish the first tune, I announce to the audience what I will play next—and when I heard this again, it brought me back with a shiver to the reality of what I was like at that time. My voice is a fragile, raw, barely audible whisper, and I am struggling palpably to get each word out. The second tune, also an original, was "Still Here," my dedication to saxophonist and composer Wayne Shorter, who is still creating amazing music, even now in his eighties. The title seemed to encapsulate the moment.

The set is a surprisingly long seventy-five minutes—four originals; Jimmy Rowles's ballad "The Peacocks"; "Work" by Monk; and, as the finale, a slow, bluesy version of Sonny Rollins's "Doxy." John Hébert had yet to become part of my working trio, and the rhythmic hookup between him and Richie was iffy; they had never played together. Still, putting aside a few flubs and some ambiguous sections, the music is creative, fresh, and deeply felt, as if I were playing these pieces for the first time. In a real sense, that is exactly what was happening, because I was a different person now. The new me was, in fact, playing this music for the first time.

After a terrific standing ovation, I played my short solo ballad "Valentine," a song of romantic yearning that always makes me think of Scott. As I played it, I felt connected to each person in the room. The performance of that song was my thank-you to everyone who had helped me get to that point in one piece.

After "Valentine," everyone rose to give me another standing ovation, and I took a bow and nodded in thanks. I was visibly choked up, and I knew the audience could tell, but I didn't care. I had gotten my share of standing ovations before, and I have gotten plenty of them since. But I've never gotten one with the pure and raw emotional energy of the ovation that night. It couldn't have been clearer that people who cared about me were thrilled to see me and to hear me making music again. It was obvious from the applause I received when I walked in that people were simply happy to find me alive and alert. In the end, though, it had to have been the music that brought them to their feet. Leaving behind every consideration of technique, I made no effort to impress anybody. I just wanted to make music for my friends and for myself, show that I could do it again in a meaningful way. Playing from my heart, I hardly needed my fingers.

Over the years since then, nearly all the people who were there have told me that the show was unique in their musical experience. Charlie Hamlen recalled, a couple of years later, "The music that night was the most moving music I had ever heard in my life." Several others used almost the same words. There was indisputably something profound about the performance. You can almost hear my musical spirit fighting to rise above my body.

At home, the battle with my body was ongoing. I was still on a liquid diet, fed through a machine into the tube embedded in my stomach. In the night, I would have to urinate into a bottle, since I couldn't get myself out of bed, sometimes filling three containers due to all the liquid I was taking in.

For long stretches during this period, and for a good year or more after I would begin eating again, I couldn't always control my bladder or my bowels, and Scott would have to help clean me and the mess. I was humiliated and felt terrible for Scott. (Once I began going out of the apartment, I was always fearful that I would have an accident, and I did, many times.) I don't know how Scott handled it. When he was in the loft with me, he was always on nurse duty. One of his jobs was to clean and disinfect the area of my stomach where the feeding tube entered my body. It was a disgusting mess of pus and liquid. Scott, who had always been more than a little squeamish, had to breathe deeply to stay calm every time he did it. He was heroic.

Scott's hardest task was surely putting up with my impatience and my stubbornness. I wanted so badly to get better fast. The feeding machine was mounted on a rolling IV pole and pumped a set amount of canned liquid food into my stomach per minute. I kept turning it up to take in more. Scott would catch me, turn it down, and scold me, saying that I was exceeding the recommended amount. Then I would turn it back up as soon as he was not around. But both Scott and I wanted to condition my stomach to get used to real food again—and I wanted to gain weight as fast as possible—so we started buying cans of high-calorie Campbell's Chunky soup, pureeing it in the blender, and then forcing it into my stomach several times a day. (I had, unbeknownst to Scott, been sneak-eating chocolate pudding and canned peaches even before I was officially cleared to swallow. I just had to taste *something*.)

About a week after the Smalls gig, on my fifty-third birthday, I was given my second swallow test and had high hopes of being ready to have the feeding tube removed. In a swallow test, you drink a barium preparation with the consistency of a milk shake that enables the technicians to watch it go down your throat on an X-ray device. If that goes well, you try to swallow a thicker liquid. If that is successful, they watch you eat a cookie—in real time. If you can do that successfully, you're cleared to eat.

I failed at the first stage. The test was stopped, and I was devastated. Yet, even if I had passed it and could start taking food orally, I would have had a high risk of aspirating, because I still had only one working vocal cord.

My doctors recommended a novel surgery by which my nonfunctioning vocal cord would be moved alongside the working one, so the one could vibrate the other, with the inert cord held in place by a plastic shim. Through this technique, I would be able to speak at something close to full voice, though not with the vocal resonance I used to have, and after more swallow therapy to strengthen my oral muscles, I hoped to be able to eat and drink again. I had this surgery, called medialization thryoplasty, done in November 2008. After three more months of therapy, I finally passed my third swallow test in February 2009.

The feeding tube was then removed, painfully yanked out, and I was cleared to eat and drink again, at first with some restrictions to get my system used to solid food. Since our experiments with pureed canned soup (and my illegal snacks), I was more than ready to celebrate the end of this seemingly endless abstinence from food and drink. Scott and I went to Bouley, the TriBeCa restaurant that was our favorite "big-deal meal" place, the night following the day of the test, which happened to be the evening before Valentine's Day. We ordered the five-course tasting menu and a bottle of champagne, a gift from my mother. I ate it all, my senses overwhelmed by the delicious and varied tastes and aromas—poached egg with truffles, Dungeness crab, sea bass, mille-feuille—and we polished off the champagne. It was the most memorable meal I have ever eaten, though I couldn't wait to go home and eat chocolate pudding again, legally. I would have preferred Scott's homemade crème brûlée, of course.

Although I recovered the power of speech, my voice will never be quite the same. If I speak for too long or get fatigued by talking in a noisy environment, my voice conks out. I can't sing very well anymore, either. This is no great loss to the audience for vocal music. Still, it's a minor disappointment to me. I've always enjoyed singing for pleasure, and it has been useful in working as a composer or occasional vocal coach to be able to sing through a passage, to demonstrate what I have in mind. That's one thing I've had to give up, along with a notion I've always had in the back of my mind but have never discussed publicly. Ever since my days at Bradley's, when I would watch Jimmy Rowles and enjoy the way he would occasionally break into song with that unassuming, unpolished, gravelly non-singer's singing voice of his, I thought it might be fun to sing just one song on very rare occasions late in my life. That's not going to happen now.

Fortunately, I could still play the piano, if not with my old technical ability—not at first, though it came back before long. Indeed, I think my playing is better in many ways today than it was before I got so sick. I have found my left-to-right-hand independence to be looser and more interesting, and my general facility is much improved. Most important, I believe I am playing with more freedom and creativity and less judgment—just putting one phrase or idea after the next, telling continuous musical stories, being comfortable with my music making without needing to prove anything to anyone.

As I found at Smalls, I have come away from the coma experience with a deeper sense of myself as well as a heightened appreciation for the gift of the opportunity to make music. After my recovery I took more satisfaction in playing than I had ever taken in my life. I didn't micromanage my improvisations. I became much more forgiving of any little errors I might make from time to time. The internal judgmental chatter that can occur when playing in public seemed to have gone away for good. I found myself sitting down and playing for pleasure for the first time in years. It felt eerily wonderful to run through a basic tune or play some Bach. The simple act of making chords was a thrill, and the notes sounded fresh and exciting to me.

I played and played some more, lost in the experience and enjoying the process, as my muscles grew stronger. By January 2009 I felt good enough about my playing to return to the public eye in a significant way. I honored a week's engagement at the Village Vanguard I had booked long before, playing with a quintet billed as the Fred Hersch Trio + 2 after the 2003 album of the same name. With me was John Hébert on bass and Nasheet Waits on drums, along with Ralph Alessi on trumpet and Tony Malaby on tenor saxophone. We drew from the book of my compositions and arrangements for quintet that I have added to over the years, and it was a pleasure to present that material at the Vanguard. Candidly, it helped me to have four other musicians to share the solo duties.

We played two sets a night for six nights straight, and there was a lot of love in the room. Word of my coma and recovery had gotten around, of course, so quite a few people came to cheer me on. A few probably came more out of a morbid curiosity as to whether I was really okay. I think everyone in the club had to have walked away surprised that I was fully intact and, in some ways, playing better than ever—or at least more deeply. I remember Lorraine Gordon, the Vanguard's notoriously irascible owner, being especially sweet, saying, "We love having you here—where you belong." It felt great to be back.

THE dreams that I recalled in such details were still swirling around in my head. After all, they were all I retained of my two months on the brink of death. I read over the accounts of the dreams I had initially typed out just to have a recollection of them, and it seemed to me that they had dramatic resonance. I started thinking of making something from the material of the dreams—*something*, though I wasn't sure *what*. From the beginning I wanted to use an evocative visual component. I didn't simply want to compose an instrumental suite based on the dreams, where the dreams would just be written up and appear in a printed program. But I had no idea about how to go about it at all.

So I showed the short accounts of the dreams I had written to Herschel Garfein, the librettist who had helped me shape *Leaves of Grass,* and he was so moved that he offered to collaborate with me to create a theater piece with music, inspired by the dreams. We agreed that Herschel would conceptualize the piece, write the text (drawing from interviews he would conduct with Scott, my doctor Michael Liguori, and me), and—from my written recollections of the dreams—I would compose the music, mostly instrumental selections, though with one lengthy song that we envisioned as the centerpiece of the whole work. The song drew from my dream about "The Knitters" with lyrics by Herschel, adapted from my written account of the dream. I didn't want to do another *Leaves of Grass,* which was so completely focused on Whitman's words. I wanted to express each dream in a unique musical or visual way without it being another song cycle.

The piece took form as a hybrid performance/multimedia work, *My Coma Dreams.* Herschel, a gifted dramaturg, took my vivid but terse recollections of my dreams, added monologues and other dramatic material, and crafted a cohesive 85-minute work of what we ultimately called "jazz theater." He added a couple of sequences that I wouldn't have thought of, including an account of the life of St. Vincent de Paul, the namesake of the hospital, who, as Herschel described him, was "the first social activist saint." To bring a leavening dose of lightheartedness to a grimly serious piece about illness and mortality, he wrote a flat-out funny section about the preposterous portrayal of comas in movies and TV medical dramas, where patients miraculously awaken with perfect hair, bright eyes, and big smiles.

One actor/singer, Michael Winther, who had performed in an earlier iteration of *Rooms of Light,* played all the roles in *My Coma*

Dreams: Scott, me, and a few incidental characters. The two major parts were Scott and I, and Michael captured us both with a simple costume change, by wearing a T-shirt when he was I and slipping on a long-sleeved shirt when he was Scott. He also made tiny, meticulous actorly adjustments in his body language and voice—and those who know us both were amazed at the way he channeled each one of us with little obvious effort. Michael is a superb actor as well as a singer who has the rare ability to sing in character in a theatrical setting with the utmost unfussiness, sincerity, and commitment.

I worked on the music during a four-week residency at MacDowell in August 2010. I arrived at the Colony with the libretto and not much else. But I knew instinctively that "The Knitters" had to be the first thing I tackled—I wrote it in three feverish days. For the dream of Thelonious Monk, I wrote the music using my kitchen timer so I could simulate the panic that I went through in the dream, writing a tune as fast as possible to get out of the cage.

The result was a set of thirteen instrumental pieces arranged for a mixed ensemble of eleven players, including a full string quartet, trumpet, trombone, two woodwinds (doubling on saxes, clarinets, and flutes), bass, drums, and piano. The musical language is for the most part what one would identify as jazz, though highly personalized, but some of the pieces were informed by my extensive knowledge of classical music so they were in that musical world. As I said to the woman at BMI all those years ago, it was "Fred Hersch Music." I didn't limit myself to any genre or style; I just tried to respond in a truthful musical way to the essence of each dream. There is much more improvised solo space in the piece compared to *Leaves of Grass*—though everything was precisely scored by me in pencil. But this time, I ultimately had the parts computer-copied and then edited for performance by my music director and conductor Gregg Kallor.

My original desire for animation proved more complex than any of us could have imagined. I hired a gifted young animator, Sarah Wickliffe (the daughter of Paul Wickliffe and Roseanna Vitro), but we realized in short order that there was going to be a need to use much more than hand-drawn animation for such a massive piece. Through a recommendation, we engaged Eamonn Farrell, who had worked on many experimental theater pieces that had a visual component. Using the amazing computer-graphic program Isadora, he ultimately became the thirteenth member of the ensemble. Since there was so much improvisation, nothing could be exactly timed, so he had to run the computer images (which he had helped design and generate) along with us in real time—and he had to know the piece inside and out. There were hundreds of video cues, and the images were projected on a giant screen at the back of the stage behind the ensemble. Aaron Copp was our imaginative—and patient—director of lighting and production. It was a labor of love on everybody's part.

My Coma Dreams had its premiere in May 2011 at the Alexander Kasser Theater at New Jersey's Montclair State University, where my suite of jazz portraits, *Dedications,* had been performed three years earlier. It was commissioned once again by Peak Performances, with generous additional funding from my close friends Linda and Stuart Nelson. Performing it—at the piano with the ensemble on stage, visible to the audience the whole time— was the most wrenching and strange experience I had ever had as a musician, with the singular exception of my first set back in the public eye, at Smalls. There I was on stage, playing music that by all rights I shouldn't have been alive to write, and Michael was portraying me a few feet away—and my piano playing was itself a central character in the story. Herschel wrote an account of the moment in the exercise room at Rivington House when I saw a reflection of my frail, hobbling self in the mirror. At the very end of the show, as Michael described that moment, without speaking I rose from the piano bench, faced the audience for the first time, and mimed clumsily trying to walk using the parallel bars in tandem with him. I felt so faint from the emotion of the moment that I could have used a walker again. The audience gasped.

After its premiere in Montclair, *My Coma Dreams* was presented in a series of well-executed and very well-received performances, including for the European Society of Intensive Care Medicine in Berlin, as well as a staging at the Miller Theater at Columbia University, sponsored by the school's innovative Department of Narrative Medicine. This performance was captured for a DVD release. In Berlin, more than one doctor came up to me after the show and said, "This is going to change the way I practice medicine." These ICU doctors may have realized that they had not been giving enough attention to the extraordinary effort of the loved ones and caregivers who needed to be better informed and more than occasionally reassured. A patient is a whole person, not just numbers on a medical chart.

At the end of the year of the premiere of *My Coma Dreams*, I was voted Jazz Pianist of the Year by the Jazz Journalists Association. I gave David Hajdu a brief speech of thanks to read on my behalf at the award ceremony, because I couldn't be there. I was on the road again, busier than ever.

CHAPTER 18

TOGETHER AND ALONE

I was different now—slapped down, knocked out, brought back, humbled, and, in the end, recharged by my lengthy incapacitation and difficult recovery. I felt different, too—lucky, grateful, and awestruck by the unpredictability of life. My music seemed freer, less effortful, more open to the unexpected. Not that I'm less proud of the vast amount of music I had made before my coma—it's all *me*, made with care, and done for a reason. I'm pretty happy with all my output, or nearly all of it. Still, something *happened* to me—and my music—after my coma, and it was something positive.

Other people, including critics, seemed to treat me differently, too. I've been fortunate to get a great deal of favorable press since my first years as a professional musician in New York, from *Down-Beat* and the other jazz magazines to the *New York Times* and *The*

New Yorker. For the music I made after my recovery, the reviews got almost embarrassingly effusive. The critics who had always liked me said they liked me even more now, and the ones with reservations in the past said they were hearing qualities in my music they had never heard or noticed. And my calendar was even more full, with performances around the world both with my trio and as a solo pianist.

In February 2012 I played a week at the Village Vanguard with John Hébert and Eric McPherson, my now steady trio. Eric, who has been best friends with Nasheet Waits since they were in fifth grade, had filled in for Nasheet on drums a few times, and I felt that he, John, and I clicked in a different way. As a drummer trained as a classical percussionist, Eric is a great listener as well as a deeply creative player—he's playing *with* John and me at all times, always at the right dynamic level, never under us or over us. John, who has one of the great bass sounds in jazz today, is as capable of playing a ballad with wisdom and patience as he is of creating something with a spontaneously generated structure. We had already recorded *Whirl*, my first studio album after my illness, but I was itching to record us at our "home club."

Palmetto Records had all six nights of sets at the Vanguard recorded for a live album. We played things I like from every realm of jazz territory, mingled with quite a few of my own pieces, new and old: "Segment," a lesser-known Charlie Parker tune that, as far as I know, is his only composition in a minor key; a sloweddown take on Sonny Rollins's bluesy "Doxy"; a medley of Ornette Coleman's "Lonely Woman" and Miles Davis's "Nardis"; a few standards such as Cole Porter's "From This Moment On" and Jule Styne and Sammy Cahn's "I Fall in Love Too Easily"; and my tunes "Dream of Monk" from *My Coma Dreams* and "Tristesse," a new number I had written in dedication to Paul Motian, the wonderful drummer, who had died just three months earlier.

Paul had played the Vanguard so often that he was practically the house drummer. He was part of the original Bill Evans Trio—along with bassist Scott LaFaro, who died in an automobile accident at age twenty-four in 1961. They pioneered the conversational style of trio playing that has been so influential. Paul and I worked together once for a week at the club in a trio with Drew Gress, and though we didn't always click musically—Paul's musical personality was so strong that it could be overpowering—I admired his music and was glad to experience making music with him firsthand. I knew he suffered from myelodysplastic syndrome, a debilitating blood disease, which he pushed his way through in his final years, and he knew what had been going on with me.

The magical drummer Billy Higgins had a similar story. He and I never got the chance to play together, one of my great regrets, as he was among my all-time favorites. He was on dialysis and suffering with liver problems when I saw him play his heart out at the Vanguard not long before he died. After the set I went back into the kitchen that serves as the musicians' hangout to pay my respects. He seemed weak, completely exhausted, and he was sweating from the effort of the set. But he mustered the energy to get up from his chair when he saw me and give me a warm embrace. Then he held me at arm's length, smiled, and said softly in my ear, "It's good to be *alive*." Though we never discussed it, he knew of my health situation and he was giving me some of his precious life energy.

For that whole week with my trio at the Vanguard, John, Eric, and I were beautifully connected. We were all full of ideas and really attuned to one another. When I listened to the recordings Palmetto made, I couldn't bear to cut tunes to meet the running time of an album. Generously, the label agreed to release a double CD. In recognition of how good it felt to be where I was after what I had been through, we called the project *Alive at the Vanguard*. As there have been so many albums titled *Live at the Village Vanguard* (including my own in 2001), I was very deliberate about the choice of the word "alive."

The intensifying recognition of my work after the coma had a strange retroactive effect. In 2011, two years after my coma but a year before *Alive at the Vanguard*, Palmetto recorded me at the club as a solo pianist. I was now established as the only musician in the eighty-plus-year history of the Village Vanguard to be presented regularly as a solo pianist. (If it sounds self-congratulatory to say that, I'm sorry. It's true, and I can't help but be proud of it, as I am of having my photo hanging prominently on the wall of the club.) It had all started by accident. Once, back in 2005, when I was slated to play at the Vanguard with Drew Gress and Nasheet Waits, I got a call at the last minute from Drew, saying that he was stuck in California and wouldn't be there in time for the first set. I immediately reached out to John Hébert, and he too was en route from California. So as the lights went down at nine, and just as the owner, Lorraine Gordon, was walking into the club, I was making my way onstage to play a solo set with the blessing of the club's manager, Jed Eisenman. The set was a mix of original tunes, some jazz classics, something Brazilian, and I ended, as I always do, with a ballad and a Monk tune. Though Lorraine might not have agreed with this solution had she gotten there earlier, she and the crowd were very enthusiastic and I think she could imagine a week of it. In 2006, Palmetto released a solo recording from a live concert in Amsterdam, *Live at the Bimhuis*, and I persuaded the club to give me a solo week to coincide with the release. The response was terrific.

And in 2013, as the label had done for the *Alive* trio release, Palmetto recorded a full week of sets at the Vanguard from my second solo engagement there. Originally intending to select the best performances from individual shows, I decided in the end to release only the complete last set from the final night in the run as *Alone at the Vanguard*. The set had a flow and a cohesion that made it feel like not only a set but an *album*. The sequence was perfect, I was in the zone, and I thought that pulling one definitive set made a bold statement that picking and choosing wouldn't have.

I remain appreciative of the good notices that have come my way since my emergence from the coma. I feel like I have been playing more deeply at this point in my life, whatever the reasons— age, experience, maturity, not caring as much what people think, and/or the wisdom and enhanced clarity of purpose that often comes to people forced to face death at close range. At the same time, I want my listeners to appreciate my music on its own terms, as music, and not as something secondary to the drama of my survival narrative. Just as I've never wanted to be defined solely by my sexual orientation or my HIV status, I don't want to be known merely as the coma survivor. I don't want praise out of pity or congratulations for my good fortune.

This is a complicated matter, because jazz is an art that prizes personality. To express yourself from within, saying something true to your being, is an essential tenet of the genre. In my music, specifically, I have drawn deeply from my own feelings, beliefs, and experience. I'd like to think there's truth in the proposition that no one else sounds quite like me and no one else could have written the music I've composed, for better or worse. My identity as a gay man, someone with AIDS, and a coma survivor has informed the music I have made over the years. Everything in me has gone into my music. In the end, though, it's the music that matters—not what went into it but how it came out. Besides, a great deal of my music—in fact, the majority of it—has nothing to do with the particulars of my sexuality or my health.

By the week of trio shows that led to *Alive at the Vanguard*, I had recovered all the technical facility I'd had before the coma while gaining quite a bit emotionally. I wrote a song about the coma and its consequences for me, centered on the comment that the ICU doctor had made to Scott at St. Vincent's Hospital, "Good things happen slowly, but bad things happen fast." The song, which has lyrics by David Hajdu, takes a positive turn, just as my life did, and ends with the thought that good things may happen slowly, but good things often *last*. David used the metaphor of floating at sea, lost in the dark, submissive to the fates: "Close the compass, fold the sail, and maybe we'll land in a different place." As a man and a musician, I landed in a new place after the coma, and it was a great place to be.

I tend to think of the years after the coma as the period when I reached full maturity as a musician, with no slight to the hundreds of recordings and thousands of hours of playing jazz in live performances earlier in my life. I listened recently to one of the first albums I ever made, *As One*—the duo project with Jane Ira Bloom,

who after decades of making brilliantly individualistic music remains underappreciated. I was surprised to find that album still
exciting to hear. Jane is magnificent, of course, and I don't sound
much different than I sound today. Not *much*—still, I *do* sound
somewhat different now, and I certainly don't *feel* the same as I
felt in 1984, when I was young and hungry and working overtime
to prove myself. I won't disagree with any of the people—critics
and agents and music presenters and fans and friends—who have
told me that since the coma I'm playing better than ever. But the
factors underlying my development over the years are manifold
and can't be explained completely by my illness and recovery.

Throughout the second decade of the twenty-first century, I've
been working primarily in my favorite three formats—solo, duo,
and trio—and I think my approach to all three has deepened. I've
been offered more and more opportunities to play solo and have
become closely associated with the format since my prodigious
solo output at Nonesuch and breaking ground at solo piano at the
Vanguard. As I've said, I've been interested in solo performance
since my early days at NEC, when I was studying with Jaki Byard.
I love the freedom that being alone at the piano provides. Keith
Jarrett, in his early solo recordings, seemed to revel in that freedom, and so did Cecil Taylor. Keith seems to thrive in the freedom
of playing alone. Cecil *demands* it. My solo playing may sound
more structured than either of theirs, but as it goes down, I am
constantly taking chances, playing on the edge, phrase to phrase.

It took me years of experimenting with solo piano to understand
that freedom isn't a mandate for dizzy extemporizing. The framework of the composition is not an encumbrance, it's a mechanism
for applying the creative imagination. Rules can be oddly freeing—

and most artists need some kind of limit, subject, framework, or focus in order to create. Stravinsky said something like, "If you gave me everything I could possibly require to compose and told me I could write whatever I wanted, I would just stare at the music paper. But if you asked me to write a piece for one piccolo and twelve tubas, I would be inspired and get to work at once."

I'm reminded of the respect for compositional form that I learned in my early classical training. Over the years I've never stopped listening to classical music as well as contemporary improvised music and music from around the world. When I play solo piano now, I draw on everything I've learned as a student, a music educator, a musician, a composer, and a listener, as well as a pianist in at least two genres. I'm working in a certain language of my own that draws from multiple traditions but retains the bedrock principles of theme and variation.

I value storytelling above all else in art forms. This way of thinking is applicable to group playing, naturally, but it's especially valuable in solo piano, where you're the whole orchestra. I use varying registers, varying dynamics and articulations. I spread my hands from one end of the keyboard to the other, lowest note to highest note. I use multiple independent contrapuntal voices, all of which are responsive to the rhythm. It's jazz, so there has to be a good time feel. When I'm done, I'd like to be able to say, "That's *time*." It's taken me years to get to a place where I can do all that without thinking about it.

IN 2015 I turned sixty. It's an age that people often dread. For me, making it to sixty felt close to miraculous. I had been diagnosed with AIDS in my thirties and never expected to reach the age of forty. To have lived another twenty years of highly productive life, in a wonderful relationship, working and learning and growing musically the whole time, is a gift I marvel at every day but still cannot fully grasp. In Japanese folklore, when you turn sixty you are reborn—I certainly feel that way as I enter my seventh decade.

In October 2015, the month of my sixtieth birthday, I was on the cover of the iconic jazz magazine *DownBeat* for the first time; that December I was on the cover of *POZ*, the AIDS magazine, for its long-term survivor issue. I am quite sure I am the only person so honored by both of these publications. I marked the occasion musically with an album simply called *SOLO*, the tenth solo album of my career. Released by Palmetto shortly before my birthday, it's an archival recording of a concert I had given in August 2014 at the Windham Civic Center Concert Hall, a converted church in the Catskill Mountains of Upstate New York. I was unaware that the concert was being recorded and just played following my intuition without a set list—as usual. I remember really digging the recording when I first heard it—but I disregarded it for potential release, as most of the compositions had already been recorded by me on other projects or in other musical configurations.

But alone in my car a month later, I put on the Windham recording and thought, *Well, this is about as good as I can play.* Everything just came together for me that night—my connection to the piano, to the tunes themselves, and to the audience was extraordinary. And Miles recorded "Autumn Leaves" God knows how many times. In the end it's not the material that matters, it's the performance. The vibrant church acoustics with great natural reverberation had led me to play "Caravan," the deliciously rhythmic and angular piece of swing-era "exotica" by Juan Tizol and Duke Ellington, as a very slow and spacy tango—you can hear my punched-out high notes ricochet from the back of the hall. I played my signature dedication piece, "Whirl" (for ballerina Suzanne Farrell), my classically influenced tribute to Robert Schumann's "Pastorale," and one of my favorite Monk tunes, "In Walked Bud," his tip of the hat to the great bebop pianist Bud Powell, a colleague of his from the early days of bebop at Minton's Playhouse in Harlem.

The tracks are presented in close to the order I played them at the concert, but I eliminated a couple of performances and sequenced the album ending with Joni Mitchell's "Both Sides Now." Though I've loved Joni's music since my high school days and was tickled to see her at the bar at Bradley's once or twice, I had only played "Both Sides Now" once, many years ago, on a concert tour of the United Kingdom. But she was on my mind at the time of the show, which took place not long after word had gotten out that Joni had collapsed in her home from a brain aneurysm and was now hospitalized. With no plan to do the tune but a memory of the melody and chord changes intact from my teenage years, I played it in my own way, slowly, soberly, and in three-quarter time—and I've been doing it in concerts, on and off, ever since. When I play it today, I not only feel the music, I connect to the words, having lived a life that I've often seen as having two sides.

At this point, though, I no longer see my life—or much of anything—in such simple terms. I've learned that there are many, many sides to most things and to most people, myself included.

The only things that have two sides are flat, and the life I have experienced has been anything but that. I know how fortunate I've been to have had the experiences I've had, from hanging out and playing with the legends of jazz to achieving more success as a musician than I had ever imagined when I was hanging around the jazz clubs in Cincinnati. I'm profoundly blessed to have survived what I've endured physically, and I'm humbled to have the opportunity to give back as both a teacher and an activist.

I look at life from many sides now. I'm still trying to make sense of it and draw from its lessons—and its mysteries—to make Fred Hersch music.

TO BEGIN

started this book much like I start a piano lesson with a new student. I sat down with myself and said, *I'd like to learn about you. How would you describe yourself?*

This is what I wrote that day:

I'm a jazz musician. I have always made my living at it and these days, I can play whatever I want with whomever I want.

I have a faithful and loving partner. I can't believe how lucky I am.

I have a variety of interests in and out of music. I'm a big fan of professional tennis. I enjoy visual arts.

I toggle between massive insecurity on one hand and feeling like I am a badass on the other.

I have battled with compulsive behavior for much of my adult life, and I'm still fighting that fight. I am currently obsessed with computer mahjong solitaire, which I find more addictive than cocaine.

I'm never sure what or how to practice, so I rarely do. But I seem to pull it together when the lights go up. Occasionally I don't, but I move on and pretend the next day like that concert never happened. Life is more than my last gig.

I read a lot. I still get a kick out of Charles Dickens.

I have a love-hate relationship with New York, which has been in a bit of a hate phase recently. I also love the country and the woods.

I have been HIV positive for more than thirty years. I said this already, but I can't believe how lucky I am. I take thirty-three pills a day.

I am still in psychotherapy—perpetually trying to figure myself out.

When I listen to music, it isn't always jazz. I put on classical music or Brazilian music or R&B. I prefer to hear jazz live and go out as often as I can to hear other people play.

I love crème brûlée but can't eat it—as I am diabetic.

I still get a thrill out of playing spontaneous music in front of an audience.

I'm not a saint. There are times when I am angry, insensitive, and lacking in self-awareness.

I am disposed to strong opinions and intense feelings. I think both have been assets to me as a musician, though they don't always help me in personal situations.

I've learned a lot over the course of my life. I hope I'm a more patient person since my coma, and I think I'm a more relaxed and generous musician.

I have learned that gratitude is better than entitlement.

I feel like I still have a great deal to learn.

After one month of working every day at it, I can now touch my toes.

I'd like to try to write a book. Here goes.

ACKNOWLEDGMENTS

My sincere thanks to: David Hajdu, my close friend and full collaborator since the inception of this project; Kevin Doughten, who brought intelligence and passion to the editing of this book; Chris Calhoun, the best (and musically hippest) literary agent imaginable; Jamie Bernstein, Marilyn Fabe, Hank Hersch, Peter Katz, Peter Kountz, Linda Nelson, Esperanza Spalding, and Johannes Weidenmueller, who saw this book in its early stages and made valuable comments; Ethan Iverson, whose interview with me on his blog *Do the Math* got me thinking about writing a book; Jesse Aylen, Molly Stern, Tricia Boczkowski, Mark Birkey, Elizabeth Rendfleisch, Jon Darga, Stephanie Davis, Julie Cepler, Ellen Folan, Linnea Knollmueller, Maya Lane, and Christopher Brand at Crown Books; all the photographers who captured the wonderful images for the insert; everyone at the MacDowell Colony, Peterborough, New Hampshire; Lorraine and Deborah Gordon and Jed Eisenman at the Village Vanguard, New York City; Herschel Garfein; Robert Rund; my piano teacher Sophia Rosoff; Dr. Michael Ligouri, Dr. Mark Astiz, Dr. Linda Kirschenbaum, and the entire staff of St. Vincent's Hospital; and especially to Scott Morgan, for always being there for me in every possible way.

SELECTED DISCOGRAPHY
(RELEASES AS OF SEPTEMBER 1, 2017)

* Original composition(s) recorded on this album
+ Album produced by Fred Hersch
Δ Album or selections arranged by Fred Hersch

AS LEADER

Open Book (Palmetto PM 2186)*+ Δ

Sunday Night at the Vanguard, The Fred Hersch Trio (Palmetto PM 2183)*+ Δ (2017 Double Grammy Nominee)

SOLO, Fred Hersch (Palmetto PM 2081)*+

Floating, The Fred Hersch Trio (Palmetto PM 217)*+ Δ (2015 Double Grammy Nominee)

Alive at the Vanguard, The Fred Hersch Trio (Palmetto PM 2159)*+

Alone at the Vanguard, Fred Hersch (Palmetto 2147)*+ (2012 Double Grammy Nominee)

Whirl, The Fred Hersch Trio (Palmetto PM 2143) *+ Δ

My Coma Dreams (DVD), Fred Hersch, directed by Herschel Garfein (Palmetto PM 2175) *+ ∆

Fred Hersch Plays Jobim (Sunnyside 1223)+

Live at Jazz Standard, The Fred Hersch Pocket Orchestra (Sunnyside SCC 1222)*+ ∆

Concert Music 2001–2006, Fred Hersch (Naxos 8.559366)*+

Night and the Music, The Fred Hersch Trio (Palmetto 2124)*+ ∆

In Amsterdam: Live at the Bimhuis, Fred Hersch (Palmetto 2116)*+ ∆ (2006 Grammy Nominee)

Leaves of Grass, The Fred Hersch Ensemble (Palmetto 2107)*+ ∆

The Fred Hersch Trio + 2, The Fred Hersch Trio (Palmetto 2099)*+∆

Live at the Village Vanguard, The Fred Hersch Trio (Palmetto PM 2088) *+

Songs Without Words (Nonesuch 79612-2) *+ ∆

Let Yourself Go, Fred Hersch at Jordan Hall (Nonesuch 79558-2) *+

Thelonious: Fred Hersch Plays Monk (Nonesuch 79456-2)+

The Duo Album, Fred Hersch & Friends (Classical Action 1002)+

Fred Hersch Plays Rodgers and Hammerstein (Nonesuch 79414-2)+

Passion Flower: Fred Hersch Plays Billy Strayhorn (Nonesuch 79395-2)+

Point in Time, Fred Hersch (with Drew Gress, Tom Rainey, Dave Douglas, and Rich Perry) (Enja ENJ-9035 2)*+

The Fred Hersch Trio Plays (with Drew Gress and Tom Rainey) (Chesky JD-116)*+

I Never Told You: Fred Hersch Plays Johnny Mandel (Varese Sarabande VSD-5547) (1995 Grammy Nominee)

Live at Maybeck, Volume 31, Fred Hersch (Concord Jazz CCD-4596)*

Dancing in the Dark, The Fred Hersch Trio with Drew Gress and Tom Rainey (Chesky JD-90)+ (1993 Grammy Nominee)

Red Square Blue: Jazz Impressions of Russian Classics (Angel/EMI 54743)+∆

Forward Motion, The Fred Hersch Group (Chesky JD-55)*+∆

Heartsongs, Fred Hersch Trio with Michael Formanek and Jeff Hirsh-field (Sunnyside SSC 1047)*+

Evanessence: A Tribute to Bill Evans, featuring Gary Burton and Toots Thielemans (Evidence ECD 22204-2)*$_\Delta$+

The French Collection: Jazz Impressions of French Classics (Angel/ EMI 49561)*$_\Delta$

Sarabande, Fred Hersch, Charlie Haden, Joey Baron (Sunnyside SSC 1024)*+

Horizons, Fred Hersch Trio featuring Marc Johnson and Joey Baron (Concord Jazz CCD-267)*+

AS CO-LEADER

Free Flying, Fred Hersch and Julian Lage (Palmetto 2168)*+ (2014 Grammy Nominee)

Songs & Lullabies, Fred Hersch and Norma Winstone (Sunnyside 1108)*+

Live at Jazz Standard, Nancy King with Fred Hersch (MaxJazz 122) +$_\Delta$ (2006 Grammy Nominee)

Songs We Know, Fred Hersch and Bill Frisell (Nonesuch 79468-2)

As One, Jane Ira Bloom and Fred Hersch (Winter & Winter JMT Edition 919-003-2)*+

Thirteen Ways, Fred Hersch, Michael Moore, Gerry Hemingway (GM 3033-CD)*+

Slow Hot Wind, Janis Siegel and Fred Hersch (Varese Sarabande VSD-5552)+

Beautiful Love, Jay Clayton and Fred Hersch (Sunnyside SSC-1066)+

Short Stories, Janis Siegel and Fred Hersch (Atlantic 81989)*+$_\Delta$ (1989 Grammy Nominee)

E.T.C., Fred Hersch with Steve LaSpina and Jeff Hirshfield (Red Records RR123233)+

AS FEATURED SOLOIST

Haunted Heart, Renée Fleming with Fred Hersch and Bill Frisell (Decca 4406-02)

Tightrope, The Three Cohens (Anzic Records) *

Build a Bridge, Audra McDonald (Nonesuch 79862-2) ᴬ

Two Hands, Ten Voices, Fred Hersch with ten vocalists (Broadway Cares 1002)+

Last Night When We Were Young: The Ballad Album (Classical Action 1001)+ᴬ

The Richard Rodgers Centennial Jazz Piano Album (Broadway Cares 1001)+

Dawn Upshaw Sings Vernon Duke (Nonesuch 79531-2)ᴬ

Dawn Upshaw Sings Rodgers and Hart (Nonesuch 79406-2)ᴬ

The AIDS Quilt Songbook (Harmonia Mundi/Nightengale HMU 907602)*

Maiden Voyage, Leny Andrade featuring Fred Hersch (Chesky JD-113)+ᴬ

In a Sentimental Mood: Mathis Sings Ellington (Columbia 46069) (1991 Grammy Nominee)

AS SIDEMAN

WITH JANE IRA BLOOM

Chasing Paint (Arabesque Jazz, AJ0158)

The Red Quartets (Arabesque Jazz AJ0144)

The Nearness (Arabesque Jazz AJ0120)

Mighty Lights (featuring Charlie Haden and Ed Blackwell) (Enja 4044)

Slalom (CBS 44415)

Modern Drama (CBS 40755)

WITH GARY BURTON

Departure (Concord CCD-4749-2) (featuring John Scofield, John Patitucci, and Peter Erskine)

WITH MICHAEL CALLEN

Legacy (Significant Other 50951)

WITH EDDIE DANIELS
To Bird with Love (GRP 9544)+∆ (1987 Grammy Nominee)
Breakthrough (with the London Philharmonia) (GRP 9533) (1986 Grammy Nominee)

WITH ART FARMER
Mirage (Soul Note SN-1046)*
You Make Me Smile (Soul Note 21076-2)
Yama (with Joe Henderson) (CTI 9000)
Warm Valley (Concord CJ-212)*
A Work of Art (Concord CCD-4179)* (1982 Grammy Nominee)

WITH BILLY HARPER
Quintet in Europe (Soul Note 1001)

WITH LEE KONITZ
Round and Round (MusicMasters 60167)

WITH MICHAEL MOORE
Home Game (Ramboy #02)
Chicotoumi (Ramboy #06)
Bering (Ramboy #11)

WITH LUCIANA SOUZA
North and South (Sunnyside SSC 1112) (2003 Grammy Nominee)

WITH TOOTS THIELEMANS
Only Trust Your Heart (Concord CJ-355)*+∆
Do Not Leave Me (Stash STCD-12)

WITH ROSEANNA VITRO
Softly (Concord CCD 4587)*∆

PHOTOGRAPH CREDITS

ABOUT THE AUTHOR

Jazz pianist, composer, activist, and educator Fred Hersch is a ten-time Grammy nominee and the recipient of a 2003 Guggenheim Fellowship in Composition. He was named a 2016 Doris Duke Artist and has twice been awarded Jazz Pianist of the Year by the Jazz Journalists Association. He concertizes worldwide as a solo artist, as a collaborator, and with the Fred Hersch Trio. He was a longtime member of the Jazz Studies faculty of New England Conservatory and currently teaches at Rutgers University. He is the subject of the feature documentary *The Ballad of Fred Hersch*. He lives in New York City and Pennsylvania with his partner, Scott Morgan.

www.fredhersch.com